Vocational Education in Correctional Facilities

An Anthology of Personal Perspectives

EDITED BY
ROBERT MATTUCCI

Published by

CALIFORNIA STATE UNIVERSITY
SAN BERNARDINO

CALIFORNIA STATE UNIVERSITY
SAN BERNARDINO

Published in San Bernardino, California,
by California State University, San Bernardino.

Special thanks to Robert Mattucci for the support that brought this book project from its inception through to actual publication.

Image credits

Photos: "Father and Son" by Meg Mattucci; "Bob and his dog Danny" by Rose Freeman; "Bob in the trench" by Joe Walsh. All owned by Robert Mattucci.

Cover design by Charlotte Garvey and Deanna Dunn.

Printed in the United States of America by
Wirz & Company Printing
444 Colton Avenue
Colton, CA 92324

ISBN 978-0-9776008-5-4

This book is printed on permanent/durable paper.

DEDICATION

This book is dedicated to my father, Benny Mattucci (1922-2009), a World War II veteran who served in the Burma Conflict, 1943-1945. He was my friend and my mentor, as well as my father.

Robert Mattucci

CONTENTS

By Robert Mattucci

This anthology has been a dream of mine for several years. In July 2006, I became the Chair of the Special Interest Group in vocational education for the Correctional Education Association. I had a purpose in taking this position—getting the word out about vocational education in jails and prisons in the world of correctional education. I had many different ideas but the most concrete and viable one was to compile personal experiences in this field that would help to reveal the true nature of vocational education. I also wanted to explore the important role it has played in the lives of many former incarcerated adults.

Why is this anthology so critical? How could I, as one person, tackle such a huge task with credibility and honesty?

To begin with "I" could not do this alone. The immediate concept for this anthology went from "I" to "we" or "us." In this journey I needed help putting this inspirational idea together. Believing in the value of "us" opened many new doors, helping to take the concept of vocational education in corrections to a whole new global level.

In starting to put this whole idea of a "we" approach to vocational education in corrections, I talked to people who actually did this—administrators, educators, teachers and skilled tradesmen who worked on site. This book is about the men and women who have worked in the field diligently, trying to bring about change.

Change in correctional education comes about very slowly. Reading the classics by Thomas Mott Osborne and Austin MacCormick provided real insight. I am a plumber. I have built pipe systems in houses and commercial buildings for over 30 years. Change in the plumbing field is quick and fluid. I have been teaching plumbing in four county jails for almost eleven years and did not comprehend how slowly change occurred in correctional education. Reading the classics of prison reform and correctional education fueled my enthusiasm to undertake this critical book project.

The cooperation of the writers of the critical pieces was amazing. This book is a "WE" success story. I phoned each person and talked at length of my ideas and the goals of this project. Each said YES without reservation. This was very exciting; it kept me energized throughout the whole process. Their positive energy and enthusiasm brought this important correctional education anthology into existence.

I want to thank Ann for her editing skills that help guide this process along, Dr. Young for her encouragement to go on and follow my heart over the years, and Dr. Thom Gehring for inspiring me to climb the mountain and put these ideas together. Special thanks to those who wrote chapters: Bob, Dwight, Norris, Jeremiah, Donna, Bill, Richard, Mark, and Judy. In addition, the book includes parts of Dr. David Snedden's chapter on Industrial Education in Reform Schools from his 1907 *Administration and Educational Work of American Juvenile Reform Schools* and Austin MacCormick's groundbreaking chapter on Vocational Education, which first appeared in his 1931 *The Education of Adult Prisoners.*

I hope this anthology gives all who read it a clear understanding of the role that vocational education can play in the lives of incarcerated men and women and adjudicated youth, and how vocational education fits into the whole continuum of correctional education. I am grateful to you for giving me the opportunity to work with each of you—the contributors who wrote the book and the readers who will make it all worth while.

Thank You

Robert Mattucci
Correctional Educator
Member Local 267 Plumbers and Steamfitters Local
rmstoneage@yahoo.com

INTRODUCTION

by Diane S. Young

A book solely dedicated to correctional vocational education is needed and exciting. There is increasing empirical evidence that rehabilitative programs, when tailored to the specific needs of individuals and of sufficient duration, decrease recidivism. As the public and our political leaders turn greater attention to addressing community reentry needs, in an effort to reduce recidivism rates that have been too high for far too long, correctional vocational education has the opportunity to play a critical role as a vital component of rehabilitative programs.

It is abundantly clear that the vast majority of men, women, boys and girls that comprise the well over two million incarcerated in the United States are poor, undereducated and unskilled, with poor employment histories. They stand to gain significantly, as do the families and communities to which they return, through the acquisition of marketable skills, productive work as part of a team, increased self-confidence in their ability to make positive contributions, and satisfaction in the fruits of their (legal) labors.

It is true that the problems of some incarcerated individuals are complex and multifaceted and cannot quickly be fixed. Many of the problems are embedded in our societal structures (e.g., neighborhoods devoid of jobs that provide a living wage and affordable and safe housing, lack of drug treatment beds) and beyond the capacity of any one vocational education program to address. On the other hand, there are factors that correctional vocational education programs are uniquely positioned to address. Several ideas are offered by the authors of the chapters that make up this book.

Vocational education has a long history within corrections. Its programs have been more or less visible and available, depending partially on whether they operate within a rehabilitative or retributive era. Some of the authors in this book write about aspects of this history and of the people who helped to shape correctional vocational education. All are in agreement about the importance of vocational education for present-day offenders and the families and communities to which they will return. Although it is harder to implement vocational education programs within an era focused on "just deserts" and punishment, the importance of the task is no less vital. This book provides a tool for thinking about the current state of correctional vocational education, what it ought to be, and how to move it in that direction.

One of the strengths of the book is the variety of perspectives involved: those of tradesmen, administrators, and educators, many with extensive years of experience in correctional vocational education. The breadth of topics is another strength. Theoretical underpinnings, research findings, practical applications, historical examples, and pressing current-day issues are all included. Each author, through the respective chapters in the book, conveys his or her own perspective on correctional vocational education.

Bill Muth creates a context for thinking about the policy and pedagogical issues that prison-based vocational education would do well to address as it strives to provide effective and relevant vocational education programs. David Snedden, from his *Administration and Educational Work of American Juvenile Reform Schools* (1907), shows how closely institutional and educational influences were aligned when industrial education developed throughout the nation. Snedden's work had a major impact on vocational education, urban education, and correctional education. Austin MacCormick, in the chapter on vocational education from his book *The Education of Adult Prisoners* (1976/1931), describes the state of vocational education for adults in correctional facilities in the early 1900s. He discusses several possibilities for the content and structure of vocational education programs and applies them to prisons. Both Snedden and MacCormick responded to John Dewey, and many have seen them as practitioner-researchers who applied Dewey's approaches to the issues of correctional education. Although prison conditions and vocational education programs have changed significantly since the time in which they wrote, some of the same problems with implementation remain (e.g., lack of adequate funding) and much can be learned from their thorough examinations. Robert Mattucci takes the words and work of Austin MacCormick and applies them to his own experiences teaching vocational education programs in correctional facilities. Through illustrations, Mattucci conveys present-day applications of MacCormick's ideas.

Robert Holtz and Donna Shea, in their chapters, provide a theoretical focus for vocational education. Holtz presents an introduction to the historical work of John Dewey and Anton Makarenko, education theorists that he believes have important lessons for today's correctional educators. Shea reminds us of the importance of assessing, understanding and accommodating the learning styles of adult learners and touches on theories and research relevant to learning styles of adult students. Richard Dackow emphasizes the essential role of correctional education in helping students change and improve their self-images. He suggests some behavioral therapies that can support this focus and provides an inspiring real-life example. Bill Muth's presentation of the European Prison Rules for correctional education gives us an idea about the opportunities for change and improvement that the European Union nations have been pursuing, thereby suggesting directions that might be pursued in North America.

Jeremiah Gee, through his study of rural jails in Pennsylvania, forcefully reminds us that diverse geographic areas have different levels of programmatic resources available to them and may have different vocational training needs. Vocational education programs are shaped by the availability of resources and local interests and "one size fits all" approaches will not benefit the various vocational education programs that operate within Federal, state, local, adult, youth, men's, and women's correctional facilities. Diane Young and Robert Mattucci, in their chapter, provide one example of a plumbing program for jailed women. Program description and program outcomes illustrate one possibility for vocational education in this type of correctional setting.

Dwight Stecker and Norris Williams bring historical and personal perspectives to the book, drawing on their work experiences over several years with correctional vocational education. Stecker's work took place primarily at the county level and Williams' at the state level. Both offer suggestions for today's vocational education programs. Mark Dearing's contribution is based on his personal experiences teaching prison workshops. He enthusiastically conveys his belief that treating all students with unconditional positive regard has its rewards for both students and instructors.

Judy Porter reminds us of the importance of evaluating our vocational education programs through rigorous and methodologically sound research approaches. This is necessary to develop a body of knowledge about what works with various types of offenders, and to make a case for fiscal support of effective programs. Finally, Diane Young, while focusing on vocational education for incarcerated women, reminds us that excellent vocational education programs are one component of what is needed for successful community reentry to occur for previously incarcerated individuals. Correctional vocational education is viewed in a broader context of individual, societal and correctional system changes that contribute to positive outcomes for all of us.

Diane S. Young, Ph.D., MSW
University of Washington Tacoma, Social Work Program

CHAPTER I

PAST, PRESENT, AND FUTURE PROGRAMMING IN RURAL JAILS: A SNAPSHOT OF PENNSYLVANIA

by Jeremiah C. Gee

Abstract

This chapter presents an overview of programming available in rural jails in the Commonwealth of Pennsylvania. It is pertinent to the discourse on vocational education in that it shows where vocational education "fits" within the broader scope of programming altogether. When reading the chapter, you will notice that the vocational programs mentioned are not necessarily what one might find in a state prison, where particular skills are taught. Some county jails reported life skills, parenting skills, or computer skills classes being offered—but none reported training for a specific job skill or vocation as such. So, "vocational" in this chapter is taken in the broadest sense, meaning anything related to skills training.

Pennsylvania county jails are characterized by a variety of traits that they do not share with state prisons—for example, their funding sources draw from the county tax base and their populations turn over quickly. This presents a constraint on the opportunities that can be offered within county jails. As you read, consider what the inherent differences are between (a) vocational and other types of programs and (b) county jails and state institutions. How do programs' logistics and facilities' characteristics shape the opportunities that can be offered?

Introduction

While research at urban, state, and Federal facilities is relatively frequent, our nation's small and rural facilities are rarely the subject of targeted research. This survey was designed to answer the question: What is the extent of programming opportunities currently available to inmates in Pennsylvania's rural jails? The survey was administered as part of a master's thesis; it provides an idea of "what is out there" as a step toward evaluating program effectiveness in small correctional facilities. A brief introduction to the historical context of correctional programming is presented first, followed by the details of the current survey and its results. The final section discusses the future direction of correctional programming, with a focus on the need for more research in small facilities and a call for programs to be evaluated by asking about their sustainability.

I—Historical Context: Programming in the Past

The earliest correctional education program is believed to have started in Pennsylvania. Gehring cites clergyman William Rogers as the first provider of organized instruction in a United States correctional facility. He began teaching in Philadelphia's Walnut Street Jail in 1787. Gehring & Wright (2003) consider it the beginning of the "correctional education movement." One hundred years later, correctional instruction in Elmira, NY, was oriented toward so-called "handicapped" learners. Gehring lists some of the features of the Elmira, NY, facility as follows:

a. Systematic linkages between academic, social and vocational learning experiences;

b. Early morning individually tutored remedial instruction;

c. Individual diets and calisthenics, prescribed by the institutional physician;

d. Completely individualized student education files.

In this description of early programming, attention is paid, in detail, to the person. Gehring notes that even the physical measurements of each inmate were recorded. Aiding in the classification of inmates, and thus accepted for its efficiency, this system was the precursor to individualized prescribed instruction in today's public schools (commonly referred to as an Individualized Education Plan or IEP).

Correctional programming by facilities since then has become less individualized. Presumably to keep up with a growing inmate population, the programming tactic has been to "stack" one approach on top of another. This has resulted in a host of singular services to be provided; there is not an integrated system of delivery to correlate concepts from one program to another. As will be seen in the survey results below, a variety of programming is currently offered in Pennsylvania's small jails by a range of service organizations. Each program comes on-board with the correctional facility to serve the population, but they do not plug into an established conceptual framework, per se. While associations and agencies in correctional education do exist to unite programming efforts, usually for providers in Pennsylvania State facilities, the average program volunteer in a small county jail is unaware of or unaffiliated with these associations.

Programming in the Present

This background information begs the question, "Where are we now?" To round out the historical context of the current research, there are few reviews of correctional programming that are already published with direct relevance to rural and small populations. The first is from an unpublished manuscript by Ruddell (2005). In this literature review, Ruddell summarizes the problems that small jails face as challenges of geography, size, and economics. Regarding sustainability issues, Ruddell addresses the fact that small communities simply cannot afford extensive programs in their jails. He also notes that administrative problems are those common to many small businesses—making ends meet and making sure a competent staff exists. (This stands in contrast to what most people think of as "problems" in jail—i.e., gangs, riots, the severe adversity highlighted on, for example, MSNBC's "Lockup" TV show.)

The second research review was presented at the Academy of Criminal Justice Sciences conference by Patchin and Keveles (2004). This review assessed the integrity of the research base behind a spectrum of programming categories in correctional facilities. The authors noted that programming was accessible in small and rural facilities. Several of the areas defined by Patchin and Keveles were also found through the current survey, including community service, work release and substance abuse treatment. Patchin and Keveles specifically note recommendations for the rural Wisconsin area of their sample. "It is unclear the extent to which all of the programs are suitable for a small rural county. It may be advisable to coordinate efforts with adjacent jurisdictions so that resources can be pooled and more offenders can be served." (p. 12).

Patchin and Keveles note three goals for program delivery. Specifically, they highlight the need for awareness of risk factors "such as antisocial values, aggressiveness, academic failure, and weak family bonding" (p. 10). In order to target these behaviors, they write that cognitive behavioral and social learning strategies should be used. Finally, they call for an effective staff which "matches modes of treatment to the learning styles of offenders" (p. 10). This idea of "matching" needs and opportunities echoes the concept of individualization found in Elmira's first programs.

II—The Survey: A Closer Look at Present Programming Background

To limit the scope of the survey and facilitate comparisons between community demographics, only rural county jails were surveyed. The designation of rural was determined by consulting the Center for Rural Pennsylvania, which defines rural based on population density. In Pennsylvania there are 19 urban counties and 48 rural counties. Rural Pennsylvania counties have a range of population density from 11.6 people/sq. mile (Forest County) to 262.5 people/sq. mile (Lawrence County). Four counties do not have jails; they are Cameron (15.0 people/sq. mile) Fulton (32.6 people/sq. mile), Forest (11.6 people/sq. mile), and Sullivan (14.6 people/sq. mile). The would-be inmates of these counties are housed at other county facilities, most of which are also rural. These are four of the five least-populated counties in the Commonwealth. The remaining low-density county, which does have a jail, is Potter (16.7 people/sq. mile). Table 1 shows the population densities and average daily populations of the counties in the sample. The study participants were wardens of rural Pennsylvania county jails, with the exception that three of the 22 wardens who were contacted referred me to either a deputy warden or an administrator of inmate services.

Table 1: Population Densities of the Rural Counties Surveyed, Compared to the Average Daily Population (ADP) of their Correctional Facilities

	Population, 2000	# Square Miles Land	Population Density	Mean ADP	ADP housed elsewhere
Bedford	49,984	1,014.60	49.3	154	3
Cambria	152,598	688.09	221.8	425	15
Carbon	58,802	382.57	153.7	123	4
Clarion	41,765	602.49	69.3	84	0
Clearfield	83,382	1,147.38	72.7	137	< 1
Greene	40,672	575.91	70.6	112	1
Indiana	89,605	829.53	108.0	66	15
Juniata	22,821	391.63	58.3	30	5
Lawrence	94,643	360.49	262.5	252	2
Lycoming	120,044	1,234.93	97.2	317	55
McKean	45,936	981.62	46.8	71	0
Mercer	120,293	671.86	179.0	122	76
Mifflin	46,486	410.71	113.2	109	0
North-umberland	94,556	459.93	205.6	198	4
Potter	18,080	1,081.23	16.7	13	0
Schuylkill	150,336	778.61	193.1	247	Not reported
Snyder	37,546	331.23	113.4	121	0
Tioga	41,373	1,133.77	36.5	92	0
Union	41,624	316.76	131.4	34	26
Venango	57,565	675.11	85.3	155	2
Warren	43,863	883.47	49.6	110	5
Wayne	47,722	729.36	65.4	73	8
PA Total	12,281.054	44,819.61	274.0	138	0

Survey Instrument

The survey captured three categories of information: demographic, program-specific, and sustainability-oriented. The first category refers to questions regarding average population counts and ethnic composition. The second refers to types, frequencies, and restrictions on programming opportunities. The last refers to service providers, funding, future plans, and recidivism rates.

In order to assess the clarity of the survey questions, one local county warden completed the survey via telephone as a pilot test. It was determined that the questions were worded in such a manner as to gather the data as intended. During the course of the pilot, it was ascertained that one question, regarding variety and needs of local employers, was too time-consuming and seemed extraneous. For this reason, the question was dropped. Further input regarding acceptable wording for the survey instrument was gathered from discussion with my research mentor at Mansfield University.

Procedure

After the pilot test, the survey was administered by telephone on a Tuesday and Wednesday during the spring of 2006. The warden of the facility was requested by name; when he or she was reached, a script was followed which identified the caller as a graduate student conducting master's thesis research. The purpose of the research, its inclusion in a master's thesis, and possible uses in future research and publications were indicated as a measure of informed consent.

Initially, 21 rural counties were successfully contacted for inclusion in the convenience sample. After considering the sample by geographic location, it was determined that for a more even distribution one more county on the Maryland border should be included in the study. This raised the total sample size to 22 counties (half of the rural PA counties which have jails). The counties included in the sample are dotted on the map shown in Figure 1.

Figure 1: Geographic Distribution of Counties Surveyed

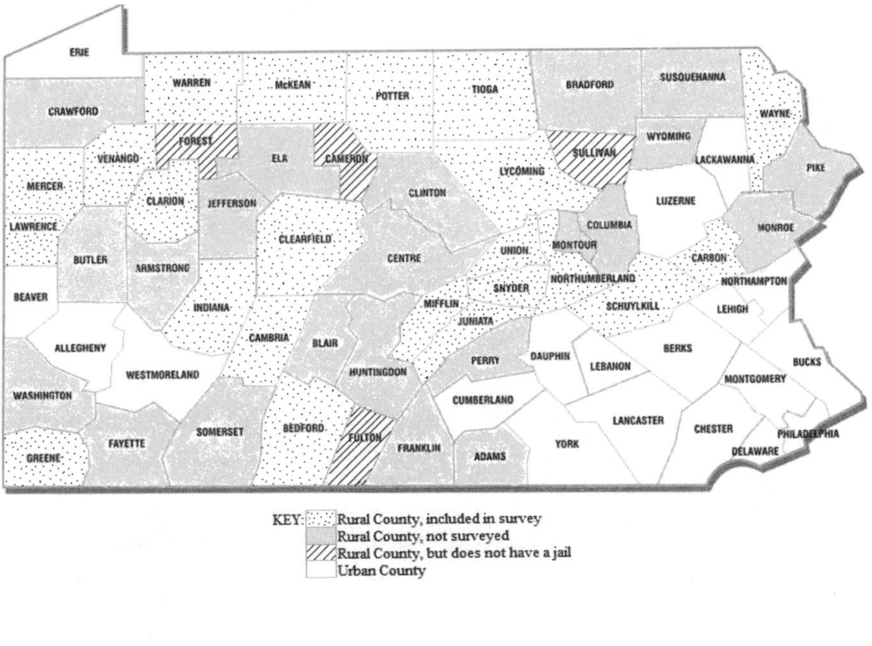

KEY:
Rural County, included in survey
Rural County, not surveyed
Rural County, but does not have a jail
Urban County

Data were summarized in a chart which appears in the results section below. Programming was thus quantified and subsequently cross-referenced with the data regarding facilities' average daily populations.

Survey results—Demographic Data

While no participant referenced data from a published report, most administrators said that White male inmates were the majority in their populations. However, two facilities, in Cambria and Northumberland counties, reported predominately Black populations. The 20 remaining counties reported estimated averages of 85%-90% Caucasian male inmates. Women, Blacks, and Hispanics comprised the remaining 10-15% of these populations.

When asked what the three most common convictions or charges were for inmates at their facilities, most respondents listed DUIs, drug or drug-related offenses (such as property crimes to obtain money for drugs), and parole violations. Several administrators offered comments regarding the relationship between different kinds of crimes which were ultimately drug-related in origin. For example, some felt that although burglary is not a drug crime, the cause of burglary is drug-related often enough for it to be considered drug-related in a broader sense. The average lengths of stay varied from three to 18 months. These data were not references to statistical research within the facilities; rather, they were estimates.

When reviewing the average daily population of each facility, it became evident that many of them house inmates in other counties. Fifteen of the 22 counties surveyed reported housing inmates in another county. The same number reported housing inmates from at least one other county. Inmates from the hosting facility are sometimes housed in exchange for the services rendered (i.e., inmates are "swapped"). If not, rent is charged per diem. Reasons given for population redistribution were (a) lack of a facility, (b) lack of room in a facility, and (c) behavior management (meaning to separate inmates from each other in order to preempt behavioral problems). Although there is a considerable amount of inmate reorganization, the trend does not seem to depend on population density as much as it does on facility capabilities. Some small counties have larger facilities than they technically need so they can rent space to other counties as a way of generating revenue.

Survey results—Program-Specific Data

The types of programming for these facilities fell into six main categories: (a) GED and literacy, (b) vocational and parent training, (c) church support, (d) counseling, (e) work release, and (f) transition skills. High-school students are supported through the local school districts or Intermediate Units (which provide selective services in Pennsylvania to several local school districts), so the first category includes only GED courses or specific programs in literacy.

It does not include post-secondary programming, as no county reported an opportunity for higher education which would result in college credit. Although college courses are offered regularly at many State and Federal facilities, they were not mentioned in the current study. The vocational and parent training category also includes job skills courses. Church support is defined as being either a Bible study or a Sunday service. The category of counseling involves all mental health-related professional services (anger management, e.g.) as well as Alcoholics Anonymous and Narcotics Anonymous. Work release experiences range from community service to in-house service to an individual's regular part- or full-time job. Finally, the category for transition skills was reserved for courses specifically focusing on pre-release inmates and the skills needed for reentry (securing housing, employment, and social support, e.g.).

Three facilities had a "director of inmate services" or coordinator for programming. One county reported that this position's purpose was to provide individualized program attention to each inmate. This county, Cambria, had the largest average daily population by far, as well as three full-time counselors. Several other counties reported having a person in charge of program scheduling. Cambria was an outlier both in its size and its extent of programming opportunities—it qualifies as a rural facility, but is not "small." Contrary to what one might assume, the chart below (Table 2) indicates that the smallest facilities are not devoid of programs. Both small and large facilities share a common trend: existent GED programs, multiple church services, and limited transition skills programs.

Table 2: Services, Ordered by Average Daily Population

Jurisdiction	People per Sq. Mile	Jail's ADP	GED	Vocational	Church	Counseling	Work Release	Transition
PA State	274.0	138						
Cambria	221.8	425	GED	Banking, budgeting, job-hunting, parenting & the Healthy Choices curriculum	Multiple groups per week	At least seven different services	Yes	Pre-release program
Lycoming	97.2	317	GED	None	Multiple groups	AA, NA	Yes	
Lawrence	262.5	252	GED	None	Multiple groups	AA, NA, by video	NR	
Schuylkill	193.1	247	GED	Alternative education program	Multiple groups	AA, NA	Yes	
Northumberland	205.6	198	GED	None	Multiple groups	AA, NA, counseling course	Yes	
Venango	85.3	155	GED	Access to County technical center; parenting class	Multiple groups	AA, NA, Counselor	Yes	
Bedford	49.3	154	GED, literacy	None	Multiple groups	AA, NA, and staff counselor	Yes	

(Continued on following page)

Table 2: Services, Ordered by Average Daily Population Cont'd.

Jurisdiction	People per Sq. Mile	Jail's ADP	GED	Vocational	Church	Counseling	Work Release	Transition
Clearfield	72.7	137	GED	Job skills, budgeting, garden program	Multiple groups	AA, NA, Counseling	NR	
Carbon	153.7	123	None	None	Multiple groups	AAA, NA, Tri-county Agency	NR	
Mercer	179.0	122	GED, literacy	None	Multiple groups	AA, NA	Yes	
Snyder	113.4	121	GED	Life skills, arts & crafts	Multiple groups	AAA, NA, full-time counselor & four-county agency		
Greene	70.6	112	GED	Parenting, with individualized & group classes	Multiple groups	AA, NA	Internal & com. service	
Warren	49.6	110	GED	Healthy Relationships program through county Human Services mandatory after 90 days	Multiple groups	AA, NA, County MHHS	Yes	
Mifflin	113.2	109	GED	Career Link, parenting	Multiple groups	At least six different services	Yes, inside & outside	
Tioga	36.5	92	GED	Computer skills, parenting, & a rehabilitative block	Multiple groups	AA, NA, contracted counseling in-house	Yes	
Clarion	69.3	84	GED, literacy	Economics skills, nutrition, self-empowerment	Multiple groups	AA, NA	NR	
Wayne	65.4	73	GED	None	Multiple groups	AA, NA	Yes	
McKean	46.8	71	GED	Parenting plus classes for life skills	Multiple	AA, NA	NR	
Indiana	108.0	66	Tutors	Healthy Choices, sex education, business mentorship, parenting, life skills class	Multiple groups	AA, NA, Counseling	NR	Transition program
Union	131.4	34	None	None	Multiple groups	Access to four-county agency	NR	
Juniata	58.3	30	GED	None	Chaplain	AA, NA	Yes	
Potter	16.7	13	High school on furlough	Computer skills	Multiple groups	NA inside AA outside	Yes	

Note: "NR" means No response.

Wardens noted that attendance frequencies for the first five categories were high (GED, Vocational, Church, Counseling, and Work Release); they gave estimates that about 50% of their general populations participate in at least one program. Almost every program is offered at least once per week. One restriction on eligibility for programs was mentioned by two counties—they would not permit an inmate in solitary confinement to begin enrollment in a new program.

However, they did not necessarily prohibit attendance in programs for which the person had already enrolled.

The counties which offer GED programs are serviced on a volunteer basis through collaboration with local individuals, universities, and literacy councils. The intensity of programming extends from "handing them a book" upon request to more-or-less formal class settings. The survey results suggest that facilities with higher average daily populations offer more intense GED and literacy programs. All counties, regardless of size, are provided service by their local school district or Intermediate Unit for high school-aged individuals in their populations. These students have the opportunity to attend programs offered at the GED level as well as those offered through school districts or Intermediate Units (they are not limited to either one or the other).

Regarding programming as a whole, many respondents commented that participation both "passes the time and looks good" for inmates. Wardens made it clear that they offer programs because they perceive that people need them. When asked about programs that had closed, only two references were made to past programs. The overall attitude toward programming was summarized by several respondents in the statement that "a good inmate is a busy inmate." In some cases, participation is court-mandated. No matter why a particular program is offered, it is generally welcomed by the administration, especially if it is cost-free. Regarding potential new programs, one warden said, "I'll try anything once." This welcoming attitude is typical of what was heard from wardens of the other counties as well.

Survey results—Sustainability-Oriented Data

Finally, questions regarding service providers, funding for programs, future plans, and recidivism rates were taken as indications of overall sustainability of program efforts. All counties surveyed reported partnerships with at least one (and, in some cases, several) community-based efforts in supporting their programs. Inter-county providers were identified in addition to Pennsylvania Department of Education's Intermediate Units. These providers are human service agencies similar to those which many counties have individually; they offer counseling services to inmates at more than one county facility. Several counties currently contract for counseling support rather than hiring a full-time counselor as a corrections staff member.

The survival of programming is dependent on the tax base of the county and on some Federal funding, but mostly on volunteer efforts. It was reported that little, if any, funding for the facilities' administration of programs came from grant-funded resources. Two participants listed obtaining grants to expand programming as a goal for their facility. Others noted that outside providers sometimes obtain grants to work inside correctional facilities, and that these monies are not tied to the jail's income or expenses.

To be fiscally sustainable, an investment ought to have a return. In corrections, this translates into decreased recidivism rates and changed lives—neither of which is easy to measure or validate. When asked about this component of sustainability, administrators had little hard evidence to share regarding current recidivism rates. One participant referenced an unpublished study at his facility about two years ago, and the recidivism rate of that county was 79%. Gee (2005) reported a recidivism rate of 83% in one northern Pennsylvania county. Of the 19 participants who made an educated guess at their recidivism rate, six reported 70% or higher, eight said between 50 and 70%, and the remaining five said between 25 and 50%.

Conclusion

Overall, programming for the sampled Pennsylvania counties follows a shotgun approach, meaning that it has a broad scope viewed globally and that programs operate independently of each other. Providers do not necessarily have an awareness or understanding of each other's efforts. The programming does not result in holistic applications, meaning that individuals do not participate in a set of programs tailored to their individual needs. While some jails have program coordinators, and some have counselors, it is not apparent that the Commonwealth of Pennsylvania provides adequate monies to fund individualized program participation in small jails. There is also a lack of individualized program service providers who have ample resources to fund and maintain assessments of correctional programs.

In spite of these constraints, rural Pennsylvania counties are able to offer their inmates a range of services to address educational and personal counseling needs. Vocational and religious needs are provided through community endeavors, and work release is available to some inmates. To their credit, wardens have managed to successfully maintain collaborative partnerships with community resources, and they remain open toward future improvements in programming.

III—Implications for the Future of Programming

The Need for More Research

If there is such a variety of programming, then why is there still so much recidivism? Do we really know which programs work and which do not? How do we define a successful program? The answers to these questions tie together the need for program assessment and the importance of what is meant by being sustainable. In order to determine where a system of programming excels (or falls short), it must be assessed along some axis or in relation to some standard. Here, the standards are tacit. Recidivism is discussed as a measure of success, but its definition is not standardized—and comparing rates from jail to jail is a complicated procedure (Lyman & LoBuglio, 2007). Furthermore, small jails do not have the monies to track and compare recidivism rates. Even if they did, whose definition would they use? Would they all use the same standards for data processing?

Without a more comprehensive research base at the county level, programming will not be evaluated systematically and assumptions will go unchallenged. A substantial change must occur in the way programming at the rural county level is assessed as a whole, for it simply is not being assessed as a whole. Researching state-level facilities alone is a major undertaking, and research in small jails seemingly falls by the wayside. The high rates of recidivism, as estimated by the sampled respondents, imply a lack of "correction" in the counties surveyed. Further—because of a lack of research—instructors, administrators, and service providers at the county level are limited to a few assumptions about inmate needs when they plan programming. Research, properly coordinated, will provide an assessment of program effectiveness and highlight best practices for meeting inmates' specific needs.

The Need for a Sustainable Community Effort

In the end, we are faced with the reality that it is the responsibility of the community (not simply the job of its warden) to "correct" socially undesirable behavior. So, what is a warden to do? Pennsylvania's wardens are to be commended for setting the standard by involving the community in their programming and being open toward research in their facilities (such as the survey presented here).

One logical next step would be to integrate transition skills into the programming curricula in our local county jails. Sustainability is directly tied to transition skills: To sustain the personal changes that begin in jail, a program participant must be able to re-enter the community with the requisite competencies and disposition, and with follow-up support. The sampled wardens had positive attitudes toward enhancing the programming in their facilities, and several mentioned desire for transition programs.

Research suggests that educational programming is a cost effective way to combat recidivism (Steurer, Smith, & Tracy, 2001), but funding projects is a constant battle. The proceeds from work release and commissary funds are not enough to fund a network of service providers throughout Pennsylvania. Jails that charge inmates per diem housing costs do not profit enough to fund community-based transition programs. Moreover, a decline in recidivism would not immediately affect the financial status of a facility or community; it takes time for the economic impact of lower corrections-related costs to be felt.

To this end, programming that is sustainable must be designed to generate opportunities rather than to (only) consume them. A truly sustainable program would not require a continuous influx of tax-payer or grant money. The sustainable curriculum is defined by its holistic nature. It embraces the needs of learners, institutions, and communities by offering the most economical and effective opportunities. While some states have seen trends toward regionalization of jails, the question arises as to whether the actual physical facilities need to be regionalized, or if one set of programs can be administered centrally.

Community involvement is crucial for successful re-entry to society, as many inmates are impacted by short lengths of stay. Simply put, one tentative explanation for high recidivism rates is that periods of incarceration are too short to result in a life pattern or behavior change without continued community involvement. In a rural community, a citizen's crime and subsequent incarceration creates a proportionately larger ripple effect than does an urban counterpart's, much like a boulder dropped in a mud puddle would create a bigger washout than one dropped in a pond. Programming that will work specifically for small communities is needed.

In short, it behooves us to study the results of programs, specifically those in rural and small facilities, so we can use the results to improve programming and discern best practices. The future direction of correctional programming ought to be sustainable; it must (a) parsimoniously bridge the gap between the correctional facility and the community, and (b) cause enduring change rather than a temporary interruption of behavior cycles. Programming must be community-based and "follow through" with the inmate after release. Without high levels of pre- and post-release community-based involvement, it is impractical to believe that recidivism in small communities will decline.

Biographical Sketch

Mr. Gee instructs a GED class at a local county prison through a grant managed by Mansfield University of Pennsylvania's Center for Lifelong Learning. This chapter is drawn from his master's thesis, which researched the needs and opportunities available to inmates in rural county correctional facilities. It originally appeared in the 2007 September/October issue of *American Jails* and is reprinted here with permission.

CHAPTER II

VOCATIONAL EDUCATION IN PRISON: FIVE POLICY AND PEDAGOGY ISSUES

by Bill Muth

Vocational education (VE) is a broad term that applies to a range of programs and approaches to learning. Technical literacy, soft skills, computational proficiency, written and oral communication, information management, cultural knowledge, apprenticeships (explicit and tacit learning), related trades, and participation in discourse communities share this big tent with specific hard skill content areas like carpentry framing, word processing, and certified physical trainer programs. Add to this wide topic the complexities of prison and re-entry systems, and we begin to grasp the multitude of themes related to prison-based VE.

This chapter will address selected broad issues related to two dimensions of VE—policy and pedagogy. These issues are not meant to be comprehensive, nor is my coverage of them exhaustive. However, I do hope to stir things up and provoke reactions and reflection. The chapter is intended to assist busy practitioners—including teachers, administrators, and policy makers—with some key questions to guide discussion (with our colleagues or ourselves) to inform our personal and collective philosophies of practice. Given the dynamic state of our world, and the extraordinary potential of VE to adapt to and transform it, an on-going process of critical reflection seems not only timely, but urgently needed.

The first section, Context, raises issues related to globalization. Five issues—three associated with policy and two with pedagogy—are then presented. The Policy Issues section addresses selected issues related to program scope, delivery models, and re-entry. Next, in Pedagogy Issues, I address social-reflective learning and digital technology.

I am not a VE teacher. However, for almost 20 years, in past roles as School Principal and Education Administrator for the Federal Bureau of Prisons (FBOP), I managed vocational training and advanced occupational education programs. At both the school and system levels, I have been responsible for setting VE policy, establishing program goals, working with accreditation agencies and trade organizations, hiring staff, defending and establishing budgets, and evaluating program performance. I currently teach adult learning and literacy courses at Virginia Commonwealth University. Thus the chapter is confined to those VE dimensions I know something about—policy and pedagogy. I wish to thank Robert Mattucci for inviting me to contribute to this much needed book, and congratulate him for having the wisdom, knowledge and energy to take up this project.

Context Issues

The United States' economy has rapidly shifted from an industrial base to an informational one (ACTE, 2008). Accordingly, the Association for Career and Technical Education (ACTE, pp. 1-2) notes that

> The globalization of business and industry requires workers to acquire core knowledge and skills that can be applied—and quickly upgraded and adapted—in a wide and rapidly changing variety of work settings. Unfortunately, the skills of Americans have not kept pace. More than 80 percent of respondents in the 2005 National Association of Manufacturers Skills Gap report indicated that they are experiencing a shortage of qualified workers overall – with 13 percent reporting severe shortages. The U.S. Chamber of Commerce also reports a growing skills gap. In the 2002 Keeping Competitive report, 73 percent of employers reported 'very' or 'somewhat' severe conditions when trying to hire qualified workers.

These two issues—the need for skills that transfer (allow for flexible retraining) and a generally under-skilled workforce—present enormous challenges and opportunities for correctional educators. Unlike community-based training and educational programs in which adult learners frequently cannot persist because of work, transportation and dispositional barriers (Comings, Parrella & Soricone, 1999), prison-based VE accomplishes extraordinary results. Where prison VE programs exist, they are well attended, achieve high completion rates, reduce recidivism and pay for themselves by reducing the costs associated with repeated incarcerations.

Numerous studies have documented the effectiveness of VE in terms of reduced taxpayer costs and reduced recidivism (Aos, Phipps, Barnoski & Lieb 2001; Saylor & Gaes, 1997). Nevertheless, Lawrence, Mears, Dubin and Travis (2002, p. 1) report that "Few states come close to providing the levels and quality of programming that research indicates are needed to positively impact employment or other outcomes." In fact, the Mears team note that participation in prison-based VE declined from 31 to 27 percent between 1991 and 1997. This failure to invest in VE is a failure of correctional policy in the U.S.* But it also is a failed economic policy, given the effects of globalization noted above. It is within this context of urgent challenges and opportunities that the following policy and pedagogical issues are presented.

---

* One noteworthy exception is the Federal Second Chance Act, which allocated $5 million for technology careers training demonstration grants in 2010 (Reentry Policy Council, 2010).

Policy Issues

Where is VE located? To what extent are these programs embedded in post secondary programs, such as those afforded by the recent Youthful Offenders Grants administered through the U.S. Department of Education, that enabled learners to earn college credit? What percentage of our programs are set aside for those learners who may not be high school graduates or GED completers? What distinguishes post-secondary VE programs from other VE? Are the former more theoretical and the latter more concrete? What non-formal settings host VE learning experiences (formal or non-formal)? To what degree do VE programs address transferable skills in addition to (or in the place of) job-specific hard skills?

Transferability Issues

Workers today need the knowledge and skills to quickly upgrade and adapt to rapidly changing technologies. The Association for Career and Technical Education (ACTE, 2008) refers to these transferable, generic skills as "workforce readiness skills" (p. 4), which include such competencies as "basic employability skills, and reading, writing and communication skills" (p. 2) and "locating information, listening, teamwork and observation" (p. 4). More specifically, this "technical literacy" (p. 4) includes the ability to

> apply academic knowledge and skills to a broad field of technical studies; read, understand and communicate in the language of the technical field; understand technical concepts and principles; and use technology to complete projects in a specific career/technical field. (ACTE, p. 4).

ACTE noted that these workforce readiness skills are often measured with such national assessment instruments as the ACT National Career Readiness Certificate™ (based on ACT WorkKeys®), the National Work Readiness Credential, CASAS Workforce Skills Certificate and the SkillsUSA Workplace Readiness Certificate. They note however, that these instruments are still in early stages of development.

Given the tendency of traditional VE programs to focus on trade-specific hard skills (plumbing, guide dog training), what kinds of accommodations for generic skills should correctional policy makers consider? Policy makers might be tempted to eliminate traditional VE programs—those with a proven track record of reducing recidivism—in favor of generic, one-size-fits-all technical literacy programs. But this would not be wise for many reasons. I present two: (a) Given the profound difficulties some individuals have finding skilled work when they re-enter society (even equipped with VE certificates), will more generic or foundational skills, even if they provide a more highly valued skill set in theory, actually impede employability in a specific trade? (see Re-entry below). (b) Both the National Research Council and the National Academies

15

of Science encourage learning in context as opposed to decontextualized, academic learning (ACTE, 2008). They urge the design of engaging curricula and assessments that apply to real-world situations:

> This is critical. . .for workforce readiness skills. . .The national and state level credentials, while validating different skills, all attempt to verify that a student will be prepared to excel in the workplace, rather than an isolated classroom or testing center. Assessments that are utilized for these work readiness credentials assess workplace-related skills in as authentic an environment as possible, and include topics not typically addressed in academic environments. (p. 4).

Generic (transferable) skills, then, are still best taught within the contexts of specific, real-life trade programs. I will present further critical advantages of contextualized learning in the Pedagogy section below. It appears then that the question of transferable skills versus hard skills is not "either-or" but rather one of integration. Thus, the problem may best be framed in this way:

Issue 1. How should transferable "technical literacy" skills be integrated into VE programs that continue to lead to credentials within specific trades? Which skills should be included?

Delivery Models

Should all VE occur in formal classrooms? What role should apprenticeships and on-the-job training programs play in correctional education? Official Department of Labor-certified apprenticeship programs have maintained a small but relatively stable place in prison education for decades. However, on-the-job training (OJT)—as an officially recognized correctional educational program—seemed to fall out of favor in many systems during the 1970s. They were often viewed as poorly defined and difficult to structure in ways that protected the learner's ability to acquire skills.

With the advent of business-government-trade organization partnerships that are leading to new nationally standardized assessments for technical literacy (job readiness skills), perhaps it is time to reconsider OJT. The Encyclopedia of Business (2006) describes two types of on-the-job training—structured (planned) and unstructured (unplanned).

> Unstructured is the most common kind and refers to loose on-the-job training programs. . .Unstructured training is designed based on work requirements (e.g. manufacturing products), not on imparting job skills needed by new workers (e.g. the

specific skills needed to manufacture products). Consequently, unstructured on-the-job training often fails to impart needed skills fully or consistently, because experienced employees sometimes are unable to articulate clearly the proper methods for performing a job and they sometimes use different training methods each time they train new workers. In contrast, structured on-the-job training involves a program designed to teach new workers what they must know and do in order to complete their tasks successfully. (5th paragraph).

What may be noteworthy today is the structure afforded by the previously mentioned new national assessments. By articulating generic-level (transferable, technical literacy) skills embedded in specific prison job assignments, and aligning them with national standards, it may be possible to leverage some prison work assignments by converting them to structured OJT programs which, with the addition of formal assessments, could lead to certificates of completions and transcripts that document nationally recognized skill sets.

This up-front work might be costly, and might have to be implemented incrementally, perhaps starting with the highest skilled prison jobs. A genuine commitment from staff at all levels—warden, case manager, detail supervisor— would be required to ensure that skill assessments were conducted in credible ways, documents were authenticated and housed in prisoners' central files, and processes did not devolve into paper programs. More costly quality controls might be required, but they would be less expensive than the cost of formal VE programs. Given the very limited numbers of prisoners that have access to VE, this delivery format might be worth reconsidering. The Federal Bureau of Prisons, at the time of this writing, is in fact experimenting with similarly embedded OJT training venues.

One positive side effect of this strategy is the inclusion of correctional staff into educative roles. Since job foremen and detail supervisors often mentor and coach their workers, this would provide a way to recognize situated learning and teaching that otherwise would remain tacit. A negative side effect might be the inclination to replace formal VE with on-the-job training. While tempting in times of budgetary reduction, given the documented success of VE programs and the growing political support for them, this strategy would be both shortsighted and amoral. Given these concerns, perhaps the issue could be framed this way:

Issue 2. Can structured OJT programs be established that have valid assessment and credentialing processes, and nationally accepted skill sets? Can they be implemented in ways that augment—rather than compete with—VE budgets so more individuals can re-enter society with marketable, technical literacy skills?

In many systems, including the FBOP, individuals leaving prisons are expected to get a job quickly. The time frame is often as short as two weeks to 30 days. Yet few VE completers get hired into fields for which they were trained inside when they first leave prison. This is the result despite recent prison-based re-entry innovations such as career development centers and job fairs, and model community treatment centers that include supports such as job development counselors and bonding programs for employers. Multiple reasons can be cited for this mismatch: lack of skilled jobs; state or corporate regulations that prohibit ex-offenders from licensure; insufficient time to find the ideal job; lack of bonding opportunities for employers; obsolete VE programs; and inadequate inside-outside information networks that fail to transfer transcripts, certificates, and other educational records to prospective employers and job developers.

The particularly disturbing aspect of these post-release employment issues is not the mismatch between skill learning and employment, but the fact that many prisoners, unless they return to a skilled job they had prior to incarceration, settle for unskilled, entry level work to satisfy conditions of probation or parole. Policies that work at cross purposes are costly—such as indiscriminate use of short time frames to get a job. We know that job retention for workers in skilled positions is greater than for those in unskilled positions. Further, Kling, Weiman, and Western (2000) found a relationship between wages, work, and crime. They estimated that a 10 percent decrease in an individual's wages could result in a 10 to 20 percent increase in criminal activity and incarceration. Thus, policies that pressure individuals to take unskilled jobs immediately upon release may undermine prison-based VE training investments and lead to job dissatisfaction, turnover and increased recidivism.

Should we consider post release employment as a two- (or multi-) staged process? Should we expect VE completers leaving prison to take an unskilled first job, develop soft skills such as dependability and professional courtesy, and, after a set period of time, seek skilled work? This is a particular problem for those who acquired their first marketable skills while in prison (i.e, have no skilled work history prior to incarceration). In this scenario, what extended role should be developed for community treatment professionals so continuity of support is provided until these individuals finally attain skilled employment? Will these extended efforts be worth the costs?

Conversely, could we connect the dots of re-entry programs so prisoners can apply for skilled work and set up job interviews before they are released from prison? First-generation re-entry programs relevant to this approach would include job fairs, career development centers, document transfers from prison to community, and community-based job development.

If both of the solutions above seem unattainable, I urge readers to provide alternative and more feasible ones. Leaving these issues unaddressed should not be an option. It would be tantamount to resigning ourselves to existing policies and the likelihood that across America, two-thirds of the 660,000 prisoners released from prison annually will return within three years. VE completers recidivate at impressively lower rates than those who have not been in VE programs; but there is still much unrealized potential. Undoubtedly there are great complexities faced by ex-prisoners, probation officers, community treatment specialists, receiving families and community employers. The young field of re-entry has made many promising starts, such as the career development centers and job fairs mentioned above, as well as more intensive community corrections services. But it will take public support, political will, and enormous perseverance to achieve the goals espoused by the re-entry community.

In this section I focused on re-entry policy issue (employment) among many (drug abuse, housing, family re-entry, etc.) realizing that no single issue exists in isolation. Nevertheless this re-entry issue is quite difficult enough. It is:

> Issue 3. How can we build to scale a continuum of support that spans from inside VE to post-release skilled employment?

Pedagogy Issues

To what extent are VE curricula based on established adult learning principles? Many vocational teachers are experts in their trades, and their love for teaching and their trades is contagious and admirable. Experts are gifted in many ways. They know what to attend to, what to ignore; they know how to spot problems quickly; they know how to remember important facts in orderly ways, and are efficient in retrieving relevant information from their memories. But Bransford, Brown and Cocking (2000) observed that experts often are not very good at explaining their craft to others. Perhaps this is because so much of what they do is on a tacit, or automatic, level, they never have to "think" about it. So an important pedagogical question needs to be asked here: As correctional educators, how does our pedagogical knowledge match with our content knowledge? In this section I take on two issues: one directly related to pedagogy (social learning), and one that is grounded in both pedagogy and policy (digital technology).

Social-Reflective Learning in Prison

Andragogy (Knowles, 1998; Lindeman, 1926) roughly means pedagogy for adults. I have deliberately not used this term throughout the chapter for two reasons. First, I anticipate that some readers may work with younger students, and the term pedagogy is more universally applied to all learning (children and adults), despite its root, ped. Second, claims that andragogical learning principles apply exclusively to adults have been contested. Nevertheless, andragogy has made important contributions to pedagogy over the years. For example, Knowles (1987) studied the way prior experience forms the base for new learning in adults, and Brookfield (1987) emphasized critical reflection as a method for identifying one's own mature purposes for learning. The idea of social-reflective learning is implied in these ideas (building on prior experience, reflective self-awareness).

Social-reflective learning refers to the ways learners construct ideas about the world and their own identities through dialogue. The term reflective learning does not emphasize the social dimension to the act of reflection. (Even if reflection is done in private, one carries on a conversation with one's self, and this conversation is often nourished by past and future conversations with significant others.) This may seem exotic to VE, but I will argue that especially in VE the potential for social-reflective learning is great.

Unlike some prison academic literacy classrooms, where instruction is usually individualized, VE often affords learners opportunities to work on projects in small groups. In these small group experiences, under the tutelage of the vocational teacher, students learn trade community discourses (ways of expressing, thinking, acting). This learning is often tacit—it goes on unconsciously, without planned instruction—and that is appropriate. Much socialization into new communities (entering into a new church community or going back to school and fitting in on campus after many years away) is done at the tacit level, yet we learn well how to carry ourselves in these new communities. By constructing authentic, real-life contexts for learning, traditional shop classes can be outstanding contexts for learning how to participate in new trade communities. That is why I agree with others about the need to maintain traditional VE programs (see Transferability above).

Compare this situated, social learning to an individualized, decontextualized literacy classroom. In these literacy rooms students often learn how to "do school." But they may not learn how to draw on academic skills to help them with real-life matters, such as using journals to reflect on the mistakes of their past, or writing letters home to help their children solve problems at school. In VE shops, students learn the social aspects of the trades as well as novice level cognitive and motor skills.

Many VE classes afford great authentic opportunities for tacit social learning. But how many VE courses are structured to take advantage of these social networks by building opportunities for dialogue and personal reflection? When a cohort of learners moves through the VE program together, a strong social community of practice sometimes develops. When it does, a space may open before them unlike any other place in prison: a psychologically safe environment. It is within these safe spaces that meaningful dialogue can (and does) take place. Whether the conversations are sanctioned by the instructor or not, students in these safe spaces will share their hopes and dreams, fears and concerns with each other.

Some teachers believe we should simply be teaching trade skills. However Gehring (1988) argued that, unless we concern ourselves with the whole student in correctional education, we will likely end up with a skilled criminal rather than a transformed person. What separates instrumental teaching (concerned with skill acquisition) from transformative teaching (concerned with attitudes, beliefs, habits of mind, and world views)? This question is related to teaching roles: when we wear our teachers-as-experts hat, we are the authorities and our knowledge counts; when we wear our teacher-as-facilitator hat, students become authorities and their knowledge counts. Having the judgment to know when to switch from expert to facilitator may have to do with knowing when and how to use safe spaces to guide dialogue. Prisoners often do not possess the reflective skills necessary for self-examination, realistic self-appraisal, goal setting, etc. If we do not afford them opportunities to reflect rationally and critically on their lives, or, put another way, to take stock of the situation, when will they have a chance to develop the capacity to reflect, come to terms with their lives and themselves, and transform?

Not all social-reflective experiences are constructive. Sometimes conversations can become too personal for the teacher's or the student's comfort. The degree to which shared personal experiences lead to healing and helpful reflection depends, in a large part, on the comfort level and motivations of the teacher. Three specific conditions seem essential to this: (a) the student is not coerced to participate, (b) the teacher is comfortable knowing when and how to respectfully draw the student out and how to draw a line, and (c) the purpose is based on student needs (not the curiosity of the teacher or others). Where these conditions exist, constructive social reflections have a chance of emerging naturally, often in modest, spontaneous, and deeply meaningful ways. Many correctional educators are quite comfortable facilitating social-reflective dialogue. They cultivate spaces in the classroom for students to work through personal problems when the issues are related to the broad goals of the program—such as negotiating their criminal history in a letter to a prospective employer, thinking through possible parenting strategies to meet a specific crisis at home, or developing release plans. But other caring and talented teachers find this level of dialogue unmanageable. We each have our own ways of building rapport with students, and what works for one teacher might not for another.

No matter how we approach the issue of rapport, we never forget they are prisoners and we are, in effect, their keepers. We cross borders (Wright, 2008) every time we reach out to help a student, no matter how impersonally this contact manifests itself. Each teacher negotiates this differently, and these differences must be respected. However, as a profession we can, and need, to do more—in VE and in literacy—to design safe spaces for dialogue. Reluctant teachers will develop confidence and competence in facilitating reflective dialogue if these skills are formally taught. Those teachers who already possess the facilitation skills and dispositions should be recruited to conduct (facilitate) staff development programs in social-reflective learning. These programs should address both skills—like learning how to conduct role plays, how to implement a journal writing program, how to listen, or how to set group boundaries and norms—as well as dispositions (confidence, tolerance, respect).

Keeping in mind both the need to expand our use of social-reflective learning and respect for individual educators to establish their own limits in its use, I suggest this way of framing issue four:

> Issue 4. How can we expand the use of social-reflective practices to support learners' abilities to voice their hopes and fears, confront their pasts, and plan their futures? How can we do this in a way that respects the personal boundaries of teachers and students and strengthens, rather than weakens, institutional security?

Digital technology

There is little argument that computer and information literacies are essential. In 2004 alone, over five exabytes of new information were generated (the equivalent of 32 Libraries of Congress), and the world's information is now doubling every 20 months (Merriam, Caffarella, & Baumgartner, 2007). Computer skills are "critical to employability" (Comings, Garner, & Smith, C., 2004, p. 119). Stites (2004) claimed that learning how to navigate and use the internet is now a basic skill:

> Learning how to learn with computers and the Internet are important basic skills for life in the 21st century. . .The new learning technologies are well suited to learner-centered, goal-driven, socially interactive, and authentic applications in support of adult literacy and life long learning. (p. 110).

Technology education also can augment transferable learning, such as "higher order thinking, problem solving, creativity, and integrated skills development" (Stites, p. 114) as well as discipline-specific skills such as drafting. However, Stites (2004) noted that not all computer-assisted instruction is effective. Successful technology instruction embodies careful planning, authentic learning contexts (see Transferability), social-learning opportunities (see Social-Reflective Learning), and frequent feedback from the instructor.

Yet the digital divide between the haves and have-nots—like the socio-economic gap—is growing. Lack of access to the digital world has both an economic impact (i.e., accelerating the deterioration of the U.S. workforce) and a social justice impact (i.e., causing more peoples and whole-communities to slip into—or further into—marginalization and poverty). To date, adult education policy in the U.S. has failed to keep up with this daunting problem.

While all demographic groups are gaining access to computers and the internet, Stites (2004) cautioned that, "disparities remain, and the digital 'have nots'—minority groups (particularly Blacks and Hispanics), and older people (especially those not in the workforce)—continue to lag far behind national trends in computer and Internet use" (p. 120). In 2001, about 40 percent of Black households and 32 percent of Hispanic households had internet access. Of those who lacked a high school education, only 11.7 percent had internet access in 2000, compared to 49 percent of those with just some college experience. Most incarcerated adult literacy learners may not have had Internet access at home prior to prison, and, in the vast majority of cases they do not have access to it while in prison.

D'Amico (2004) argued that without courageous moral action at the institutional level in the information age, the SES (socio-economic status) gap between low-literacy and high literacy adults in the U.S. will continue to widen. Since 1980, earnings of 25- to 34-year old men who had not completed high school dropped by 30 percent, while college graduates' incomes rose by 60 to 133 percent. It is hard to deny D'Amico's argument regarding the lack of access to quality education, that "class, race and gender. . .act in concert in their effects on our institutions. . ." (p.19). She understood that adult educators want their programs to improve social equality, but cautioned that they "may be mandated to teach in ways that reinforce rather than transform differences of class, race, gender, and sexual orientation" (p. 18).

D'Amico (2004) directly challenged us to action by ". . .questioning and challenging the status quo" (36). Taking up this challenge, I argue strenuously that it is time to rethink responsible internet access for prisoners. There are numerous, though isolated, models of internet use in prison today.

- Intranet based law-libraries, housed in central-office file servers, download new content from venders periodically; the electronic materials are then distributed to the field via the intranet system.

- Universities provide secure on-line access to incarcerated students enrolled in their courses.

- Incarcerated parents maintain ties with their children through secure video-conferencing.

- Prisoners receive and send e-mail, screened by staff, to those who are on their approved correspondence list.

I respect the important security issues related with this topic, particularly in post 9-11 America, where terrorist networks are of primary national security interest. That is why I advocate responsible and cautious growth in internet use. I make this argument for all the social justice and economic reasons above, and also for the following ones: (a) Almost all correspondence courses are now on-line access only. Since the loss of Pell grants and the elimination of hard-copy correspondence courses, VE in prisons has been drastically reduced. (b) As noted above, digital technology is a basic skill, like reading and writing. To prohibit it by policy is to institutionalize a huge educational barrier that impedes higher-level technical learning of critical, transferable skills. (c) Internet-based educational resources are often inexpensive and can be used quite effectively to leverage precious correctional programs budgets. However, as noted in the Social-Reflective Learning section above, access to digital technology should never replace face-to-face learning in prison. Further, as Stites (2004) warned, quality technical instruction requires careful planning and attention to sound educational principles such as social learning, frequent feedback and real-life experiences. I frame issue five with these pedagogical, policy and security cautions in mind:

> Issue 5. How can the internet be accessed by prisoners in ways that maintain security, enhance the quality and relevance of learning, and leverage instructional budgets?

Conclusion

In this chapter I framed five broad issues that concern prison-based vocational education. For each issue, background information was provided that may serve to inform relevant discussions. It is my hope that teachers, administrators and policy makers will find some of these (or related) issues useful and the chapter format appropriate for creating discussion groups, planning retreats, or instigating other forms of dialogue. Each of the five issues is complex and some may be beyond the capacity of individuals or even individual systems to resolve. Perhaps the issue-based structure will support efforts to bring diverse stakeholders together. The concerns in this chapter in no way are meant to demean VE as a discipline. In fact, there are few educational programs more relevant and equipped to address the complex societal, moral and economic problems we face today. It is because of the extraordinary potential of VE to address vast societal challenges that we should embrace the five issues raised above so that VE's full potential can be realized.

Biographical Sketch

Bill Muth is an Assistant Professor of Adult and Adolescent Literacy at Virginia Commonwealth University. Until August 2005, Bill was the Education Administrator for the Federal Bureau of Prisons. Other positions with the FBOP included: reading teacher, principal, and Chief of the Program Analysis Branch. In 2004 Bill earned his Doctorate in Adult Literacy from George Mason University. His research interests include Thirdspace and Reading Components theories, especially as these apply to prison-based family literacy programs and children of incarcerated parents.

CHAPTER III

FREEDOM TO DREAM:
RECOLLECTIONS OF VOCATIONAL EDUCATION
IN SUFFOLK COUNTY CORRECTIONS

by Dwight Stecker

What follows represents one person's memory regarding Vocational Education in New York's Suffolk County Department of Corrections. That person is me, Dwight Stecker.

Almost twenty years ago, one of our students incarcerated in Suffolk County's Riverhead Facility wrote the following:

Freedom To Dream
by W.M.

The wind blows quietly as the grass stirs softly on the other side
of Hell.
The bars on my window are only a near reality,
the fantasy that I see when I look at the road in the distance.

The days pass slowly by and the tears turn to ice as the chain on
my heart confines me.
All that I've lost is great.
All that I've found is pain.

The spirits, which pass me, cry for the freedom of the wind.
But the bars that confine me say I have no hope.

But as long as I have the freedom to dream, I have the freedom
of wind and road.

With the "Freedom to Dream," I offer other highlights—as I remember and interpret them.

- Inmates worked on the Suffolk County Farm.

I have been told that inmates worked – with no compensation – on the Suffolk County Farm in Yaphank for many years. The story is a bit hazy. Some tell me that German prisoners of war were housed and worked there in the 1940s. I do not know; however, I believe Suffolk County inmates worked on the County Farm before 1975.

- In 1975, Suffolk County Cornell Cooperative Extension established at least four Vocational Education Programs on the Suffolk County Farm: Small Engine Repair, Carpentry, Meat Processing, and Landscaping.

In 1975 I met with two representatives of Suffolk County Cornell Cooperative Extension at the Career Guidance Center of the Board of Cooperative Educational Services (BOCES). They told me that Suffolk County had asked Cooperative Extension to manage the County Farm. Cooperative Extension agreed to do so only if they could provide educational services to inmates and other County residents. Furthermore, inmates would not "work" the farm unless that work was associated with a vocational training program. Suffolk County agreed.

Grants supplied the bulk of the initial vocational education funding. The percentage of the County's share increased over time.

These programs—especially meat processing—became so successful that it was not unusual to see a former inmate working at a maintenance shop, home improvement company or behind the meat counter in Suffolk Food Markets.

- In 1977 Eastern Suffolk BOCES introduced a Life Skills / Career Counseling Program for inmates participating in these programs.

With Sharon Fagan, I developed and implemented that service. The Adkins Life Skills Series formed the foundation of our Career Counseling / Life Skills service.

Less than one hundred inmates were housed at the Minimum Security Facility in Yaphank. That facility was frequently called "The Farm" because most of the inmates housed there participated in vocational programs at the County Farm.

The inmates and I had a ball! We enjoyed our time together! Because most were convicted of, relatively speaking, minor crimes (such people in Suffolk are now placed on probation, not in jail), they knew their release date and expected to obtain employment. They earnestly participated in the vocational education and Life Skills classes. I doubt any college student would have been more dedicated and appreciative.

- In 1979 Re-Rout, a Transition Counseling Program was introduced by the Suffolk County Sheriff, Eastern Suffolk BOCES, Suffolk County Community College, Department of Labor, and the Department of Probation.

By 1979 we realized that even though our incarcerated students did well in the academic and vocational programs we offered inside the correctional facilities, most could not function outside. Inside they were housed, clothed, fed, protected, counted (four times a day), offered medical care, education, religion, recreation, and predictability. Outside they were on their own. Suffolk County Correctional Facilities became the most comprehensive community service provider in the County. After a few weeks, most inmates—especially those adult males sentenced to Yaphank—began to feel comfortable, and to fear release.

After one of my toughest inmate-students broke down crying two days before his release and then returned smiling two weeks after his release, I began serious efforts to replicate a transition program operating in Fairfax County, Virginia. Suffolk's Transition Program—Re-Rout—is now 31 years old.

Based on many studies, I believe that an inmate-student who participates in Re-Rout and one of our other educational-vocational programs will be 50% less likely to return to jail than an inmate who chooses not to participate. Furthermore, I believe this observation can be valid in any county correctional facility offering educational-vocational programs along with transition counseling.

- In 1980, Eastern Suffolk BOCES and Suffolk County Community College joined Cornell University in providing Baking and Food Preparation (inside the Correctional Facilities), freshman level College Courses (at Suffolk County Community College), Office Practice Skills, and Computer Literacy and Commercial House Wiring (at BOCES facilities).

From Monday through Friday at 8:00 in the morning vans carried about thirty inmate-students from the Yaphank Correctional Facility to classes at the County Farm while a dozen other inmate-students attended baking and food preparation courses inside the Yaphank Facility. At about 3:00 P.M., yellow school buses carried about forty male and female inmate-students to Suffolk County Community College or one of the BOCES vocational education schools in the nearby towns of Riverhead or Bellport. The educational facilities were generally not serving other students in the late afternoon so the buildings were available. Incarcerated students filled several classrooms!

It was simply fantastic. Suffolk County tax payers were helping Suffolk County inmates become Suffolk County tax payers.

- All those programs shrank after crack cocaine entered Suffolk in the early 1980s and financial aid for inmates attending college stopped.

Incarcerated persons accused of selling crack cocaine were generally un-sentenced and classified at a level that denied them permission to attend vocational programs at Suffolk Community College or BOCES. Suffolk County jails had no room to incarcerate sentenced inmates previously eligible to attend educational-vocational programs outside the jail. Those inmates were now placed on probation.

Crack cocaine seemed like an equal opportunity drug. African Americans became the predominant sellers of crack, so the dealers arrested and incarcerated were predominantly African American. The incarcerated population of Suffolk County became 50% or more African American.

At about the same time, financial aide for inmates attending college stopped. I hope it was a coincidence.

- Between 1982 and 1986, the Suffolk County Sheriff and Eastern Suffolk BOCES joined with New York State (NYS) Commission of Corrections and the NYS Education Department to write and advocate legislation to fund the Incarcerated Youth Education Program. Suffolk's Jail Education Program for Youth began in February, 1987.

Quite frankly, young inmates had by and large been, and probably still are, "pains in the neck." As students they had as little interest in education as they had when they attended school outside jail. Like other educators, I much preferred the older inmate-students. Indeed, I dreaded working with the 16-18 year olds!

However, Suffolk County Sheriff Jack Finnerty was both morally and legally correct when he initiated efforts in New York State to ensure educational programs for incarcerated youth. I am very proud of having the opportunity to work with him and others to write, promote and pass the appropriate legislation. Incarcerated youth who have not yet graduated from high school and are less than twenty-one years of age are entitled to attend a minimum of fifteen hours each week of educational-vocational programs (three hours, five days per week) paid for by the school district in which they claim to live.

The Suffolk County Educational Program is adequately funded to provide superior academic, art and vocational programming, as well as comprehensive career and transition counseling. Indeed, incarcerated youth make tremendous academic gains, possibly because there are few better ways to pass time, and possibly because there are virtually no discipline problems in the school.

- In late 1991, Eastern Suffolk BOCES and the Suffolk County Sheriff created Freedom To Dream—a program designed to introduce inmates to others who are struggling or have struggled but who refuse to "throw in the towel," who refuse to live a life of incarceration. Initially the encounters were half a day in length. In the early 1990s well-known artists and artisans began to develop and present vocational training programs lasting more than one day inside Suffolk County Correctional Facilities.

Mr. Mark Mathabane, the world famous author of Kaffir Boy, inaugurated our Freedom To Dream series on December 9, 1991.

Four speakers contracted through BOCES Arts-in-Education addressed inmates at the Riverhead and Yaphank Facilities:

- Dr. Betty Shabaaz, the distinguished professor at Medger Evers College and widow of Malcolm X, visited the Suffolk County Correctional Facility in Yaphank on September 9, 1992.

- Mr. Steve Tomecek (better known as "Dr. Dirt"), the distinguished scientist and educator, visited the Riverhead Facility on September 14, 1992.

- Mr. Mark Mathabane revisited Suffolk County Correctional Facility in Riverhead and Yaphank on September 17, 1992.

- Mr. Willie Houston, Director of the African-American Museum in Hempstead, New York, spoke to the incarcerated students in Riverhead and Yaphank on September 21, 1992.

Later we contracted with Fred Morsell (of "Frederick Douglass," typically the season opening event for the Freedom To Dream Series) and invited many well-known artists and artisans to develop and present programs lasting more than one day to our incarcerated students.

- In March, 1994 the Sheriff and BOCES joined Suffolk County Probation and more than ten other Suffolk County agencies in national efforts to develop and implement a Day Reporting Center (DRC) program for non-violent offenders. It opened for probationers under intensive supervision. The Center provides physical and mental health care services; substance abuse and career counseling; academic, art, and vocational education. Probationers are assigned to the Center as an alternative to incarceration.

More than sixty persons attend daily. All would have been incarcerated at least a year if the DRC were not available. Thus, society saves at least $65.00 per participant per day.

The Center tests for substance abuse every day. Attendance in all classes is mandatory. It is a demanding program (about half choose to leave and go to jail). However, if a probationer attends more than one month he or she can expect to have a significantly lower recidivism rate.

I am very pleased to be associated with the Suffolk County Day Reporting Center. Keeping someone out of jail—where all too frequently his or her ability and confidence to function outside disappears—is a great thing.

- Sometime during the 1990s I attended a meeting called by James Kademus of New York State Education Department (NYSED). The topic

29

was "The Decline of Vocational Education in Secondary Education." I suggested that NYSED help build vocational educational schools inside the fences of county correctional facilities. There would be no shortage of applicants.

Since that time, the New York State Department of Education has encouraged the State's community colleges to provide vocational education to post-high school students. May I humbly suggest that extensions of community colleges be built inside the fences of County Correctional Facilities?

- During the new millennium vocational programs have experienced a renaissance, principally a result of encouragement from the Suffolk County Sheriff's Office. These programs have been offered by Suffolk Cornell Cooperative Extension, Eastern Suffolk BOCES, and the Sheriff's Department. They include horticulture, sewing, carpentry, landscaping, plumbing, and baking.

Life is good. However, it would be better if we fully re-instituted the Freedom to Dream Series and the Suffolk County Community College Programs.

Closing Observations:

Adult inmates are fantastic students. Any educator loves to feel appreciated. These students appreciate educators. It is a "win-win" situation.

Inmates above the age of eighteen who enroll in the programs are competitive with the best university students, and they work as hard and are as dependable and likeable as anyone. However, upon their release they face a new set of frustrations and very frequently revert to their previous coping behavior—alcohol and drug abuse.

Adult inmate-students (especially those around 22-24) seem to have the best chance to change their lives and make a good transition. Yet as these students become older, they lose the confidence needed to survive outside. They are more sure of their ability to serve and survive inside than outside. It is cruel to force them to leave!

All incarcerated persons have the freedom to dream; however, almost none have the self-confidence to realize those dreams outside the prison wall. After a short time, incarcerated persons learn to survive and dream, and believe they are better off within prison walls.

Sheriff Finnerty said, "Careful! If you break it, you own it! Our job is to not break it," not to break a person. I believe our job is to help inmates become fully functioning human beings—hopefully, for life outside the prison walls.

Biographical Sketch

Dwight Stecker worked with the United States Peace Corps in Costa Rica (1966-1969), and with the Suffolk County Anti-Poverty Program (1970-1975). He earned two Master's degrees: one in Foreign Affairs from the Fletcher School of Law and Diplomacy at Tufts and Harvard Universities in 1966, and another in School Counseling, with a professional degree in School Counseling from C.W. Post University in 1974 and 1975. Dwight has been a correctional educator in Suffolk County, New York since 1976, employed by Eastern Suffolk BOCES until October, 2006. He helped create Re-Rout, a nationally recognized transition program for incarcerated and released offenders, and worked with New York State education and corrections professionals to establish legislation for educational services to incarcerated youth. Dwight joined other criminal justice professionals to establish alternatives to incarceration including Suffolk's successful Day Reporting Center in 1994. Since retiring from Eastern Suffolk BOCES, Dwight contributes time to the education, medical and counseling services of Suffolk County's Sunshine Youth and Family Center; The New Life Center for recently released offenders; Mather Hospital's Institutional Review Board; and The Art of Mathematics, a tutoring program providing Supplemental Education Services in math.

CHAPTER IV

VOCATIONAL EDUCATION FOR INCARCERATED WOMEN: ONE PIECE OF THE PUZZLE

by Diane S. Young

Vocational education programs for incarcerated women can contribute to the successful reentry of women to their communities upon release from prison or jail. They are best seen as one component, or one piece of the puzzle, fitting together with other vital components so that successful reintegration occurs. Not all incarcerated women can or will benefit from vocational education, but when one considers the characteristics of the vast majority of women in correctional facilities in the United States it is clear that many require additional skills and resources to make it on the outside. As the number of imprisoned women increases, the pressure to develop strategies to promote their positive reintegration also increases.

In 2006 there were just over 103,000 women incarcerated in state and Federal prisons. This number represents a 4.5% increase from the previous year. Additionally, approximately 98,000 women were held in jails at midyear 2006. This represents a 40% increase between the years 2000 and 2006 (Sabol, Minton, & Harrison, 2007). Although women make up a much smaller proportion of the incarcerated population than do men, their growth rate has increased at a faster pace for several years.

At some point, almost all incarcerated women are released. Sadly, a significant number return, evidenced by the relatively high recidivism rate. In a large study on the recidivism of state prisoners released in 1994, 58% of women were rearrested, 40% were reconvicted, and 39% had returned to prison within three years of release (Langan & Levin, 2002). Because the sheer number of incarcerated persons has increased significantly over the last few decades, many more women are facing the challenges of reentry.

Participation in vocational education programs has been associated with reduced recidivism in some recent studies (see Young & Mattucci, 2006, for a brief review), although the relationship is less clear for women. This may be in part because women comprise a small proportion of incarcerated adults, and studies examining the effects of vocational education have not included them in sufficient numbers. It is clear that women in prisons and jails are predominantly poor, under-educated and unskilled, with poor employment histories. Economic marginalization is a significant hurdle to overcome. A study of women at one of the nation's largest county detention centers found that 54% of the women reported being homeless within the 30 days prior to entering jail (Goswami, 2002). Thus, vocational education programs that equip women with marketable skills, particularly in areas of labor market shortages and sufficient to provide a living wage, show potential for easing economic difficulties upon release and consequently reducing illegal behaviors.

Vocational education programs for women do exist in prisons and jails, although their availability and accessibility are severely limited. In addition, programs offered are not typically responsive to labor market shortages (Lahm, 2000) or intensive enough to fully equip women with the skills needed to satisfactorily perform job tasks. The Bureau of Justice Statistics reported that about 30% of women in state prisons in 1997 were enrolled in a vocational program, but information was not provided on the types of programs (Harlow, 2003). Erisman and Contardo (2005) gathered data from 46 state and Federal prison systems in 2003-04 about postsecondary correctional education programs. Altogether only about 5% of prisoners were enrolled in postsecondary educational programs, with almost two-thirds of these enrolled in for-credit vocational certificate programs. Even in the 15 highest enrollment prison systems, only 54% of the facilities offered postsecondary educational programs; in the rest of the states, only 35% offered such programs. The report does not provide any gender comparisons. Even fewer programs are available in jails. In 1999, only 6.5% of jails offered vocational education (Harlow, 2003).

As other authors have pointed out, stronger research designs that can establish causal links between vocational education and recidivism as well as other positive outcomes such as employment, ability to earn a living wage, and participation in advanced education continue to be needed. In the meantime, because the empirical evidence regarding the effectiveness of vocational education to bring about positive outcomes for incarcerated women is limited, it makes sense to draw upon theory when considering what contributes to successful reintegration for women and how vocational education is a part of that.

One theoretical approach that explicitly considers complex relationships and interactions between persons and their environments is the ecological perspective (Hernandez & Franklin, 2008). Addressing a problem from this perspective, such as the complex needs of incarcerated women as they face community reentry, requires a focus that is much more than "fixing" a person (Kirst-Ashman & Hull, 1993). Rather, the focus is on the reciprocal interactions between people and their social environments. People are in constant interaction with the contexts within which they live, including societal policies, communities, organizations, and families. For incarcerated women, this environmental context includes the correctional facility in which they live. Mutual interactions between a woman and her multiple social environments influence individual behavior. To understand and appropriately intervene in constructive ways requires a holistic view of and multi-faceted response to the circumstances faced by incarcerated women.

The purpose of this chapter is to examine individual, societal and correctional system factors that, as a whole, are required for the effectiveness of vocational education programs for incarcerated women. Vocational education programs are best seen as one potentially important contributor to women's reentry experiences after release from prison or jail. Standing alone, vocational education is not likely to be effective in significantly reducing recidivism. When joined with other individual, societal and systemic changes, however, women's opportunities for successful reintegration will be greatly enhanced.

Individual Factors

Individual or personal factors that affect the reentry process for women released from correctional facilities and that also affect the ability of vocational education programs to "work" in the long run include mental and physical health; ability to meet basic needs such as housing, food, childcare, and transportation; and recovery from drug and alcohol addiction. (See Table 1 for a summary list of individual, societal and correctional system factors.) These concerns, so prevalent in incarcerated women's experiences, severely impede one's ability to get and keep a job and apply newly learned work skills once released (see O'Brien & Young, 2006, for an overview of these issues and their prevalence). For example, almost 24% of female state prison and local jail inmates have been identified as mentally ill (Ditton, 1999). Almost 60% of female state prisoners report experiencing prior physical or sexual abuse (Greenfeld & Snell, 1999). A high proportion of incarcerated women suffer from depression and post-traumatic stress disorder, often related to psychological trauma stemming from sexual and physical abuse (Covington & Bloom, 2006). A study of women in prison found that 75% of them reported a substance use problem, defined as daily use of alcohol or illegal drugs in the 30 days prior to incarceration (O'Brien & Bates, 2005). Left untreated, these kinds of mental health and addiction issues will hinder women's efforts to reintegrate.

The overlapping nature of these variables is supported by studies examining incarcerated women and employment issues. Alemagno and Dickie (2005) conducted a study of 110 women in two jails. The vast majority of the women reported a need for employment assistance (86%). Of the women who needed employment assistance, 81% also needed help with obtaining housing, 79% needed medical care, 76% needed drug treatment, and 51% needed mental health treatment. Blitz (2006) found that two of the strongest predictors of stable employment in a sample of 908 women in prison, if needed, were whether substance abuse treatment and mental health treatment were received.

Other individual factors logically connected to participation in vocational education and to post-release employment include social skills and self-esteem. Social skills related to performance in many jobs include communication and interaction skills, the ability to function as part of a team, willingness to follow instructions, and dependability. Self-esteem, including confidence in one's ability and a sense of self-efficacy, are often enhanced through vocational and academic programs. Spark and Harris (2005) found that a primary reason for participating in vocational education in an Australian women's prison was a desire to attend to one's mental health; enhanced self-esteem was an unanticipated and welcome consequence of participation. Fine and colleagues (2001) found that participation by incarcerated women in a college degree program resulted in self-reflection, pride, envisioning a different and positive future, and a new view of self that included a belief in one's ability to effect change. Adequate social skills and a healthy sense of self are assets when facing the difficult challenges of community reentry, including seeking and maintaining employment.

Educational readiness is also an individual factor that affects who can benefit from vocational education programs. Harlow (2003) reported that 42% of female state prison inmates had not completed high school or earned their General Educational Development certificate (GED). Among jail inmates (men and women) in 1996, 46.5% had not completed high school or their GED, compared to 18.4% of the general U.S. population. In addition to basic academic skills, women must possess a readiness to learn. Rose (2004) discussed the importance of cultural capital resources for educational achievement. This includes things like valuing learning and understanding its importance, being socialized in ways that prepare students to understand teacher expectations and follow procedures used in classroom settings, and being willing to work hard to master concepts. Literacy levels and academic skills are typically low among incarcerated individuals, and educational deficits must be overcome for women to participate in vocational education. Cultural capital resources must also be nurtured for women to fully participate in educational programs in correctional facilities.

Societal Factors

Societal factors that affect the reentry process for women released from correctional facilities and that also affect the ability of vocational education programs to "work" in the long run have been created and implemented within a context of punitiveness and reluctance to give those convicted of breaking the law a clean slate upon release (see Table 1). Numerous restrictions, referred to as invisible punishments (Mauer & Chesney-Lind, 2002), have been passed into law or made public policy and consequently affect the lives of those released with felony convictions. Pogorzelski, Wolff, Pan, and Blitz (2005) categorized restrictions in eight areas when looking at those established as public policies and applied in New Jersey: employment, public assistance, driver's license, voting and jury duty, housing, education, expunging of criminal record, and parental rights, adoption, and foster care. All individuals within their sample of over 3000 prisoners (15% of the sample were women) faced lifetime consequences in employment, housing, education, parental rights, and jury duty. For example, in the area of employment, employers may ask about arrests and convictions and ex-offenders must report felony convictions on job applications. For certain types of professional licenses applications may be denied by the government. By statute and depending on type of conviction, ex-offenders are barred from 22 categories of employment including public sector jobs, public schools, airports, and places where liquor is served or sold retail (Pogorzelski et al., 2005).

The restrictions are more severe for individuals with felony drug convictions (Pogorzelski et al., 2005). For example, individuals with drug convictions may be ineligible for public housing for life, and those receiving public housing benefits may be evicted if they allow a convicted drug offender to live with them within two years of release. Ex-offenders with drug convictions are not eligible for Federal financial aid for education for one or two years after their first or second offense, and for life after the third offense. Ex-offenders with a drug distribution conviction have a lifetime restriction from general public assistance. Those with non-distribution drug convictions are only eligible for Temporary Assistance for Needy Families (TANF), general assistance or food stamps if they are enrolled in or have completed drug treatment. Eligibility for TANF is especially critical for women because they often rely on public assistance to provide for themselves and their children as they struggle to make a fresh start. More mothers than fathers reported living with their children prior to prison (64% of women compared to 44% of men), and more mothers than fathers were the only parent to live with their children prior to arrest (46% of mothers compared to 15% of fathers) (Mumola, 2000). Almost 29% of incarcerated women in state prisons were sentenced for drug offenses in 2004 (Sabol, Couture, & Harrison, 2007), and the most common nonviolent felony conviction for women in the New Jersey study was drug-related (Pogorzelski et al., 2005). These legal and policy restrictions are much more far-reaching than New Jersey. Many states and the Federal government have passed legislation that severely restricts the opportunities for ex-offenders in these areas (Harrison & Schehr, 2004; Smith & Young, 2003).

Compounding these restrictions are the "regular," difficult, societal circumstances that many face, including poverty, racism, and an inability to access mental health care or treatment for addiction in the community. Incarcerated women are overwhelmingly poor, and many have unmet or ongoing treatment needs with limited access or ability to afford care. Incarcerated women are also disproportionately women of color; 53% in 2006 (Sabol, Minton, & Harrison, 2007). Blitz (2006) found that a predictor of pre-incarceration employment for women was race, with Black women faring worse than White women, even when the women had equal education and treatment histories. When one considers the aforementioned legal and policy restrictions and the effects of poverty and racism on women exiting prisons and jails, the obstacles to successful reentry are significant.

Correctional System Factors

Correctional systems provide the immediate contexts within which vocational education programs are offered and profoundly affect what programs are available, who can participate, and how these programs are received (see Table 1). Erisman and Contardo (2005) found that lack of funding for postsecondary educational programs was perceived by correctional education administrators as a significant obstacle to their ability to make vocational education more widely available to prisoners. Federal Pell Grants were available to eligible prisoners prior to 1994, and the funding from these grants supported academic and vocational programs. However, when Congress denied Pell Grants to prisoners, many college programs did not continue their correctional programs; this funding has not been replaced or restored although the Federal Incarcerated Youth Offender block grants have provided funds for some postsecondary educational programs for offenders younger than age 26. Currently, the proportion of prisoners enrolled in postsecondary correctional education programs has returned to what it was prior to the elimination of Pell Grants for prisoners, but still only about 5% of prisoners are enrolled in such programs (Erisman & Contardo, 2005). Lack of funds severely limits the number and types of programs that are available to prisoners.

Funding levels are not completely within the control of correctional systems. Societal factors, such as the public and politicians' willingness to pay for these programs, and the prevailing opinion about whether offenders deserve these services, are directly related to decisions about resources. This is a good example of how interactions between multiple systems shape the environmental contexts within which people live.

In addition to funding, several characteristics of correctional systems shape the viability of vocational education programs (Erisman & Contardo, 2005). The remote geographic locations of many prison facilities make it difficult for prisons to develop collaborations with community colleges and trade schools that could provide vocational education programs. Remote locations also limit the hiring of qualified instructors for the facilities. These conditions are not as much a problem for jails located in urban areas, but are a reality for jails in rural areas. Safety and security concerns limit the types of programs that correctional facilities are willing to offer. There is a reluctance to allow prisoners access to the internet, and the types of supplies and materials allowed in the facility may be very restricted. Learning a trade often requires the use of tools, and the fear that tools will be used as weapons is a concern that correctional administrators must address. Space for classrooms in overcrowded facilities, and in facilities not built for educational purposes, is also scarce. Prisoner transfers between correctional facilities, which often occur with little warning, make it almost impossible for prisoners to complete courses they have begun.

Another correctional system factor that has an important impact on vocational education programs is the level of administrative and staff support for these programs. If administrators or staff persons do not value vocational education programs, believe in the rehabilitative possibilities of such programs, or feel prisoners deserve them, there are numerous ways they can sabotage them. Officers are relied upon to release prisoners from their cells so they can attend classes, transport them to classes, and determine what materials prisoners can have or carry with them. Correctional personnel make determinations about what programs prisoners may participate in and when. Correctional administrators have final say about what programs will be allowed in their facilities and what times they will be offered. If vocational programs are placed during limited visiting hours, for example, prisoners may be forced to choose between a program and an opportunity to see a family member. Staff members can also play a role in encouraging prisoner participation in programs or discouraging it by making disparaging remarks about the program or belittling those who attend.

One correctional system factor that is receiving attention recently but that has far to go in implementation is the development of prison and jail environments that are nurturing and empowering for incarcerated women. Covington and Bloom (2006) discussed the importance of gender responsive treatment and services in correctional facilities. Relational theory informs gender responsive approaches and is a theory about women's psychological development. A basic assumption of relational theory is that women's growth and development is intricately bound to mutually empathic connections with others (Covington, 1998). Connections are so crucial that psychological problems can be traced to disconnections or violations within relationships. Women's sense of self and self-worth are tied to connections with others. Incarcerated women's histories are replete with severe relational disconnections, evidenced by the large proportion of incarcerated women that have been physically and sexually abused, as children or adults. One outcome of this absence of mutually empathic relationships is the use of substances to minimize the grief, loss, and pain associated with disconnection (Covington, 1998). The typical correctional culture is one of "power-over-others"; this environment contributes to the alienation that women are already experiencing and does not promote positive personal growth and change (Covington, p. 123). Examples of power-over-others include practices such as referring to prisoners by their numbers rather than names, enforcing petty rules that are not related to the security and safety of the facility, prohibiting natural expressions of friendship among prisoners, interacting with prisoners in demeaning ways, and severely restricting opportunities for meaningful and collaborative activities.

Benda (2005) examined gender differences in recidivism for individuals being released from a boot camp, offered as an option to prison for eligible offenders. He found that the following problems were predictors of increased recidivism: childhood and recent physical and sexual abuse, feelings of depression and fearfulness while in boot camp, and stress. Also for women, positive relationships with family, friends, and partners facilitated law-abiding lifestyles (Benda, 2005). Vocational education programs can be implemented in ways that nurture and support women and work to counteract the traumatic relational experiences that many women have experienced. Spark and Harris (2005) found that the women in their sample of vocational education program participants reported improved relationships with staff, appreciation for the opportunity to be part of a supportive community of women, development of relationships based on mutual respect and support, and a sense of being valued. Though more empirical work needs to be done to identify and understand the links between correctional environment factors and women's psychological development, it is not hard to understand how a healthy sense of self and positive relational connections with others could enhance reintegration efforts.

Individual, societal, and correctional system factors do not operate in isolation. Societal views about what prisoners deserve affect funding for programs, which in turn affects the accessibility and availability of educational and vocational programs. Correctional environments rigidly focused on personal control reinforce relational disconnections among women, and further injure women's sense of self and self-esteem, individual factors logically related to making one's way in the community and workplace after release. Public policies that restrict employment and educational opportunities for previously incarcerated women affect women's ability to provide for their own and their children's basic survival needs (an individual factor). Because these factors are inter-related and all impact women's reentry experiences, a multi-faceted response is required.

So what can be done? How can correctional administrators, staff members, and educators implement effective vocational education programs for incarcerated women, knowing that multiple factors shape reentry experiences? Advocacy is needed to change societal policies that severely impede women's abilities to be successful during post-release, such as eliminating invisible punishments and making community-based treatment accessible and affordable. At the same time, correctional facilities must work to create policies and environments that address individual and correctional system factors, working to change factors that are within their control (see Table 2).

Vocational education programs, as well as other rehabilitative programs, must be encouraged and made a correctional priority. The warden or chief administrator has the capacity and responsibility to set the tone within the facility, one that is supportive and sees quality programmatic opportunities for prisoners as essential rather than nonessential. With this view endorsed at the top, staff members will be encouraged to act in ways that promote rather than impede prisoner participation in vocational education. Community collaborations should be explored and developed with educational programs, such as community colleges, trade schools, or four-year universities. Many educators and educational institutions would likely respond positively to genuine requests for partnerships initiated by correctional administrators. Collaborations with educational institutions would help ensure quality vocational education curricula. Prisoner transfer policies also need to be scrutinized. If program participation and completion are considered correctional priorities, then prisoners should not be transferred to other facilities prior to program completion unless the program can be completed at the transfer facility or there are other critical reasons that require a transfer. Given the overcrowding in facilities and other security concerns, transfers cannot always be avoided. However, transfers are currently made with little attention to program disruptions that may result for prisoners. Creating opportunities for long distance education is one possibility for easing disruptions through transfers and also for making programs more accessible in remote locations and at more facilities.

Correctional staff should receive training about the needs of female offenders (Covington & Bloom, 2006). Information is vital to creating a context within which vocational education programs can be ultimately effective, especially about relational theory, the psychological development of women, and strategies for working with women in ways that maintain safety and security and also promote women's personal growth. In addition, staff can be provided with empirical information that demonstrates the positive links between educational accomplishment in correctional programs and ex-prisoners' longevity in the community. Correctional staff that value education and understand the needs of women will help create an environment where positive changes can occur. This training will need to be provided because it is not typically part of standard officer training programs.

Shifting the correctional culture in ways that are better informed about and responsive to the needs of women is likely to positively impact some of the individual factors that promote women's success, such as their self-esteem. For example, female prisoners are seldom asked for their suggestions for change. Creating a forum for women to offer suggestions about ways that correctional environments can become more supportive of women's needs is one way to acknowledge that they matter. Related to vocational education, women could offer suggestions for types of programs to be offered, how limited program slots can be fairly allotted, guidelines for conduct in the classroom, and information on ways they learn best. Allowing women a voice would not only recognize them for their contributions, thus enhancing self-esteem, it would also give them ownership in the resulting decisions and strengthen their motivation to complete the program.

Recognizing that women's healthy psychological development and self-esteem are tied to mutually empathic connections with others suggests that the use of peers and mentors can be an effective way to enhance academic skills, improve literacy, and foster cultural capital. Vocational programs can utilize teaching strategies such as working in small groups or in teams, calling upon those who have a good mastery of concepts to tutor those who struggle, and, in general, encouraging women to develop supportive relationships as they learn together. In correctional facilities this would mean allowing small groups of inmates to congregate outside of class for study together. Collaborative learning strategies have been useful with adult learners, and these approaches fit well with the needs of women.

Women's reentry is indeed complex. Multiple individual, societal and correctional system factors influence the outcome. Vocational education is one piece of the puzzle, and must be combined with other pieces for a reasonable expectation of long-term success. There is much that correctional administrators, staff members and educators can do to shift the correctional culture to one that fosters positive outcomes for incarcerated women. Joined with other individual, societal, and systemic changes, correctional vocational education programs can be partners in significantly improving the opportunities for women's successful reintegration.

Table 1: Individual, Societal and Correctional System Factors Affecting Reentry Experiences for Women

<u>**Individual Factors**</u>

Ability to meet basic needs
Mental and physical health
Drug and alcohol addiction/recovery
Social skills
Self-esteem
Literacy and basic academic skills
Cultural capital resources for learning

<u>**Societal Factors**</u>

Prevailing view about what offenders deserve
Legal and policy restrictions:

    Employment
    Housing
    Educational aid
    Public assistance

Racism
Poverty
Accessibility of treatment

<u>**Correctional System Factors**</u>

Funding
Geographic location
Safety/security concerns
Facility space
Transfer policies
Administrative and staff support
Facility culture

Table 2: Recommendations for Changing Correctional System Factors Affecting Reentry Experiences for Women

Make rehabilitative programs a correctional priority.
Develop collaborations with community educational institutions.
Change prisoner transfer policies.
Develop long distance education opportunities.
Provide training for correctional staff about the psychological needs of women.
Provide training for staff related to the effectiveness of educational programs.
Create a forum for women prisoners to offer suggestions.
Utilize teaching strategies emphasizing teamwork and small groups.
Utilize peer tutors and mentors.

Biographical Sketch

Diane S. Young, Ph.D, MSW, is an Associate Professor at University of Washington Tacoma's Social Work Program in Tacoma, Washington. She teaches courses in criminal justice and social work. Dr. Young has several publications related to the health and mental health needs of incarcerated individuals, the families affected by incarceration, social work practice in criminal justice settings, and correctional education. Her practice experience includes over 10 years of working with incarcerated adults in Washington State.

CHAPTER V

ENHANCING THE VOCATIONAL SKILLS OF INCARCERATED WOMEN THROUGH A PLUMBING MAINTENANCE PROGRAM

by Diane S. Young and Robert F. Mattucci

Abstract

Vocational education programs show promise for reducing recidivism among adult offenders, measured most typically through re-arrest and re-incarceration data. Yet such programs for women in U.S. correctional facilities have more often provided training in gender-stereotyped and low-paid professions when compared to vocational programs in men's facilities. As the number of incarcerated women continues to climb, programs are important for both the women and society if they help women develop marketable skills that will enable them to support their children upon release and overcome the economic marginalization that is so closely tied to offending.

This chapter describes a 16-hour, pre-plumbing program designed to prepare individuals for basic plumbing maintenance in settings such as hotels and hospitals. The program was taught by a plumber to seven groups of women (N = 60) from four different county correctional facilities in New York State. It incorporated hands-on work and evaluation, and emphasized collaboration, a positive attitude, and confidence building, all qualities that are necessary in the work force and to women's self-esteem. Across all groups, the mean gain on a 100 point post-test assessing understanding and mastery of course concepts was 32 points (SD = 18), a statistically significant difference. Lessons learned and suggestions for future research and program and policy reform are also described in the chapter.

Introduction

In the United States, approximately 12% of jailed adults are women, with just under 87,000 women in jail at mid-year, 2004 (Harrison & Beck, 2005). For ten years the average annual rate of growth in the adult female jail population has been increasing faster than that of men (7.0% compared to 4.2%) (Harrison & Beck). Women in jail typically have multiple and complex problems that must be addressed to enable reentry and sustained success in the community after release.

Economic difficulties are often an important part of this challenge. Women in jail are predominantly undereducated and unskilled, with poor employment histories. About 60% of these women are unemployed prior to arrest (James, 2004). A snapshot study of women at one of the nation's largest county detention centers found that 54% reported being homeless (defined as residing in an emergency or transitional shelter, doubled up with family or friends, staying outside, or in cars)

43

in the 30 days prior to entering jail (Goswami, 2002). In addition, the majority of incarcerated women are mothers, had lived with their children prior to arrest, and intend to reunite with their children upon release (Bloom & Steinhart, 1993; Greenfeld & Snell, 1999; Hairston, 1991). Overcoming economic marginalization is thus important for both the women and their children.

Vocational education programs in correctional facilities show potential for easing the economic challenges of reentry and for reducing recidivism. After a review of the literature that examines the outcomes associated with vocational education in correctional facilities and the current state of these programs for incarcerated women, this chapter describes a plumbing program provided to women in jail. Implementation issues and recommendations for future work in this area are also discussed.

Literature Review

Vocational Education and Recidivism

Vocational education has been defined as the acquisition of skills that are directly transferable to a workplace (Bazos & Hausman, 2004, p. 4) with the emphasis on "skills development in a particular trade or industry" (Lawrence, Mears, Dubin, & Travis, 2002, p. 12). Unlike educational programs that focus primarily on increasing literacy and assisting students to complete Adult Basic Education (ABE) and General Equivalency Diploma (GED) requirements, vocational education seeks to directly prepare individuals for specific sectors of the workforce.

Recidivism has been defined in different ways in studies examining the impact of vocational programs on recidivism; measures of re-arrest, technical violation, re-conviction, and/or re-incarceration are typically used, with re-incarceration being the predominant definition. Despite this variation, recent studies generally support the association between participation in correctional vocational education programs and reduced recidivism (Lawrence et al., 2002; Steurer & Smith, 2003; Wilson, Gallagher, & MacKenzie, 2000). Wilson and colleagues (2000) conducted a meta-analysis of evaluations of educational programs, including vocational programs. Their analysis included 17 vocational program comparisons, utilizing studies dating from 1976 through the 1990s containing experimental or quasi-experimental designs. A primary focus was to determine whether program participants fared better than non-participants on any measure of recidivism. Based on their meta-analysis, the authors found that participants were less likely to recidivate; if a 50% fixed recidivism rate is assumed for non-participants, the corresponding recidivism rate for vocational program participants is 39% (Wilson et al., 2000). Lawrence and colleagues (2002) found similar results from their review of evaluation research, as did Steurer and Smith (2003) in their three-state recidivism study (Maryland, Minnesota, and Ohio) utilizing a quasi-experimental design with a release cohort. Their sample of 3,170 was followed for three years after release. Prior to incarceration, many sample participants had characteristics clearly indicative of their need for academic and vocational education. More than 62% of participants in educational programs had not completed high school, about 50% were unemployed for at least six months in the year prior to incarceration, and less than 50% of the sample said they had a job waiting upon release (Steurer & Smith, 2003, p. 10).

Participation in academic and vocational programs while incarcerated has also been associated in some studies with improved employment outcomes after release (Lawrence et al., 2002; Wilson et al., 2000). Steurer and Smith (2003), however, found that program participants were statistically not significantly more likely to be employed than non-participants, although program participants did earn higher wages. The nature of this relationship is particularly important for formerly incarcerated individuals because employment has been linked to reduced recidivism (for a review of this literature, see Saylor & Gaes, 1997).

Not all studies have found that participation in vocational education is associated with decreased recidivism. Brewster and Sharp (2002), in their examination of academic and vocational-technical programs in Oklahoma, found that vocational education participants returned to prison more quickly than non-participants, demonstrating shorter survival times. Although this finding seems inconsistent with other evaluation findings, researchers (Lawrence et al., 2002, Wilson et al., 2000) note that the lack of methodologically rigorous evaluations means that definitive causal links are not clear between participation in correctional vocational education and improved outcomes such as reduced recidivism.

The relationship between program participation and reduced recidivism seems even less clear for women. Perhaps because women comprise a small proportion of incarcerated adults, studies that examine the effectiveness of vocational programming largely overlook women's experiences. The review of evaluation research (Lawrence et al., 2002), and the larger studies mentioned earlier (Steurer & Smith, 2003, Wilson et al., 2000) do not report findings specific to gender, although at least some of the samples included women. Saylor and Gaes (1997) reported that, of the 904 women in their sample of more than 7,000 individuals previously incarcerated in Federal prisons, only 52 women were re-incarcerated for a new offense during the entire eight-12 year study period. Perhaps because of this small number, no significant effects related to program participation were found for women, whereas men who participated in vocational education were significantly less likely to recidivate during the same time frame. Thus it remains uncertain whether the relatively solid established correlation between participation in correctional vocational training and reduced recidivism also exists for women.

Vocational Education Programs for Incarcerated Women

Historically, when provided to incarcerated women, vocational education programs focused primarily on preparing women for traditional, gender-stereotyped roles (see Lahm, 2000, for an informative review of this topic prior to 1990). Although alternative career programs are becoming more available to women in some correctional facilities, thus far most programs continue to promote traditional training opportunities and in sheer number fall far short of addressing the level of need. This seems to be true outside of the United States as well as inside. Researchers examining vocational education in women's prisons in England, Australia, Canada, Germany, Denmark, Finland, Norway, and Scotland reported that incarcerated women had significant deficits in education and employment skills when they entered prison, few vocational programs available to them while incarcerated, particularly programs that address labor market shortages, and difficulties overcoming employment deficits upon release (Bertrand, 1996; Cameron, 2001; Hamlyn & Lewis, 2000). Lahm (2000) conducted a comprehensive study of the availability of vocational programs in the United States in 1996. Inviting all 50 states and the District of Columbia to participate, 30 states responded, representing over 460 correctional facilities (47 female). Lahm categorized each program according to the U.S. Census Bureau's six career categories: managerial and professional, technical/ sales/administrative support, service, production, operator/fabricator/laborer, and farm/forestry/fishing. She concluded that the same types of vocational programs were not available to both men and women. Women's facilities were 604% more likely to offer technical and sales training (e.g., sales associate, clerical staff, health assistant), 208% more likely to offer training in service occupations (e.g., cleaning, food service), and 100% more likely to offer training in the operator/fabricator/labor category (e.g., sewing) (Lahm, 2000, p. 43). Men's facilities were more likely to offer training in farm/forestry/fishing and production (e.g., masonry, automotive, building trades).

It seems reasonable that for vocational opportunities to benefit women re-entering their communities after incarceration, institutional programs will need to provide education in areas of labor market shortages, for jobs sufficient to provide a living wage, and be widely available to women who want to take advantage of them. The trades are one such area. For example, with aging plumbers beginning to retire and high schools closing their vocational-technical programs, which channeled young adults into the building trades, the need for plumbers and pipe fitters is increasing, and unfilled openings numbering in the thousands are anticipated (MacGillis, 2001).

Researchers have reported low participation rates in correctional vocational programs (Brewster & Sharp, 2002; Lawrence et al., 2002; Rose, 2004). Rose (2004) conducted trend studies examining women's participation in academic and vocational prison programs from 1979 to 1997. Using Department of Justice data, Rose found that there was never a time in the period studied when the majority of women in prison were participating in vocational or academic programming. Participation in vocational programming dropped slightly between 1991 and 1997 (Rose, 2004). One reason for this drop may be the denial of Federal Pell Grants to incarcerated individuals, passed by Congress in 1994. Although Pell Grants primarily supported academic programs, community college instructors would also provide vocational instruction, and when this source of funding stopped, many colleges did not continue their correctional programs (Lawrence et al., 2002). Low participation rates can be attributed to many factors, but lack of available program slots is an important structural limitation.

Personal Factors Related to Vocational Training for Incarcerated Women

Rose (2004) discussed the importance of both structural (e.g., funding availability for programs, quality of available training) and personal factors (e.g., positive peer influences, exposure to the importance of education) when attempting to break down the barriers associated with non-participation in vocational and academic prison programs. Indeed, understanding how to do the functions of a particular job is usually not enough to obtain and keep employment, and vocational educational programs for incarcerated women may be more effective in producing long lasting positive outcomes if they attend to personal factors that enhance not only program participation but also the cultivation of characteristics that employers value.

Tonkin, Dickie, Alemagno, and Grove (2004) studied the employability skills, including teamwork and interpersonal qualities, of 52 women in jail. Utilizing the women in their sample, they compared the skills of women who had worked 35 hours or more a week prior to coming to jail with women who did not meet this criterion. They found no statistically significant differences between previously employed and unemployed women on measures of interpersonal and teamwork skills, with all women in their sample generally demonstrating deficits in these areas.

Building on the work of others and thinking theoretically, Bazos and Hausman (2004) suggested that the inverse relationship between education and recidivism has two primary explanations. Correctional educational programs provide the technical training that increases the likelihood of employability and increases legitimate income, and they also provide incarcerated individuals with the opportunity to learn pro-social norms and feel accepted. The former explanation relates to structural factors and the latter to personal ones.

Method

Program Description

A plumbing maintenance program, designed to introduce individuals to the trade, has been developed and implemented in selected correctional facilities throughout New York State. The 16-hour program was developed and is currently taught by an experienced plumber who has a master's degree in vocational education. The program prepares its students to provide basic plumbing maintenance in settings such as hospitals, schools, hotels, and apartment complexes, and positions them to apply for admission to trade schools and apprenticeship programs. (See Mattucci and Johnson, 2003, for a description of the origin of the program and its implementation with male inmates.)

The program incorporates instruction about the basic theories associated with plumbing maintenance, and students learn techniques and problem solving skills through demonstrations with fixtures and tools, videos, and hands-on practice. A textbook/workbook and homework assignments are utilized to reinforce concepts learned in the classroom. During the program, students learn to set and repair all moving parts contained within a toilet and its fixtures; to assemble, install, and repair lavatory and kitchen sinks, faucets, and drain mechanisms; and proper and safe operation of closet augers and a hand-held power snake. Student progress and understanding is assessed with the use of quizzes and exams. The hands-on final exam consists of students working together in teams to be able to: (a) set a toilet, (b) set a kitchen sink, including installing faucet and drain mechanism, (c) cut, measure, and run copper for a full bathroom, following a blueprint, and (d) cut, measure, and lay out the fittings for a wasteline pipe for sink and bathtub. The instructor brings in all tools and fixtures, and instruction takes place in a typical jail classroom. For safety and security reasons, all tools are carefully inventoried upon entrance to and exit from the correctional facility.

The program has been provided in three different formats. In the most common format, class meets two hours a day for eight days, usually spread over four weeks. On the last day, a graduation ceremony is held and certificates of program completion are given out. In one alternate format, the class meets two hours in the morning and two in the afternoon for two days in a row, and then repeats this the next week. In this format, the last afternoon is the graduation ceremony. In the third format, the 16 hours of plumbing instruction are taught along with 10 hours of construction math and 10 hours of Occupational Safety and Health Administration (OSHA) safety construction with certification over a period of four weeks. This final format has been implemented with two groups of women, and is more inclusive of what construction contractors and trade unions look for from entry-level employees. In the facility where it has been offered, the jail had been looking for a way to connect a program provided at the jail with community college credit. Inmate students who successfully complete the 36 hours are awarded 3.6 units toward vocational education training. Because all formats include only 16 hours of plumbing instruction, and thus can only cover basic maintenance issues, students are informed about the limitations of their plumbing knowledge and when to call in a technician or someone with more expertise.

In addition to teaching basic plumbing maintenance skills, the program emphasizes collaboration and teamwork, a positive attitude, and confidence building. These qualities are necessary in the work force and essential for women's healthy self-esteem. A sense of respect for others and how they think and work in group settings is cultivated during each session through the instructor's encouragement and activities that utilize a team approach and require collaborative problem solving. For example, during one of the hands-on sessions, four or five women will work together to set a toilet. Some will watch, and others will work on the task, and then those who have completed the task first will teach the rest of their group through a process of mentorship. The women are especially responsive to this empowerment approach to learning.

Participants

Seven women's groups were conducted in four different county correctional facilities in New York State. One of the four facilities is located in a large urban city, two are located in mid-size cities, and one is located in a smaller city. Three of the four facilities are sentenced facilities, housing individuals who are serving out their jail sentences. Women were pre-screened by correctional staff for program participation at two facilities (five of the groups). Factors considered were reading ability, appropriate group demeanor and behavior, and progress in other rehabilitative programs. At the facilities where screening did not occur, women housed in general population were invited to participate, and whoever wanted to did so.

The women's groups ranged in size from three to 12 participants (see Table 1 on following page). Group 2, the smallest group, was conducted at a facility for offenders who were not yet sentenced. In these facilities, inmate turnover is rapid and inmates often live with much uncertainty and stress about the outcomes of their criminal cases and their families' situations on the outside, making it difficult to concentrate on learning. All of the non-completers (see Table 1) dropped out after beginning the group, with the exception of two inmates. One was released from jail and one was removed from the program at a facility counselor's request. Other than for Group #2, the non-completion rate was relatively small. The total number of participants to complete the program was 60, across all seven groups.

The mean age of the 60 participants is 34.4 (SD = 8.4), with ages ranging from 16 to 50. (Age was not reported by three of the women.) The majority of the women are Caucasian (53.3%), with the rest African-American (43.3%) and Hispanic (3.3%). Although a small number of women had completed some college, including one with a master's degree, some women had not completed high school, and the majority had either completed high school or earned their GED. Most of the women who previously had been employed listed occupations such as nursing assistant, food service worker, maid and hairdresser, with a couple women listing construction work.

Table 1: Group Size and Mean Scorre Improvement

Group	Number of Completers	Number of Non-Completers*	Point Difference (post-test – pre-test) Mean (SD)	
1	6	1	18.5	(13.0)
2	3	4	25.9	(19.4)
3	9	0	20.7	(8.1)
4	12	0	28.0	(8.0)
5	10	2	45.6	(18.9)
6	10	1	30.2	(14.4)
7	10	0	46.7	(23.0)
All	60	8	32.3	(18.1)**

*Non-completers were removed from the point difference calculations because post-test scores were not available for them.
**p<.0001.

Results

A pre- and post-test was used to assess change in knowledge about basic plumbing concepts. The pre-test was administered during the first hour of class and consisted of 27 multiple choice and fill-in-the-blank questions for a total of 100 points. The exam includes questions such as, "What plumbing fixture requires the use of a temperature and pressure relief valve?," and "How many inches is a standard closet flange roughed in from a wall?" This same exam is given as a post-test just before the graduation ceremony. Although this pre-experimental design does not allow for the drawing of causal connections, it is useful for determining whether participants' level of knowledge changed. The same instrument was administered to all seven groups.

Table 1 provides the mean score change from pre-test to post-test for each group of women. For all 60 participants, pre-test scores ranged from four to 88.5, with a mean of 54.4 (SD = 15.6). Post-test scores ranged from 67 to 100, with a mean of 86.7 (SD = 9.1). The point difference between pre- and post-test scores ranged from a one (one individual scored one point lower on the post-test than she did on the pre-test) to an 80 point improvement. Mean improvement was 32.3 points (SD = 18.1). This is a statistically significant gain according to a paired samples t test (t = -13.8, df = 59, p < .0001).

At the end of the course, women were asked to fill out an evaluation form, responding to questions such as, "What were your expectations of the class?," "What part of the class did you find most helpful?," and "What would you suggest to make the class more beneficial?" The women's responses were overwhelmingly positive. They reported that they benefited most from the hands-on approach to material and what they suggested for improvement is more—more time working hands-on, more time for class so that additional material could be covered, and another more advanced course to follow. Based on the pre-test, post-test comparison, it is clear that the women gained in their knowledge about basic plumbing maintenance. However, in addition it seems that many women gained other important benefits from the program, based on written comments they provided and staff observations. Some women commented that they felt included by the instructor in all activities, how their confidence increased as they progressed through the class, and that learning was made fun. One entire class created and signed a poem speaking of the hope they had been given. Another participant wrote, "You have definitely broadened my horizon. I not only learned how to 'set a toilet' or 'install a faucet' but also about 'life' in general. You taught some very important lessons. Also, you've helped my self-esteem." Both the instructor and correctional staff observed the women working successfully together during the hands-on final in groups of two or three, moving among four different stations to accomplish plumbing tasks.

One is left with the impression that this program is not just about plumbing, but about learning to work together, instilling confidence, and reawakening potential. Just recently, one woman from the 36-hour program was admitted to a pre-apprenticeship program offered by the local plumbing union. It is very unlikely that this would have occurred had she not participated in this correctional education program.

Discussion

Vocational educational programs such as plumbing maintenance have the potential to prepare women for areas of employment that address labor market shortages and provide a livable wage. Many incarcerated women are sorely in need of this kind of assistance. The program described here is a brief intervention, implemented in correctional facilities in the hope that women may be empowered to move forward in positive directions.

Lessons Learned

With the implementation of seven women's groups, lessons have been learned along the way that have helped to strengthen the program and that will continue to be a focus when future groups are conducted. Of foremost importance is support from the administration of the facility where the program takes place. Physical space must be made available for a classroom; this is often challenging in a jail where there is typically very limited space for programming. In addition, corrections employees' cooperation and support is vital for the smooth running of the program because they often assist with selecting participants and transporting inmates to and from the classroom. Offering the program in a sentenced facility, rather than a pre-trial facility, seems to allow for the greatest participation and retention rates.

During the first few groups it became apparent that many of the women were reluctant to use the textbook and were not completing the reading and homework assignments. This may partially be explained by the limited reading ability of some of the participants. Nonetheless, the women progressed more slowly because of inadequate preparation outside of class. Since that time, a new textbook has been introduced with larger font, several pictures and plumbing diagrams, and a review at the end of each chapter. This textbook is much easier to use and focuses on hands-on work rather than on general plumbing information. More women complete the assigned work outside of class now. The low literacy levels also highlight the importance of offering academic, as well as vocational, programs in correctional facilities.

One of the most helpful strategies for promoting learning has been the use of peers as mentors. Researchers have noted the importance of peer relationships among incarcerated women, and it makes sense to draw on this resource to promote learning and positive social connections within the program (Morash, Bynum, & Koons, 1998; Rose, 2004). For example, women who have grasped the math concepts are paired with women who have trouble in this area, and they can work together in class or outside of class on assignments. In one of the groups the participants all came from the same housing unit, and this group bonded together well, working long hours outside of class to master the concepts. They were able to motivate each other to continue to completion. Finding ways to consistently nurture such positive relationships in future classes will continue to be a focus of implementation.

Recidivism and Future Research

The pre-experimental design utilized to assess this program did not allow for the drawing of causal connections between completion of the plumbing maintenance program and recidivism. It is interesting to note that for the 28 women for whom recidivism data were obtained (46.7% of the participants), only three had been re-incarcerated by their respective counties at the time recidivism data were examined (six months to two years post-program participation). As other authors have pointed out, strong research designs continue to be needed that can establish causal links between vocational program participation and recidivism as well as other desired outcomes, such as employment, ability to earn a livable wage, participation in advanced education or training, and enhanced self-esteem. Future work could pursue the approach recommended by Wilson and colleagues (2000). Derived from theory, intermediate variables between program participation (cause) and recidivism (effect) are examined as links in the causal chain. If empirical support for the links exists, then even in the absence of true experimental designs, the case for causation is strengthened. For women, important mediating factors might include the development of pro-social bonds and enhanced self-esteem and problem solving skills, as well as more concrete outcomes such as post-release employment and voluntary participation in other educational or training programs.

Related Program and Policy Issues

In and of themselves, brief vocational education programs are often not enough to help many women overcome the multiple and complex challenges that they face upon re-entry to the community. Additional programmatic supports and policy changes will be needed to significantly impact recidivism rates. Simple solutions are not enough. Vocational educational programs should be part of a multi-faceted response to the needs of incarcerated women. Indeed, Bazos and Hausman (2004) determined that educating inmates is a cheaper method of crime control than expanding prisons. Based upon their review of studies on the costs of prison education, the number of crimes committed by offenders, the number of crimes prevented through incarceration, and the lower recidivism rates among individuals completing prison education programs, they estimate that the cost of preventing one crime through education is about $1,600 and about $2,800 through incarceration (Bazos & Hausman, 2004). Both vocational education and literacy programs were included in their examination.

Other programmatic considerations have been recommended to enhance vocational education programs in correctional facilities. These include certifying programs by the appropriate industry or state board and increasing interaction with employers in the community (Winifred, 1996). The more closely the learning objectives of vocational programs are tied to the expectations and skill requirements of employers, the more likely it is that real job possibilities will result from the learning. In addition, follow-up in the community after release with treatment and services has been found to be a characteristic of effective correctional programs (Lawrence et al., 2002). Finally, providing opportunities for pro-social connections through pro-social activities, such as correctional programs, may be especially relevant to the developmental needs of women (Rose, 2004).

Even positive programmatic changes inside correctional facilities will likely not be enough to significantly reduce recidivism rates unless corresponding policies that affect women returning to their communities are changed. Recently policies have become more punitive, particularly toward individuals convicted of drug offenses (Bloom, Owen, & Covington, 2003; Harm & Phillips, 2001; Smith & Young, 2003). For example, many states impose a lifetime ban on welfare cash assistance for persons convicted of felony drug offenses. Students may be excluded from Federal educational grants because of a prior felony drug conviction. In addition, public housing is becoming less accessible to individuals with criminal records. Women returning to their communities from terms of incarceration often need just these kinds of housing, education, and welfare assistance as they attempt to become self-sufficient. These policies should be reconsidered with a focus on what is needed for the long-term success of released women.

Employers are often reluctant to hire an individual with a criminal record. Expanding policies to provide incentives for employers to hire previously incarcerated individuals, such as tax credits and bonding insurance, may help increase the likelihood that women who have successfully completed vocational education programs will be able to utilize their newly gained skills.

Biographical Sketches

Diane Young, Ph.D., M.S.W. is Associate Professor at University of Washington Tacoma's Social Work Program. She is the author of several peer-reviewed publications on the health and mental health needs of incarcerated adults and the services needed to respond to those needs.

Robert Mattucci earned his Masters in Vocational Education degree in 2002 and has been an experienced plumber for 24 years. He developed and implements the curriculum described here, and published the corresponding textbook.

CHAPTER VI

LEARNING STYLES ASSESSMENT AND ACCOMMODATION

by Donna Shea

Introduction

An in-service workshop presented in 1990 at Skadron College, a private post-secondary career and technical school in San Bernardino, California generated the initial interest in this topic. Methodologies outlined during that workshop provided the impetus to delve deeper into this fascinating area. From 1990 to present, continued investigation into learning styles resulted in gravitation toward the subject matter ultimately selected for this chapter. Resources selected and cited throughout the chapter appeared to fit seamlessly in support of the hypothesis formulated from the original workshop. Both on-line and traditional resources were provided for the reader's reference. The identification of current trends and issues relevant to the adult learner easily generalized to correctional inmates.

From 1990 through 1998, the author applied workshop theory to students attending the Medical Assisting program at Skadron College, and from 1999 to present to scholars in the Designated Subjects Teaching Credential and Bachelor of Vocational Education Degree at California State University, San Bernardino. The available sample population was tested for learning style preference, then the author counseled students on accommodation methodologies, and incorporated strategies designed to accommodate the four styles identified in Harry Reinert's ELSIE assessment into the course materials and presentation. Also during that time the author noted a measurable improvement in academic performance, in some instances by as much as two grade points on a four point scale. This informal observation resulted from the instructor applying learning style theory to practical applications in an isolated classroom environment. Although not a structured research project, students incorporating learning style preference into their study habits reported reduced time and effort spent for greater achievement, which served as the catalyst for continued research. Figure 1 offers a brief overview of the strategies developed from student feedback and performance.

Figure 1: Sample Learning Style Strategies

LEARNING STYLE	TEACHER STRATEGIES	STUDENT STRATEGIES
Reading	Provide written materials for all content • Reading assignments • Label all visuals and manipulatives	Read, Read, Read • Reading textbook faithfully • Read through all notes to date, once every day • Read all handouts

(Continued on following page)

Figure 1: Sample Learning Style Strategies Cont'd.

LEARNING STYLE	TEACHER STRATEGIES	STUDENT STRATEGIES
Reading Cont'd. Note: Reading learners read flash cards frequently.	• Write on board, transparency or slide show • Written reviews • Written, step-by-step instructions for all skills	• Make flash cards for review and carry them around to read often
Visual Note: Visual learners associate different colored flash cards with content.	Provide visuals for course content • Labeled diagrams or pictures • Graphs and tables showing relationships • Flow charts representing decisions • Labeled models • Pictures of step-by-step instructions for skills • Videos	Visualize course content • Use multiple colors to highlight written information and textbook • Associate colors with content highlighters and colored flash cards • Pay special attention to diagrams, pictures, tables, etc. in written materials • Visualize the content like a comic book or cartoon • Draw—it does not have to look good to help you remember
Auditory Note: Auditory learners read flash cards aloud.	Give lectures and auditory prompts • Verbalize every step during demonstrations • Verbal questions for missed test items • Host class discussions • Encourage questions and answers • Sit students where they can read test questions aloud but quietly	Listen and talk aloud • Tape record presentations; listen daily • Read aloud, or have a peer read assignments to student • Join another student to discuss lessons • Recite information presented in writing • Play soft music or TV while studying
Kinesthetic Note: Kinesthetic learners are helped by flipping through flash cards.	Use activities for course content • Develop activities that clarify course content • Provide pictures and diagrams for students to label • Role play, scenarios, videos • Games • If you cannot get the students active, be active yourself. They will remember what you were doing when you delivered the information.	Get physical • Act out content in private • Trace pictures; diagram and label them • Underline or highlight while reading—the activity helps memory • Flash cards: question on one side/answer on the other; flip to help memory • Use finger to underline, keep place while reading • Pace while reading • Associate activity with content • Doodle as listening • Write content over and over

The literature review established the relevance and effectiveness of learning styles as applied to the adult educational experience. The concepts, issues, and conclusions are especially applicable to correctional facility inmates participating in Career and Technical Education courses (MTC Institute, 2003). Sources and theories prompting this chapter originate from educational behavior psychologists. According to Neva Grant of National Public Radio, in 2006 75% of state prison inmates and 59% of Federal prison inmates were high school dropouts. In her report on the Gateway Program she stated that low income families have a high dropout rate and that remaining a dropout increases the chances of remaining poor. These dropouts face a bleak future, stated Reg Weaver (2006, p. 11). He would support Grant's later findings (2008), stating that the majority of prison inmates are high school dropouts. Based on these statistics, successful rehabilitation suggests a two-pronged approach: first, GED courses for inmates to meet high school graduation equivalency and second, career and technical education to provide a means of self-sufficiency upon reentering society. Since public education does not meet these needs, what alternative approach can correctional facilities offer?

Context of the Problem

Recorded debates about teaching methodologies trace back to Plato's Idealism, based on the Socratic method of provocative questioning, and the Sophists who focused on skills or competency-based education. These factions broadly equate with contemporary scholastic versus career and technical education (CTE), formerly called vocational education. Scholasticism adopted the traditional lecture approach to presenting information, whereas CTE education presents competency-based curricula (O'Brien, 1989; Ornstein & Levine, 1997).

Today's educational system is in a state of flux, resulting from the many academic philosophies at work in the United States in conjunction with rapid changes in our world (Gardner, 1999; Ornstein & Levine, 1997). Esler (1984) observed dichotomized opinions between Gagneian/Skinnerian behaviorists and holistic theorists like Piaget and Bruner. If one subscribed to Kuhn's Paradigm Change Model, the educational system has cycled through a state of chaos and normal science. Modern education, including that in correctional institutions, is in a state of crisis demanding a paradigm shift as part of extraordinary science. (See Figure 2 below).

Figure 2: Three Phases of Kuhn's Paradigm Change Model (Gehring, 1999)

	(1) Chaos	(2) Normal Science (NS)	(3) Extraordinary Science (ES)	(2 Again) New Paradigm
General Attributes	Occurs only once; very immature	Paradigm begins puzzle solving	Paradigmatic crisis leads to revolution	New paradigm, new NS period

(Continued on following page)

Figure 2: Three Phases of Kuhn's Paradigm Change Model (Gehring, 1999) **Cont'd.**

	(1) Chaos	(2) Normal Science (NS)	(3) Extraordinary Science (ES)	(2 Again) New Paradigm
The role of a well socialized member of the professional community	Categorize data, to make some sense of a mysterious world. Chaos ends when the community installs the first paradigm.	"Receive" the paradigm (get initiated: attend school; become qualified as a community member; read texts on the paradigm; learn its exemplars, rules); use paradigm to solve professional puzzles; ignore puzzles that cannot be solved (anomalies).	Ignore the anomalies for as long as possible, then "adjust" the paradigm to accommodate as many anomalies as possible; when the paradigm's rules no longer work (puzzles can no longer be solved), grasp urgently to any theory that may solve the most important anomalies—that may become the next paradigm.	Yesterday's extraordinary science becomes tomorrow's new normal science.
Advantages	Categorized data may lead to a paradigm.	NS is an effective strategy for solving puzzles.	ES draws out the creativity and resourcefulness of those professionals who were poorly socialized.	Possible win/win situation.
Disadvantages	Chaos limits growth; few puzzles can be solved.	NS professionals cannot predict a future that is different.	To succeed, ES professionals must be superhuman; high anxiety characterizes ES, exacerbates work problems.	Possible win/lose or lose/win situation.

The new paradigm would set the pace for tomorrow's normal science. This, combined with the many philosophies and learning style models available, led to educational inconsistency and student suffering (Billington, 1998). Research suggested that adult learners were the most vulnerable because while state regulations and district policy imposed some consistency on K-12 institutions, no such continuity existed for the myriad adult learning institutions and environments. Consequently, the adult educational model varied, almost on a classroom to classroom basis, as autonomous educators established individual protocols founded on personal preference and comfort rather than student needs (Spoon & Schell, 1998; Williamson, 1998).

This is further evidenced by the number of unskilled inmates in our correctional institutions. The drop out rate of inmates far exceeds the rate in the general populace. Statistics suggest a corollary if not causal relationship between high school dropouts, low or no income, and incarceration. If dropping out of high school is the trigger, did the dropouts fail in high school or did our educational system fail the students? This concept requires a paradigm shift from the idea that dropouts are "deadbeats" who failed to study or preferred dropping out to making an effort to graduate. The high school dropouts I contacted worked as blue collar laborers, especially in construction. They indicated regret for not completing high school and felt they lacked the intelligence to succeed. Such perceptions can be generalized to inmates in correctional institutions. This begs the question: Is the difference between the institutional group and the blue-collar group a lack of trade skills training or increased opportunities for criminal pursuits? Regardless of the answer, we are faced with a population of inmates who desire and would benefit from CTE education on the road to rehabilitation. Today we face an inverse relationship between a decrease in crime and an increase in the inmate population. CTE offers one solution to reduce the inmate population and the associated financial burden on the American public. However, an effective program must address the reason many inmates fail to complete high school and pursue post-secondary education. The required first step in attending to this problem would be an assessment of how to reach these inmates.

Adult learners acquire knowledge in ways that are different from children, which requires that educators of adults have a command of a variety of learning styles and methods to accommodate them (Spoon & Schell, 1998). Yet typical adult educators, inside and outside of correctional institutions, enter teaching from a previous career, often with little knowledge of teaching methodology and skills. Vocational educators, initially hired because of their life experience and area-specific knowledge, received little, if any, classroom presentation training (Spoon & Schell, 1998). Some attended seminars and in-service teacher training presentations to satisfy Continuing Education Unit requirements for state licensure. However, once vocational educators achieved a "comfort zone" in standards, curricular content, and presentation methodologies, many were reluctant to embrace new ideas (Williamson, 1998). Academic courses were still presented through lectures and reading assignments, leaving poor readers predisposed to failure.

The Learning Styles Approach to Education Delivery Systems

Adult learners experienced only limited success in a traditional teacher-led environment of passive learning in which information was disseminated through lectures and reading assignments, leaving poor readers predisposed to failure and poor listeners labeled as trouble makers. Visual and kinesthetic learners fell through the cracks finally dropping out of high school believing they lacked the intelligence to learn. One possible solution is to provide the learner with tools to assess and accommodate personal learning styles without intervention from an outside source (O'Brien, 1989). A successful CTE program, with instructors knowledgeable in learning style preferences and armed with tools to accommodate all learning styles in their courses, must empower adult learners to excel.

The educational community broadly recognized the validity of accommodating learning styles. However, the disparity between this recognition and the application of a teaching methodology that addressed learning styles prevents the vast majority of adult learners from benefiting

59

from this knowledge. Adult learners need to assume ownership of their educational experience. Educators in all venues, but especially in correctional institutions, must facilitate student learning by presenting information on self-assessment and accommodation of learning styles, to develop strategies that ensure academic success and reentry into society with skills that promote self-sufficiency.

Andragogy: How Adults Learn

Learning consists of increasing knowledge, remembering information, gaining knowledge for practical uses, abstracting meaning from activities, and understanding what has been acquired (Learnativity, 1997-1999). Literature reviewed included the earliest specialists in this field as well as current trendsetters and their issues with an emphasis on critical or directed thinking. Diane Halpern (1996) defined critical or directed thinking as increasing the probability of a desirable outcome by employing cognitive skills and/or strategies. Halpern further suggested that different people preferred different modes of thought and that success required "being mindful" or conscious and concerned about the thinking process. A new term, metacognition, was coined to identify knowledge about how one learns.

Increasing knowledge is a vital part of an individual's growth, which constitutes a significant element of the learning process and, as such, is inseparable from learning. Measurable growth is largely physiological in children, but in physically mature adults demonstrable growth must follow mental and emotional pathways (Billington, 1998). Cited studies addressed the next logical question: Does this also imply that adults learn differently from children? One representative study indicated young children use right-brained visual-spatial strategies to learn to read; older children shift to a left-brain linguistic approach; and by adulthood, reading becomes a balanced hemispheric function. This study suggested, and seemed to support, the theory that adults approach learning differently from developing children (Dryer et al., 1999). In summary, to increase knowledge and continue to learn, even adults must continue to grow; conversely, cessation of growth results in cessation of learning as well (Billington, 1998).

Billington (1998) further identified the following seven characteristics necessary for an effective environment to facilitate adult learning:

- A safe environment that meets learners' needs and recognizes life achievements.

- An environment that encourages creativity, freedom and experimentation.

- Faculty that interface with adult learners as peers and remain open to learning from their students.

- A program that encourages students to take ownership of the learning experience and offers the opportunity to meet individual learning needs.

- Pacing that challenges growth while maintaining a realistic tension level to avoid discomfort.

- Opportunity for proactive adult learners to participate in interactive learning.

- Feedback mechanisms that not only provide learners with consistent performance evaluations but also ensure learners a voice in classroom activities.

These seven criteria supported Carl Rogers' concept of the active learner. The learning process must be self-initiated and pervasive, the evaluation locus must reside with the learner, and the learning experience must be meaningful to the learner (Corey & Corey, 1997).

With this knowledge it became incumbent that researchers answer the question of how to alter the learning experience to accommodate adult learners. While traditional approaches to presenting and measuring information principally utilized verbal/linguistic and logical/mathematical techniques, other strategies were equally important for success in life and should be incorporated into the adult learning experience (Corey & Corey, 1997). Understanding why one person learns differently from another and accepting that both are equally valid holds great power (Martin & Potter, 1998). Initial influences on how individuals acquired knowledge included the context in which information was learned and applied. Studies indicated that adult learners preferred specific learning styles to gain knowledge. Therefore, adult educators needed to be cognizant of learning styles, defined as the method in which new information is collected, processed, internalized and retained (Dunn et al., 1995; Spoon & Schell, 1998). Rather than believing themselves unable to learn certain information, adult learners then achieved academic success by taking responsibility for identifying and accommodating individual learning style preferences (Shaunessy, 1998).

Learning Styles and Multiple Intelligences

Numerous existing learning style models were classified in three ways (Learnativity, 1997-1999):

- Perceptual modalities are biologically based methods of acquiring data from the physical environment.

- Information processing pertains to a preferred method of perceiving, organizing, retaining, and processing data.

- Personality patterns attend to values, emotions, and awareness of different situations.

In all three, the components of preferred learning styles included how the student concentrated, processed, internalized, remembered, and recalled information. Individuals could learn anything by capitalizing on the strength of their unique learning style (Shaughnessy, 1998). A study involving three middle schools supported Shaughnessy's hypothesis. Each school, employing a different learner-centered approach (multiple intelligences, learning styles, and brain-based), was equally effective because all accommodated personal preferences (Guild & Chock-Eng, 1998). Unfortunately, parents expected many average learners to follow the traditional methodology of studying in quiet, secluded surroundings. Challenging the parents' paradigm, by playing music during study for example, resulted in reprimands to the child who was then forced to comply with the parent's concept of an acceptable learning environment. The concept of digital immigrant vs. digital native coined by Marc Prensky further widened this perceptual gap. Forcing children to study using outdated strategies frequently resulted in poor performance, and a lowered self-esteem which followed the learner into adulthood. Understanding metacognitive processes empowered the student to succeed through applied individualized strategies (Martin & Potter, 1998). This became even more critical for college and adult learners who realized even greater benefits from learning style accommodation than children (Dunn et al., 1995). The correctional educator faced additional challenges relevant to disparate learning styles according to the MTC Institute (2003).

Development of various learning style models addressed the issue of learning preferences. James Bell (1998) differentiated between three learning styles: (a) visual learners, who converted sensory input into images in the brain, preferred written material, (b) auditory learners, who benefitted from verbal instructions and oral delivery systems of information, and (c) tactile learners, who frequently became restless in traditional sedentary environments and required activities that offered hands-on situations. David Ellis (1991) explained how Harry Reinert's 1986 learning style identification exercise took Bell's model one step further by dividing visual learners into those who preferred written words and those who preferred pictorial images like graphs, diagrams and charts. Reinert made his assessment tool available at http://www.newhorizons.org/strategies/styles/reinert.htm. The identification of these learning styles grew from the concept of a learning cycle. According to Indiana State University (1999a and 1999b), in 1984 Kolb established an experimental learning cycle based on four quadrants (see Figure 3 on following page).

Figure 3: David Kolb's Learning Style Grid

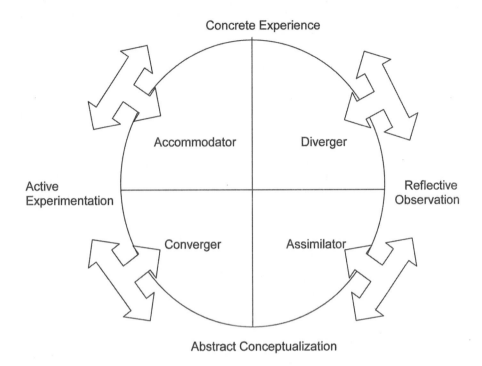

Concrete Experience

Accommodator   Diverger

Active
Experimentation

Reflective
Observation

Converger   Assimilator

Abstract Conceptualization

Kolb identified the horizontal axis as active experimentation and reflective observation. His vertical axis differentiated concrete experience from abstract conceptualization. The four quadrants separated learners into accommodators, divergers, convergers, and assimilators. Kolb viewed the educator's role as facilitating learners through all four quadrants. An adult learning model called 4MAT, based on Kolb's four quadrants, followed McCarthy's natural learning cycle (Kaplan, 1998). It identified that information can be perceived and processed four ways: connecting the information to personal meaning, obtaining expert information, repetitive application of the information, and generalizing the information to real life problem solving. In keeping with Kolb's concept of an educator, supporters of 4MAT believed in presenting all information to all learners using all four modalities (Kaplan, 1998). However, the rigidity of 4MAT did not allow for individualized instruction and methodology. In order to decide which method to employ, the individual or the institution needed to establish criteria with which to evaluate the effectiveness of these learning models as they pertained to themselves and/or their student body (Martin & Potter, 1998). For these reasons, the author found Reinert's ELSIE assessment easy to administer and implement on a daily basis with little additional preparation (Reinert, 1986; Ellis, 1991).

The Indiana State University Center for Teaching and Learning Styles Web page (Indiana State 1999a and 1999b) provided an index of learning style models based on various approaches. Social interaction models included the Perry model of four developmental stages in college, Belenky's model based on social strategies for acquiring knowledge, and the Baxter Magolda model which integrated the Perry and Belenky models into four stages including variations within each stage. In contrast, Myers Briggs incorporated Kolb's information processing model with personality types to identify world-views that influenced the learning process (see Figure 3).

Perhaps the most comprehensive was the Dunn and Dunn Learning Style Model, founded on seven principles and 23 components. This model included physiological traits, time of day, mobility, environment, sociological background, emotional state, processing preference and intake-while-concentrating preference principles, among others (Dunn et al., 1995). By incorporating biological, developmental and social factors into the model, it offered highly individualized assessment and accommodation. Correctional educators may find this model relevant and useful.

Howard Gardner (1993) took a slightly different research approach leading to the concept of seven or multiple intelligences identified as musical/rhythmic, bodily/kinesthetic, logical/mathematical, verbal/linguistic, visual/spatial, interpersonal, and intrapersonal. Gardner found that all intelligences form the core of human thought but individuals became "at promise" (highly skilled) or "at risk" (lacking ability) in applying specific intelligences. Therefore, the dominant focus on traditional verbal/linguistic and logical/mathematical presentations placed students who excelled in one or more of the other intelligences at an educational disadvantage. According to Gardner, learning styles identified a single preference regardless of content, whereas multiple intelligences addressed content-specific approaches. The wider range offered in this model suggested additional strategies for correctional educators to connect with the inmate population.

In spite of the evidence supporting learning styles and multiple intelligences, educational researchers could not reach a consensus on the validity of learning strategies. Gardner (1993) admitted to the absence of experimental testing of his multiple intelligences theory, but argued empirical evidence collected from practical applications in the classroom supported his theory. Furthermore, relevant studies identified a correlation between accommodating students' learning style and grade point average (Dunn, 1998). In opposition, McKeachie (1995) argued learning styles were habits or preferences that could be developed or changed at different times while simultaneously contradicting himself by encouraging educators to provide students with strategies to match preferred learning styles. According to McKeachie, motivation, intelligence, and prior knowledge were more important than learning styles. Conversely, Shaughnessy (1998) listed motivation as only one of twenty-three learning style elements that contributed to a positive learning experience. Shaughnessy admonished against addressing learning styles individually and suggested viewing them as a construct of variables forming a unique pattern. In further opposition to

McKeachie, Sonnier (1985) cited a number of sources that supported a holistic approach based on the lateralist theory of hemispheric information processing. Sonnier contended quantity of education was a left-brain cognitive function while quality of learning was an intuitive right-brain function.

These confounding results in adult learning style research could be attributed to an adult learner's ability to adapt years of experience in different types of learning environments to traditional teaching methodology (Spoon & Schell, 1998). Informal surveys from the author's courses supported Spoon & Schell. The ability to adapt enabled adult learners to survive traditional educational delivery systems. However, adaptive abilities did not empower adult learners to excel or gain full measure from the traditional instructional approach (Spoon & Schell). This research shed light on the murky topic of scholastic achievement or lack thereof by inmates.

Accommodating learning preferences was not a panacea for society's educational problems; however, if combined with traditional theory and methodology, learning preference accommodation increased the chance of success (Guild & Chock-Eng, 1998). Adults who found it difficult to memorize large quantities of new facts required alternatives to rote memorization and traditional instruction ("A neural network. . .," 1998). It is especially important that inmates in CTE programs assume responsibility for meeting their own needs and that correctional educators facilitate them in that pursuit. This required that the student also understood the learning process, thereby applying metacognitive strategies (Learnativity, 1997-1999). The resources below will be useful to interested readers.

Self-Assessment and Evaluation Tools

Note: The tests are intended as general indicators, and the author does not endorse them. Obtain permission where applicable to protect intellectual property.

How does learning style influence homework? (1995). St. John's University's Center for the Study of Learning and Teaching Styles. [Homework disc developed for IBM and Apple software packages].

Howard Gardner's Seven Intelligences Checklist, Adult Version, FTP: http:// www.mitest.com/o7inte~1.htm

Learning Styles Inventory (LSI). (1995). Price Systems. Lawrence, KA. [Available on Apple and IBM self-scoring discs].

McKenzie, W. (1999). Multiple Intelligences Inventory. The One and Only Surfaquarium. FTP: http://surfaquarium.com/MI/inventory.htm

---

Without resolution among the many educational factions, adult learners needed the tools to take ownership of their education. The most important thing learners could do was to identify their learning style and choose strategies to accommodate that preference (Learnativity, 1997-1999). This chapter provided correctional educators with assessment instruments and suggested strategies to accommodate inmates' preferred methods of learning

Conclusions

Growth and development is an essential element of the human condition. For adults who have reached physical maturation, growth must reside with an expansion of the mind known as learning. However, the debate on how learning is achieved rages. The following conclusions were developed during the research process.

- Adults learn differently from children and require specific environmental factors to facilitate learning.

- Numerous learning style models facilitate the academic success of adult learners.

- Research suggested that a small percentage of educators employed learning style preference in instructional methodology.

- Academic success for the adult learner is facilitated by changes in curricula and presentation and by learner applied strategies to accommodate learning style preferences.

If you want to pursue these ideas further, the following references may help.

References for Additional Reading

Corey, G. & Corey, M. S. (1997). *I never knew I had a choice* (6th ed.). Pacific Grove, CA: Brooks/Cole Publishing Company.

Ellis, D. B. (1991). *Becoming a master student instructor guide* (6th ed.). Rapid City, SD: College Survival, Inc.

Gardner, H. (1993). *Multiple intelligences: The theory in practice*. New York: BasicBooks.

Gardner, H. (1999). *The disciplined mind: What all students should understand*. New York: Simon & Schuster.

Halpern, D. F. (1996). *Thought & knowledge: An introduction to critical thinking* (3rd ed.). Mahwah, NJ: Lawrence Erlbaum Associates.

Indiana State University. (1999a and 1999b). Brief summary of select learning style models. CTL learning styles site. [Web page]. Available FTP: http://web.indstate.edu/ctl/styles/model2.html.

McKeachie, W. J. (1995, November). Learning styles can become learning strategies. *NTLF* [On-line journal], 4(6), 1-4. Available FTP: http://www.ntlf.com/html/pi/9511/article1.htm.

O'Brien, L. (1989, October). Learning styles: Make the student aware. *NASSP Bulletin*, 85-89.

Shaughnessy, M. F. (1998, January/February). An interview with Rita Dunn about learning styles. *The Clearing House*, 71(3), 141-145.

Sonnier, I. L. (Ed.). (1985). *Methods and techniques of holistic education*. Springfield, IL: Charles C. Thomas Publisher.

Walter, T. L. & Siebert, A. (1996). *Student Success* (7th ed.). Orlando, Fl: Harcourt Brace & Company.

Biographical Sketch

Ms. Donna Shea, M.A., is the Program Coordinator for the Bachelor of Vocational Education degree at California State University, San Bernardino. In addition to teaching upper division teacher preparation courses, she serves on the Science, Math, and Technology Department curriculum committee. She is a lifetime member of the Phi Kappa Phi honor society and serves as Co-Trustee in the Gamma Nu Chapter of the Epsilon Pi Tau Career and Technical Education Honor Society.

Chapter VII

Career and Technical Education

by Norris Williams

In this chapter I will give my perspective on the role of career and technical education (CTE) in correctional education. I feel that the responsibilities of CTE programs go well beyond just teaching a trade. These programs must reinforce treatment of the issues that lead to incarceration as well as prepare students for reentry. The ultimate goal of all correctional education programs has to be to prepare offenders for successful reentry into society and to teach them to become contributors to society instead of burdens.

I would like to begin with a short personal biography. My birth State is South Carolina, but I have resided in Virginia for over thirty years. I chose the electrical field as my career immediately after high school and am licensed as a master electrician. My work experience includes residential construction, commercial construction, industrial construction, naval shipbuilding, and as a specialized service technician and maintenance technician. I have always enjoyed the challenges of complex installations as well as troubleshooting complicated systems. Much of my experience has been in supervision, but I have always preferred the hands-on work. During my career I trained many apprentices and helpers. I always enjoyed teaching them, but I had never considered the possibility of being a teacher.

In 1997 I began my second career, which was in correctional education. I began this phase as a career and technical education instructor in the field of electricity. My teaching experience included approximately one year teaching men at Greensville Correctional Center and five years of teaching female offenders at Fluvanna Correctional Center. It was during this time that I came to the realization that I have always been an educator at heart.

In 1998, while I was teaching the men at Greensville Correctional Center (110 miles from my home), I was informed of a potential job opportunity at Fluvanna Correctional Center, a new facility that was being constructed near my home. This facility would be for multi-custody females and would have Virginia's first electricity program for women. I was interested in the position for several reasons. First, Fluvanna is about 85 miles closer to my home than Greensville. Another reason (and the most important one) was that I had worked with numerous women during my career in the electrical field and had nothing but good comments to make concerning their ability to work in the trade. Almost all were conscientious, hard workers who carried their share of the load. I firmly believed that the electrical field would be a good career choice for female offenders. This would give them the opportunity to earn a higher wage than traditional female jobs offer. I was sure that I would be a good choice for this job. I applied for and was selected to fill the position.

It was a pleasure to have had the opportunity to work with men and I learned a lot from that experience. However, I was truly excited about the opportunity to work with women. I found some challenges to educating female offenders in this "non-traditional" field. Most of the women had always assumed that the building trades were "men's work." It was a challenge to help them gain the self-confidence that was necessary to succeed in the classroom and in the trade. To do this, I found that it was of utmost importance to get them involved in hands-on projects as soon as possible. Developing motor skills in this new area was found to be a good motivator for them. There was also the challenge of overcoming weak math skills. Unexpectedly, I had to become a math teacher as well as an electrical instructor. This was a new challenge for me. I hired and utilized inmates who had completed the program to serve as tutors. I selected those with good math skills to assist with addressing this deficiency. The program was made to be flexible to help the students with weaker math skills remain motivated as we helped them to raise these skills to an acceptable level. This was accomplished by integrating hands-on projects with mathematically demanding course work. The goal was to get the students hooked by utilizing manual accomplishments as the motivator, which proved to be the extra push that carried them to success with the math. Successful completion of non-traditional programs gives the female offender a greater opportunity for a living wage upon release. I understand that many program completers may never actually work in the particular trade, but this success can lead to an elevated self-esteem which in itself can contribute to a successful reentry.

In November, 2003 I was promoted to the position of Apprenticeship Programs Coordinator for the Virginia Department of Correctional Education, beginning yet another career, now working in the central office. I have always been a supporter and respecter of apprenticeships. I believe that this time-tested form of teaching and learning, which is approximately 1000 years old, is an excellent means of producing a highly qualified and skilled workforce. Apprenticeships utilize trade-related instruction to complement on-the-job training.

In the last five years we have made some good advancement in our apprenticeship programs by expanding and improving them and by increasing the number of completers. The teachers and work supervisors have been encouraged to keep the learning at higher levels. Our apprentices have several strikes against them because of their pasts, therefore we want them to be as prepared as possible for the jobs they will be seeking. Apprenticeship programs give offenders an excellent, industry-recognized credential to take with them into the workforce. In correctional apprenticeships it is of utmost importance to maintain a high level of related instruction to help offset the shortfall in availability for appropriate on-the-job training. If the inmate was in an apprenticeship outside of corrections he or she would probably be exposed to a much greater variety of work experiences.

Correctional institutions are considered to be commercial facilities, with most correctional factories being rated "light industrial." Videos, trade magazines, books, catalogs, etc. can help to broaden the exposure of apprentices. Generally, corrections administrators are supportive of apprenticeship programs, as they serve several purposes for them. Apprenticeships give the institutions better trained inmate workers, and that lowers operating costs. Apprenticeship programs help raise inmate morale, which makes them easier to control. The teachers, supervisors and apprentices are continually reminded that apprentices are not students, but rather professionals who are receiving job-related training to enhance their skills. The teachers are encouraged to hold the apprentices as accountable as they would be held in programs outside of corrections.

In 2004 the Virginia Department of Correctional Education (DCE) began seeking credentials for our Career and Technical Education (Vocational) Programs. With a large percentage of our programs in both adult and youth institutions being in the area of the building trades, we decided to seek industry-recognized certifications for these programs first. Since my background is in the trades, I was given the responsibility to assist in finding credentialing opportunities for our programs. During the past few years I have been working on this initiative, being unofficially given the title of DCE Industry-Based Certification Coordinator. I believe this is a positive move for our programs. The credentials help to add credibility to our programs and to assure that they are aligned with the needs of industry. Credentialing also gives our programs portability, meaning that a student can continue in programs outside our facilities should the student be released or transferred prior to program completion.

Industry-based certifications can take several forms. In some programs, such as barbering and cosmetology, this might be actual State licensure. For other programs there may be a national certification, such as American Design and Drafting Association credentials for our Computer-Aided Drafting programs. For the building trades programs we are using both the Residential Construction Academy and the National Center for Construction Education and Research (NCCER) Credentialing Programs. This initiative has been quite a challenge for our office, as the ultimate goal for DCE is to offer the very best programming possible to our students.

I am very interested in the attention that is being given to the importance of better preparation for reentry. This should be a no-brainer. Without good reentry preparation all of the other teaching and learning do not have a high probability for success. Reentry has to be a philosophy and not a program. The preparation for reentry should begin as soon as the offender is committed to corrections. The needs for preparation for reentry have to be reinforced in all programs inside the institution, including CTE programs.

I believe that nothing should be taken for granted as offenders are preparing for reentry. It is imperative that there be a comprehensive approach to the preparation. The simplest thing may be the cause for an offender to recidivate. The offender may have never had a driver's license or held a legitimate job. It may be something as simple as not knowing how to use a phone book. It may be the inability to be considered for a job because of lack of paperwork (social security card, birth certificate, etc.). These are just a few of the potential stumbling blocks that can be addressed during preparation for reentry. Nothing should be taken for granted.

Be honest with offenders and help them to establish a realistic view of the outside world. Encourage them to maintain contact with their families, as positive family support can be an important component in a successful reentry. CTE programs should also address employability skills. This will help offenders to have an understanding of what will be expected of them on the job. Such programs should cover such topics as writing a resume, interviewing practice, how to look for jobs, etc. It should be the goal of CTE (vocational) programs to give our students adequate preparation for getting and keeping a job. If these things are done there will be a greater chance of reentry success.

Summing up my perspective in relation to CTE programs in correctional education, I believe that the role goes well beyond teaching a trade and should address every need that an offender brings into the classroom. Most vocational teachers are from the world of work. They possess a high degree of trade skills but do not, however, bring with them the skills to understand all of the needs that the students bring into the classroom. Teacher education must be available to prepare them to recognize these needs and to assist in addressing them. To meet the needs of each particular industry, we have to offer programming that fulfills the requirements of industry-recognized certifications. I believe that non-traditional programs for female offenders can be an effective means of preparing them to be self-sufficient and will contribute to a successful reentry. I also believe that apprenticeship programs in corrections can be an effective and inexpensive form of programming and preparation for careers outside of corrections.

Correctional education has been proven to positively affect recidivism. Now that we know that we do good things, it is time to fine tune what we do. Our mission is an important one. The futures of so many depend on what we do. This includes offenders, their children, their families, future potential victims, and society and communities throughout the United States and the rest of the world.

Biographical Sketch

Norris Williams
Apprenticeship Programs Coordinator
Virginia Department of Correctional Education

In April, 1997 Norris Williams began his career as a correctional educator. He is a Master Electrician and brought with him into the classroom over 25 years of experience in the electrical field. During the next six years he spent one year teaching male inmates and five years teaching female inmates. In 2003 he was promoted to the position of Apprenticeship Coordinator for the Virginia Correctional System. He is also a Past-Director of Correctional Education Association Region II and presently is Director-Elect for CEA Region II. Norris presently serves on numerous boards, including the Richmond Area Apprenticeship Association, where he serves as Director, the Board of Directors for the VA Apprenticeship Alumni Association, and the J. Sargeant Reynolds Community College Capers Oversight Committee. Other professional organizations in which he maintains membership follow: VA Association of Correctional Educators, American Corrections Association, and the Virginia Corrections Association

CHAPTER VIII

DEWEY AND MAKARENKO

by Robert J. Holtz

Abstract

This chapter provides a brief characterization of two education theorists from the beginning of the twentieth century and their impact on vocational and correctional education. American John Dewey and his laboratory model with its "progressive ideas" will be compared and contrasted to Ukrainian Anton Makarenko's model of "educational collectives." The importance the two theorists have to correctional education and vocational education will be discussed, along with a brief introduction of influential persons in correctional education in the U.S. Throughout the chapter "vocational education" and "correctional education" can be used interchangeably. Both men had enormous impact on education practices in two opposite political and social structures of their day, Dewey in the United States and Makarenko in the Soviet Union.

Background

Men and women, young and old, who are confined to the prison system are typically ill-equipped to succeed in our communities. They are incarcerated for myriad crimes and for varying lengths of time. Confinement does not eliminate the desire to continue criminal behavior once a person is returned to society. Consequently, programs to successfully reintegrate individuals should be at the forefront of correctional and vocational education research, funding, and adoption.

Vocational and academic classes are not available to all individuals paroling from prison. Does providing an education to inmates reduce the possibility of their returning to prison prior to one year of freedom? Parolees recidivate at a significant rate, typically within the first year through parole violations. Considerable legislative decisions are made based on imprisonment and its effectiveness in reducing recidivism. What level of education services should be available to inmates?

A comprehensive study of the school system within a prison setting is much needed and beneficial to the school itself. Reviews should be ongoing to ensure the school is providing for the needs of the inmate student. The school benefits by implementing effective programs and effective strategies. Educating inmates is controversial and programs may be eliminated when budgetary problems persist in an organization. Therefore, regular and thorough reviews can provide administrators the tools needed to make informed decisions when balancing budgets and when asking to keep the much needed vocational and academic programs in place.

Dewey and Makarenko

John Dewey was born in Burlington, Vermont on October 20, 1859 and is recognized in the United States as one of the most prominent educational philosophers of the twentieth century. He authored numerous books, lectures and articles and subsequent volumes were written by many other authors describing his impact on education theory. Dewey obtained his formal education from the University of Vermont and Johns Hopkins University. In 1884 he began his teaching career at the University of Michigan, then moved on to the University of Chicago, and retired from teaching in 1930 while at Columbia University in New York City. His 46 years of teaching provided him the opportunity to develop his ideas on progressive education and the laboratory school. He died in New York City on June 1, 1952.

Anton Semyonovitch Makarenko was born in Belopolye, Ukraine on March 1, 1888. He became a teacher at 17 years of age at a railway workers' school in Ukraine, under Czar Nicholas II's reign. He continued teaching there after the Bolshevik Revolution of October, 1917 and graduated from the Poltava Teachers' Institute with honors that same year. Makarenko went on to organize collective colonies for the "new" Russia from 1920 through 1935. During this time, he worked on refining an intuitive style of education theory, which he then began to write about from 1930 until his untimely death from a heart attack on April 1, 1939 in Moscow. Makarenko was not recognized as a leading educational theorist during the early part of his career, but his acceptance grew, and he eventually became the most influential education theorist in the Soviet Union.

Challenging Environments

Both Dewey and Makarenko encountered societies that were in desperate need of an education paradigm to meet existing social dilemmas. Both Russia and the United States desired to ensure students would be taught en masse, not only for the individuals' needs but also for the promotion of each country's political doctrine. This was the challenge for both countries, with Dewey and Makarenko performing their roles using parallel but contrasting methods.

The United States had suffered through the divisive Civil War. Furthermore, society was moving away from an agrarian way of life to an industrial one; from a rural to an urban lifestyle. Dewey felt the move from the agrarian setting to the factory setting played a significant role in disturbing the development of children in the United States. He felt education would have to fill the void brought about by this turmoil. Dewey believed that what the best and wisest parent wants for his own child, most of the community wants for all its children. All that society has accomplished for itself is put through the agency of the school, at the disposal of its future members (Dewey, 1907, p.19).

The family and the farm had played an important part in social development. Families and neighbors worked together to provide for their collective needs, and education was handled by societal dynamics.

This was not the impetus of the industrial production method, whereby large factories provide for society through mass production. The move to the urban environment brought about additional pressure in the development of the child by removing the influence of the cottage system, where society provided for itself. To staff factories, a large migration to cities occurred. Legislation was passed against child labor and production was removed as a way of life for the child. The importance of work needed to be taught now via the institution of public education.

Much like these severe changes in the United States, Russia was enduring extreme pressures that would change its society forever. Around the same time as the U.S. Civil War, Russia experienced the wrath of Czar Nicholas II's impunity toward the lower classes and peasants. This authoritarian murdered millions in order to exert control. Soon thereafter World War I had an excruciating impact on Russian society. Millions were displaced. Families were devastated. Up to 7,000,000 children were left to wander the countryside to fend for themselves. Industrial production was ten percent of what it had been prior to World War I. In this environment, family life was not as important as it had been in Russian society.

Education was structured so only the upper classes of society were afforded access to the best schools. Peasants and the lower classes were left with only the most utilitarian learning opportunities. Education of the masses was not a prominent priority.

These are the conditions under which Makarenko began his career. The son of a railroad worker, Makarenko overcame the predisposed notion of becoming a factory worker by being an outstanding student who graduated with honors (Judelson et al., 1976). Makarenko was described as an outstanding educator, up to and throughout the Russian Revolution.

The Russian Revolution of October, 1917 and the beginnings of the Stalinist period to 1935 can be best described as a tumultuous time, which afforded a great deal of experimentation in Russian education. This is the period when Makarenko began to develop his educational theory based on his own intuitive thoughts. He had very little specialized training in pedagogical research and therefore relied on his beliefs in Marxist doctrine (Bowen, 1965). He believed that education was the vehicle to develop the new Soviet man's role in society. Consequently, he formulated a paradigm which he applied in educating the displaced children of devastated Russia.

How They Accomplished Their Goals

Societal pressures were integral in the development of these two men. Without examining their histories, it would be easy to lose sight of what was driving each of them. A comparison of the dynamics affecting the two societies is essential to a more complete understanding.

Both men were determined to use their methods for social control. Both societies were challenged by previously unknown social problems. Integral to the problem was the large number of delinquent children that had surfaced. This would be at the forefront of the theories these two men would develop and refine over their lifetimes.

Dewey was explicit in his desire to see work, play, and education effectively intertwined, so schools could supplement families in the social development of children. He believed the radical reason that the present school cannot organize itself as a natural social unit is because just this element of common and productive activity is absent. Upon the playground, in game and sport, social organization takes places spontaneously and inevitably. There is something to do, some activity to be carried on, requiring natural divisions of labor, selection of leaders and followers, mutual cooperation and emulation. (Dewey, 1907, p, 28).

Makarenko developed a similar theory on education while head of the Gorky Colony. This institution was named after the Soviet writer Maxim Gorky, who influenced Makarenko's thinking. In the Gorky Colony (or collective), work and social order were imperative to group success. He went so far as to divide his groups into detachments modeled after a military structure. These detachments were responsible for certain activities that maintained the colony. Additionally, each detachment was encouraged to compete when it came to things like which group could chop the most wood, had the most productive acreage, assemble the most goods, and amassed quickest after a bugle call.

Dewey believed in work more than pure occupations. Through work students could learn geography, mathematics, economics, problem solving and critical thinking. Dewey felt:

> In educational terms, this means these occupations in the school shall not be mere practical devices or modes of routine employment; or the gaining of better technical skill as cooks, seamstresses, or carpenters; but active centers of scientific insight into natural materials and processes, points of departure whence children shall be led out into a realization of the historical development of man. The actual significance of this can be illustrated through actual school work than by general discourse. (Dewey, 1907, p.33).

Through his collective, Makarenko was given the task of re-educating delinquent children. His first group of a dozen charges was to be assimilated to the new Soviet order. It was an unruly group with no social skills, who would not listen to Makarenko or the other teachers. This was very difficult for Makarenko, because his ideas were not from pedagogical study, but from his own intuitive approach toward education. He had no firm foundation or application on which to draw, basing his practice on Marxist and Hegelian doctrine.

Makarenko's task was of no small order. These Ukrainian children were described as "waifs, delinquents, homeless, depraved, criminal and neglected. . .besprizorniki" (Bowen, 1965). In his book *Soviet Education: Anton Makarenko and the Years of the Experiment,* Bowen indicated a clear translation from Russian to English could not be made, so the best Russian word "besprizorniki" was left as the moniker for the children with whom Makarenko worked. Besprizorniki was a term that had no distinct definition in the Russian language; it was used as an all-encompassing term to describe Makarenko's charges.

Makarenko's work with the bespirzorniki was an experiment in Soviet education. Similarly, Dewey formulated the laboratory school to test his theories on education. Both men made it their life's work to mitigate the social woes each believed were so desperately affecting their country's children. Each felt education to be a collective process (Bowen, 1965). Makarenko held that through work, children would have connecting activities, which had been lost to society during those tumultuous times. Children must endure hard, physical, and challenging work to affect change, not through abusive means but by the pure pleasure which came from labor.

Educative activities were an essential strategy by which this would be accomplished. Each man sensed that through the process of education and labor an effective strategy of education could be developed, which consequently was adopted in each country at that time. Each man had critics. Fortunately, both worked very hard to refine their theories and define their ideas.

Initially, Makarenko's practices at the collectives were not widely accepted by Soviet officials. Actually, during the period from 1917 through 1937, Makarenko received considerable criticism from his Soviet counterparts. The twenty years after the Bolshevik Revolution through the Stalin regime were an experimental period in Soviet education. Many Soviet educators were imitating American methods of education and Dewey's laboratory schools. They believed Makarenko's ideas contrasted considerably with Dewey's. True to his communist beliefs, Makarenko refused to accept any methods from America (Bowen, 1965).

Makarenko's ideas were developed at his first Gorky colony in 1920, refined during his next appointment, then began to receive wide acceptance by 1935 when he implemented his practices at his last colony. "The main impact of Makarenko's ideas on Soviet teacher education began after his death. He became an educational idol; his portraits were hanging in each Soviet educational establishment" (Koshmanova, 1997, p.8).

Dewey's ideas were initially welcomed by education theorists of his time. It was not until much attention was directed to the laboratory schools and progressive theory that Dewey reflected on the criticism he was receiving. Many believed his theories were too progressive and not effective in educating the masses. Dewey accepted this criticism, but discounted his critics by saying his progressive school model was being introduced into traditional schools. This poor fit was the flaw, not his concepts. Schools needed to be built "from the ground up," based on his theories and practices (Dewey, 1997).

Finally, each man, out of a similar desire to educate the masses, transcended the established methods of his day. Much can be said about each man, but perhaps no one was as insightful as Bowen when he described Makarenko's and Dewey's impact on education:

> Anton Makarenko was to Soviet education what John Dewey was to education in America. Each believed education to be a group process, but placed a different interpretation upon the individual's role in society. Dewey emphasized the importance of the diversity of the individual's interest as necessary to strengthening society's growth. Makarenko felt that the individuals should be subordinate to the collective needs of the group. He sought to educate the child according to environmental psychology in which social conditioning and habituation play a prominent role. (Bowen, 1965, back cover).

Makarenko, Dewey, and Vocational Education

These men faced societies filled with delinquent children. "Correcting" the behavior of delinquents was very important to them. Both men went about it with parallel themes but contrasting methods. Each faced intense challenges, and developed ideas significant for the application to vocational education.

Correctional educators of today also encounter "the waif, neglected, delinquent, criminal, homeless, and depraved," the "besprizorniki." This is as powerful a test now as it was nearly a century ago: Meeting the needs of our students through extraordinary means. Each man led with the firm belief that he would make a difference, as we should each day as we assemble our students and classrooms. Our approach should be the same. We need to look toward our heroes who have made a difference, and utilize their techniques and theories.

As correctional educators, we desire to correct the behavior of persons who have deviated from societal norms. Makarenko and Dewey did not believe children were bad by nature, but influenced by nurture. Makarenko went so far as to discard and ignore any information he obtained on his charges. He avoided looking at an individual's past as a precursor to what was in store for that individual in the future. His emphasis was on re-education and the transformation of an individual into an effective member of society. This is an approach we can strive toward today, because our students will respond to it. They expect order and thrive on it.

We need to do this for the individuals we teach. We need to do this for the city or town these men and women are going to be released into. We need to do this for all the families, and for their hopes and dreams of normalcy. Quite possibly society has let these persons down. They became predators because they knew no better.

Perhaps they are the victims and we should show them what is right and what is wrong. Give them what humanity has to offer by making re-education the vehicle by which they can become acceptable participants in society. Engage them in activities unknown to them in the past. Provide them experiences in human interaction. Connect them to the resources that were not available as they were developing in our local schools. Teach them the positive principles of human behavior.

These methods are not always available to our students. Why give them more? Why offer them the hopes and dreams afforded to the rest of society? Many would say that our students are victimizers. They let their families, their neighbors, and themselves down. Consequently, they should be eligible for less. All of this may be undeniably true, but they are human. Give these people a purpose. Makarenko and Dewey recognized the student's humanity, overcame the ignorance, and worked for a solution. So have many of our correctional education heroes.

Makarenko and Dewey can be recognized as correctional education heroes. Vocational educators need to recognize more of our heroes. Starting around 1860 Zebulon Brockway spent 50 years in prison service, much of it at Elmira Reformatory in New York State. William George founded a democratic youth facility, the Junior Republic, also in New York State. He allowed for the democratic management of the facility by youthful wards. He was admirably recognized as "daddy George." His tenure was from 1895 to 1930. Mary Carpenter identified prison reform as a field of its own. She worked in the period from the 1850s to the 1870s. Much of Brockway's work was built on her ideas. Thomas Mott Osborne was the former mayor of Auburn, New York. He disguised himself as a prisoner in New York's Auburn State Prison to discover the conditions under which inmates lived. Osborne later became the warden of Sing Sing Prison. He made his impact in prison reform from 1913 to 1926.

Do you recognize these people? They are just a few of the men and women associated with correctional education who made a difference. Can you build upon their ideas? They too recognized the humanity, overcame the ignorance and worked for solutions under the most adverse conditions. Discover the literature associated with their impact on correctional education. Find the time to engage yourself in the methods they used to bring about change in the thousands of men and women they encountered. Identify yourself as a correctional educator, so you can do the same.

Conclusion

Anton Semyonovitch Makarenko and John Dewey showed that, given appropriate tools and direction, most individuals would overcome the circumstances that brought them to their current situations. Educators need to study the histories of these two men, and discover the heroes in their particular field of education. We need to build upon the study, the theories, the techniques, and the experiences of others. We have a huge responsibility to society, as did Makarenko and Dewey, and we need to share ideas and methods to perform a more definitive role transforming the besprizorniki of today. Our students can add to the diversity of our society or add to the turmoil that continues to plague our communities. We can make the difference and we can help them make a choice!

Biographical Sketch

Robert J. Holtz has been a correctional educator for the past 15 and ½ years. He has been a vocational instructor, a vocational supervisor, a General Educational Development Alternate Chief Examiner, a Western Association of Schools and Colleges visiting team member and leader, a Coastline Community College and Palo Verde College Proctor, a Fire Chief at a state prison in California, and is currently an assistant principal at a prison school. Robert has a Bachelors degree in Vocational Education and received his Masters degree in Education Administration and an Administrative Services Credential at California State University, San Bernardino in June, 2003. He is a strong supporter of correctional and vocational education and has worked to provide employment opportunities for students upon parole. His theory on education is: To develop a "pull system" of education rather than a "push system" thereby having industry looking to the prison system for employing ex-felons upon their release to society.

CHAPTER IX

THE STATE OF VOCATIONAL EDUCATION IN JUVENILE FACILITIES AT THE TURN OF THE 20TH CENTURY

by David Snedden
(Excerpted from *Administration and Educational Work of American Juvenile Reform Schools*, 1907)

Editor's Preface

On Feb. 12, 2010 a daily newspaper in Syracuse, New York, *The Post Standard*, printed an editorial concerning the deterioration of juvenile facilities in New York State. During the previous four years numerous documents had come to light regarding conditions that youth had been forced to endure at many facilities. The editorial content was nothing new. It focused on ongoing concerns. What was new to me was how long this abhorrent problem existed in these facilities; this sort of thing has been going on for over 100 years. The book from which this chapter was taken was written by David Snedden in 1907 while he was a faculty member at Columbia University Teachers College under dean John Dewey. It is a timeless piece concerning a continuing and hot topic in correctional education.

Vocational education has long been an integral part of any effective rehabilitation program. Written over 100 years ago, Snedden's book is an historical reference that sheds light on how far juvenile correctional education has come, as well as how much it has deteriorated. In many ways Snedden's writing on correctional education for juveniles set the pace for MacCormick's 1931 book on adult correctional education—which is the subject of the next two chapters.

Snedden was a real visionary in the care and education of juvenile offenders. One result of his book, aside from influencing MacCormick, was that urban education around the country finally found a program to replicate in what was then called the common or local public schools. Stated alternatively, Snedden's summary of juvenile correctional education practices helped set the pace for the developing local schools throughout the United States. For example, urban public schools picked up on the correctional education practices associated with compulsory education, individualized education, special education, physical education, and vocational education. Reading from Snedden's book can help remind us how we should care for youngsters so they will not graduate to a life of adult crime and prisons, and so we will not be faced with future editorials about how juvenile facilities have gotten even worse. I hope you will benefit as much as I have from the following selections of Snedden's *Administration and Educational Work of American Juvenile Reform Schools* (1907).

Robert Mattucci, Editor

(From *Administration and Educational Work of American Juvenile Reform Schools*, pp. 7-8)

1. [AUTHOR'S] INTRODUCTION

The juvenile reform school has not sprung from our public school system but has grown partly in connection with charity and philanthropy, and partly in connection with the departments of justice and penology. In a very true sense the work undertaken by these institutions has represented more fully the idea of state education than has the work of any other part of the educational system. For in these schools the entire round of educational effort must be compassed. That which in a normal society is done by home and church and shop to supplement the work of schools must here be performed by the one institution. And more: it has been the mission of these schools to take, not the normal child, but the abnormal, the neglected, the perverted; and, by educative efforts to measurably reshape the warped character and mind with which they have had to deal.

The educational work of juvenile reform schools has had few points of contact with the general system of public and private education of this country. The problems to be worked out have been so special and peculiar, as to make it impossible for the workers to find in the public school system much of suggestion. Likewise, the public schools have failed largely to cooperate with and learn from juvenile reform schools. The result is that we find in the history and present development of education for juvenile delinquents an evolution of ideals, traditions, and methods having a fairly unique character, and much suggestiveness to the educator. Hardly any other system of education is so immediately tested by results as this; for the juvenile delinquent is a marked character in society, and the effects of his contact with the school are visible and much observed. The efforts of philanthropists and the intelligence of our ablest penologists have produced the ideals under which the schools have taken shape. In many instances the supervision of voluntary agencies, as State Boards of Charity, has been superior to the supervision prevailing in public education. Under these conditions, the juvenile reform school has never been able to slight or evade the problems of what is currently termed "integral education"—education that is at once physical, moral, intellectual, and vocational. However imperfectly these schools have accomplished their work, it is nevertheless true that they represent to-day the most persistent, comprehensive, and effective experiment in the domain of education that is available to the student. Hampered by slow public recognition, inadequate and underpaid service, the traditions of the parent prison system, the evils of partisan control, and the absence of a consistent philosophy of education, they have nevertheless accomplished much of fruitful work in their own field and have produced a body of imperfectly organized educational knowledge and method which should be made available.

82

(From pp. 13-19).

The object of. . .charity is reformation, by training its inmates to industry, imbuing their minds with the principles of morality and religion, by furnishing them with the means to earn a living, and, above all, by separating them from the corrupting influence of improper associates. . . . From these conditions the evolution of the modern juvenile reform-school at its best has been a marked, but by no means a uniform process. Here and there individual schools, under the leadership of some unusually keen and sympathetic men or women, have reached high standards of excellence. A long and patiently fought local campaign has usually been necessary to secure the establishment of such schools; and it is still true that many states have as yet no juvenile reform schools. The state-controlled schools have passed through discouraging periods when they were used by the politicians for patronage. Nevertheless, as one compares the conditions of one decade with those of another, the general progress noted can hardly he said to be less than that found in the best of the other institutions of the republic.

The following are the more notable features in the development: (a) The physical welfare of the children committed to the institution has come to be more carefully attended to. Generally speaking, it would seem that to-day in the average school the pupils are well off in the matters of food, shelter, clothing, cleanliness, health, and exercise. In other words, nurture as a factor in the general education of these boys and girls has been fairly well realized in recent years. Not that conditions are ideal; the necessities of economy, the location of some of the institutions, the ignorance and inattention of many officials, prevent as full a development of the side of physical nurture as is desirable in many instances; but results attained are favorable when contrasted with the previous conditions of the institutions and frequently with the home conditions of the children themselves.

(b) Again, the change in discipline has been very marked. Relics of prison discipline have largely disappeared in the modern school and there is a tendency to approximate the conditions of the better boarding schools. Corporal punishment, solitary confinement, and various devices for humiliation and torture, while not wholly discarded, have been largely replaced by other means of procuring not only control, but also moral development. The history of the rise of the more humane spirit in the practice of these institutions is part of the larger history of the decline of severity in church, home, school, and prison.

(c) The gradual rise of the cottage system, in the estimation of the students of the subject, is also important. Very early the ideal had developed that the reform school should, as nearly as practicable, reproduce the conditions of the good home. Attempts to realize this end were difficult on account of the greater expense in land, buildings, and service required; and on account of the supposed increased difficulty of control. But after much experiment and effort the cottage system has come to prevail in various forms, and institutions not so organized are striving in that direction.

(d) With the development of the cottage system there have grown up various systems of classifying the inmates. This classification has been sometimes along lines of age and physical development, sometimes on the basis of the offence for which the child is committed, and sometimes on the basis of moral or intellectual development after entering the institution. Each system has had its defenders and is still more or less on trial; but in a general way, the system of extensive classification has greatly improved the morale and effectiveness of the institution.

(e) Another feature of the reform school which has undergone marked development is that of industrial education. The earlier institutions were workhouses, but the work was slavish, the child was conscious of no advantage to himself, and the trade learned was not one that could be followed afterwards. The manual training movement which began in this country with the Exposition of 1876 gave the schools new ideals and since then there has been a marked tendency to substitute for the old productive forms of labor those which, while making the institution more expensive to its supporters, would nevertheless give the child a better industrial education.

(f) It has always been recognized that the children committed to the reform schools were far behind the normal child in point of intellectual attainments. A notable part of the work of these schools has been the development of a system of education usually called literary which should put the inmates somewhat on an equality with children outside. In the better schools a decided attempt is made to apply the courses of study used in the public schools, but it has taken long and patient effort to reach this standard, in view of the variety of other work which the institution has been expected to perform.

(g) The older schools, affected by their prison traditions and lack of facilities, gave little attention to the discharged inmate. As a consequence, the work of the institution was frequently undone by the return of the child to a bad home, or to his failure to find a suitable home, if without parental care. Individual schools did what was possible to remedy this condition, by improving and safeguarding the conditions of indenture, by co-operating with the home, and by keeping in touch with the boy or girl after leaving. The wisdom of this policy has finally developed the general parole system which is now recognized as an indispensable part of the work of reform schools.

(h) The establishment, in quite recent years, of juvenile courts and probation has led to a more careful screening of offending or neglected children, and the present result is that the reform schools, where juvenile courts exist, get a somewhat more incorrigible class of children, and in fact the schools tend to become institutions for that residue of delinquent children who cannot be handled by the co-operation of home and probation officers.

(i) Other special devices for improving the work of the schools are the introduction of a partial wage system, and self-government. These are still in an experimental stage.

(From pp. 69-117).

2. VOCATIONS AND INDUSTRIAL EDUCATION OF 20 YEARS AGO

Because of the character of the available material it seems desirable to discuss this subject under three heads: the prevalent conditions of twenty years ago together with the ideals then held which are developed by Mr. Letchworth's inquiry of that date; the ideals and practices of to-day in girls' schools where the problem of industrial education necessarily assumes an individual character; and the ideals and practices in boys' schools. The information collected by Mr. Letchworth is primarily valuable as showing the attitude towards contract work. It has been hard in many instances for the institutions to dispense with this, owing to their inadequate means of support. But at that time (1883) it is evident that a strong preponderance of opinion existed against it [contract work] and the managers of the institutions were hopefully anticipating a time when it could be replaced by more educative work. Manual training, however, was not then widely known and understood. Field and garden work were looked upon as being the most promising alternatives. This inquiry was made in 1883, when Mr. Letchworth was a commissioner of the New York State Board of Charities. The statements were received in response to a series of categorical questions sent out by him. The substance of the replies is given here in a somewhat condensed and rearranged form.

Connecticut State Reform School: 380 inmates, averaging just over 13 years when received. Work: 120 in sewing rooms, 200 cane-seating chairs, 3 in shoe shop, 50 in laundry, dining-rooms, kitchen, bakery, halls and on farm. In spring and summer 30 boys are taken from chair-caning for work in garden. 5 hours for work, 3 for school.

Connecticut Industrial School for Girls: 185 inmates, average age 14 ¼ years. Six hours' work per day and 3 hours' school. Work: 22 box-making, 60 dress-making, sewing and fancy-work, 25 laundry, 67 housework, dairy, and miscellaneous.

Illinois State Reform School: 290 boys, average age 14 ½ years. Six hours' work daily, four hours' school. Work: shoe-making (ladies' shoes on contract) 130; cane-seating, 75; farm and garden, 20; tailoring, 16; laundry, kitchen, bakery, miscellaneous, 49.

Indiana House of Refuge: 400 boys, average age 14. "About one-third work on the farm, the remainder in the various shops. Half the day to work, half to study."

Indiana Reform Schools for Girls: 130 girls, average age14. Five hours' work daily, three for school. Work: cane-seating, 30; sewing, 20; washing and ironing, 50; and domestic service, 30.

Iowa State Reform School (Boys): 242 boys, average age 13. Four hours to labor, four to school. Work: farming, gardening, stock-raising, shoe-making, hat-making (all for use of institution).

Iowa State Reform School (Girls): 83 inmates, average age 14. The employments are domestic work, supplemented by instruction in the use of the needle.

Kentucky Home of Refuge: 247 inmates, average age 13. Six hours to labor, 4 to school. Work: cane-seating, 100; shoemaking, 10; gardening and farm, 15; housework, 54; and rest at general duties.

Maine State Reform School: 107 boys, average age 14 ½ years. Six hours' work and four hours' school. Work: farming, gardening, caring for stock, tailoring, baking, laundry, housework, and cane-seating.

Baltimore House of Refuge: 242 boys, average age almost 14. Five hours' labor, four and one-half school. Work: Basket and wicker work, 77; shoe factory, 39; tailor shop, 11; farm, 8; yards, 12; boilers and engine, 3; painting, 2; carpenter work, 2; bake-house, 9; laundry, 7; school-room, halls, and officers' departments, 12; carriage, wagon, and gate, 3; office and hospital 3; dormitories, 7. In junior department, sewing-room, 15; rooms and yards, 4; unemployed, 28.

St. Mary's Industrial School (Maryland): 442 boys, average age 15 (and inmates range from 8 to 21). Six hours' work, three for study. Work: Basket and bottle covering shops (hired by contractor) 194; tailor shop, 34; shoe shop, 26; printing-office, 18; blacksmith and engine-room, 4; farm and garden, 10; bake house, laundry, and all other domestic work, 76.

Massachusetts. State Reform School: 118 boys, average age 15 ½ years. Three hours' school, seven or eight at labor. "About half are employed at farm work, the remainder at cane-seating and domestic labor."

State Industrial School, Lancaster, Massachusetts: 72 inmates, average age 15 ½ years. Occupations: housework, light gardening in summer, sewing, knitting. Three hours daily to study.

Plummer Farm School, Salem: Restricted to 30, average age 13 ½ years. Six hours' labor, four school. Work: gardening in summer, chair-seating in winter, with some domestic work.

Lawrence (Mass.) Industrial School: Average age 12 years. Four hours for school, four to five for work. Work: farming and seating chairs.

Michigan State Reform School: 375 boys, average age 14years. Four and three quarter hours per day for school, same for work. Work: "We do a large amount of farming, making our own clothes, caps, shoes, etc., and also chair-seating."

Minnesota Reform School: 134 inmates, including 16 girls. Average age 14 years. Four hours' school, same for labor. Work: tinsmiths, 15; woodwork, 40; printing, 5; seed-growing, 10; remainder at domestic work.

St. Louis House of Refuge: 167 boys, 62 girls; average age 13 years. Seven hours' labor and three hours' school. Work: shoemaking, 90; chair making, 50; farming, 4; and the rest at sewing, baking, and domestic work. (The boys engaged in shoemaking are hired to contractors).

New Hampshire State Reform School: 108 inmates, 90 boys, 18 girls, average age 15 years. Four and one-half hours to work, five and one-half to school. Farming and chair-seating are the occupations.

New Jersey State Reform School: 344 boys, average age13. Three hours are given to school with a five-minute recess, and 6 ¾ hours to work, with two 15-minute intermissions in the shirt-making department. Work: Making shirts, 189; laundrying and ironing same, 42; farming, 24; brick making, 26; making and repairing clothing for school, 11; laundry work, bakery, waiting, and other domestic work, 52.

Girls Industrial School, Trenton, N.J.: 34 inmates, average age 14. Six hours to labor, three to School. Needle and domestic work.

Newark City Home, New Jersey: 129 boys, 27 girls. Average age, 12 ½ years. Five hours per day to work. 60 boys in brush shops in winter, 40 in summer. Farm, 16, house duties, 18. Girls are instructed in sewing and cutting clothing, and in housekeeping. Small and backward children go to school six hours per day, others 3 hours.

House of Refuge (Randall's Island, N.Y.): 694 boys, 117girls. Average age of boys, 12 to 15; girls, 14 ½ to 15. For study, four hours in winter, three and a half in summer. For work, first division, seven in winter, seven and a half in summer; second division, seven hours in winter, eight in summer. Work: making stockings, 552 (boys hired to contractor); ravelling stockings, 100 little boys, also under contract; girls do housework for their department and washing and mending for boys.

Western House of Refuge, Rochester, N.Y.: 461 boys, 105 girls. Average age 12 years. Three hours school and seven hours the limit of contract work. Work: making clothing, 154; making shoes, 140 (both occupations under contract system); seating and flagging chairs, 100 (of smaller boys); remainder do miscellaneous work, as farming, and domestic work. Girls knit hosiery by machinery, make and mend their own clothing; also make skirts, pillow-cases, towels, and stockings.

New York Juvenile Asylum: 623 boys, 160 girls. Average age, 12 years. Children under ten have five hours' schooling each day, and no labor; over ten,

3 hours school, 3 ½ hours work. Employment: shoemaking, 17; tailoring, 95; needlework, 80; fanning, 12; and housework, etc. 100.

New York Catholic Protectory: 1205 boys, 648 girls; 127 little boys. Average age, about 11 years. Children over regular school age receive two and one-half hours tuition each day; and others, five hours. Hours of labor, none for little boys; from four and one-half to five and one-half for others. Industries: shoemaking, printing, 58; caning chairs, 100; stocking factory, junior, 250; senior, 250; shoe-repairing, 28. Girls industries: glove-sewing, 68; sewing by hand and machine at shirt and dress work, 300. The girls do all the housework of the female department.

Ohio Reform School: 471 boys. Half the day to work, half to school. Work: brush shop, 115 boys each half-day; rest at blacksmithing, baking, tailoring, shoemaking, farming, gardening, flower culture and domestic duties.

House of Refuge, Toledo, Ohio: 192 boys, average age 13 ¼. Three hours daily to work, same to study. Work: sock-knitting, gardening, making their own clothing, etc. They are changed from one industry to another every six weeks.

House of Refuge, Cincinnati: 314 inmates. Seven hours to labor, 3 to school. Industries: shoemaking, tailoring, gardening, engineering, baking, cooking, washing, sewing, etc.

House of Refuge, Philadelphia: 467 boys, 148 girls. Average age of boys, 12; of girls nearly 13. Three hours school; seven hours labor in summer, six in winter. Work: brush making, 275; cane-seating, 46; tailoring, 21; shoemaking, 6; boiler room, 4; wicker work, 33; hosiery shop, 61; sewing (girls, 55; housewifery, 52); domestic work, boys, 21; remainder, odd jobs, etc. Seven are too small for employment. (The larger trades above are let out to contractors).

Pennsylvania Reform School, Morganza: 245 boys, 61girls, average age 13 ¼ years. Four hours to school, 6 ¾ to labor. Work: carpet and light saddlery and harness goods (on contract); and at agriculture and domestic work.

Rhode Island Reform School: 160 boys, average age 15. Four and a half hours each day to labor, and same to school. Work: chair making, 130; tailoring, 10; housework, 20.

Vermont Reform School: 71 boys, 18 girls; average age 13. School, four hours, work four or five according to age. Work: caning chairs, farming, gardening, making shoes and clothing, and domestic work.

Wisconsin Industrial School: 300 boys, average age 14. Work: boot and shoe factory, 100; sock and mitten factory, 120; miscellaneous work, remainder.

Industrial School for Girls in Milwaukee: 110 girls, 3 to 18 years; and 30 boys under ten. Younger children are in school six hours daily, all others four hours. Work: house work and domestic sewing; custom laundry work, custom sewing, knitting, crocheting, cutting and fitting of plain garments. Many "fancy articles" are manufactured. Older girls taught to manage sewing-machines.

The inquiry made by Mr. Letchworth brought out an interesting consensus of the ideals of the managers of these homes on the matter of industrial work and education. In 1883 the manual-training idea had not found expression to any marked extent in American education, for it is commonly assumed that the early forms of manual training arose from the Centennial Exposition in 1876. But a few quotations will show that the thought that all industrial work in reform schools must have an educational aspect, in fact must have the educational as its chief end, was beginning to be felt. Supt. Howe of the Connecticut Boys' School, with over twenty years' experience behind him said: "In regard to the employment of children in an institution similar to my own, I would say were it in my power to do so, I should have them all engage in agriculture, horticulture, and floriculture, in some form or other. Labor in the gardens, in the greenhouse, upon the lawns, the culture of small fruits, the care of stock and poultry, all conduce to health and happiness, and are much better than shop labor for reformatory purposes. That kind of shop labor which introduces machinery is best calculated to please the boy. Our sewing machines are run by steam power. The boys seek this labor through their liking for machinery."

Supt. Bond of the Connecticut Industrial School for Girls thinks that "it is desirable to employ girls and boys in institutions at industries that will fit them for honorable self-support when they leave. Girls should be instructed in the art of housekeeping in all its branches, dressmaking, plain and fancy needlework, and laundry work. Paper-box making is a good trade for girls, but we do not encourage girls to go into shops or factories. I believe in practical trades for boys, even if their labor amounts to little in the way of self-support in the institution."

The following expression is from Supt. Scouller of the Illinois State Reform School: "We have never found any employment fitted for children under twelve, either in or out of reform schools. Their work should be in school and on the playground, with ten hours in bed out of every twenty four. After that age, first work them on a farm or garden. If such is found to be impossible, then at cane-seating, bookbinding, card-printing, sock-knitting, light sewing; many other industries might be mentioned. I do not think there is anything boys or girls under the age of twelve can work at in an institution like ours, that will be of any benefit to them as a trade when discharged. Boys over twelve can be worked at light shoemaking, to better advantage than at any other occupation we know of."

Supt. Miles of the Iowa State Reform School is "of the opinion that each child capable of learning a trade should be required to do so, but it costs money to teach boys and girls trades and public opinion will not tolerate any enterprise in an institution of this kind, that will not be a revenue to the institution. Our farm of 500 acres is a revenue, and many boys are fitted for farm-hands on it and go out and do well in that capacity. Our tailor shop, shoe shop, broom shop, and straw-hat shop are satisfactory in results as far as they go, but we need more trades."

Mrs. Lewelling, the Superintendent of the Iowa Girls School says: "All our work is done by hand, with a view to better qualification for domestic service. Our younger inmates spend a good deal of time in making block quilts, and such like work; in fact, anything to keep them employed. . .If we can make of them plain, plodding people, such as are well qualified for domestic labor, we shall feel that much has been accomplished. At present we look to that end chiefly."

Supt. Farrington of the Maine State Reform School writes: "My own opinion in reference to the employment of boys in reform schools is that during the hours of labor they should be kept steadily employed at some work which will teach them a trade, whereby they may earn their own living after discharge. The work should be of such a nature, that the boys would become interested in it, and seeing it to be for their own great advantage, would strive to excel in working rapidly and well. They should in some way participate in the profits of their own labor. There would be no pecuniary profits in an employment managed in this way, except what would come from making good citizens out of bad boys; but inmates would be sent out into the world, capable of earning a good living, and imbued with the idea that labor is a blessing and not a curse. The idea of an institution earning a money profit from their labor must be abandoned. The schooling given the boys should be in the line of trade-teaching, and should include freehand and mechanical drawing and bookkeeping. The State of Maine has recently appropriated $5000 for the establishment and maintenance of manual instruction in this school: It has not been decided how that money shall be spent, or just what the instruction shall be."

From Supt. Kirkwood of the Baltimore House of Refuge: "As our object is to train boys for future usefulness, we should try to instruct them so that they may be able to secure positions in business that will render comfortable support. We have been trying to introduce other industries, so as to afford as much opportunity as possible for our pupils to learn a business for which they are naturally qualified."

St. Mary's Industrial School, Maryland, reporting through its Superintendent, Brother Alexius, says: "Institutions of this kind cannot well compete with outside skilled labor, for the simple reason that children seldom remain long enough in such establishments to learn a trade thoroughly, hence only an ordinary article can be expected from them, for which the house would not easily find a profitable and ready market. The most remunerative work done by such children, are simple and light occupations contracted for, by which habits of industry are instilled, as basket-making, caning chairs, knitting, etc. A child that has been engaged at these inferior works should, at the age of thirteen or fourteen, be transferred to a proper trade, carried on in the establishment. When a boy so employed has obtained a practical insight of the profession, he should be sent to a proper master outside the institution where he could learn his trade thoroughly, remaining, however, always subject to be recalled by the authorities of the reformatory until he is of age, in case he should fail to observe his duties. Children of such institutions should be encouraged by a certain percentage of the profits derived from their labor, and deposited in a savings-bank, to which they may lay claim when they come of age." It will be recalled that St. Mary's has established a branch called St. James' Home in which indentured boys may live, paying for the cost of their support.

"Work upon the land," thinks Supt. Allen of the Massachusetts State Reform School for Boys, "is the best employment. On stormy days and in winter, the best work we ever had is cane-seating chairs." And in similar vein writes Supt. Brown of the Girls School of the same state: "In this school we aim to keep the children busy during work hours, knitting by hand, sewing,—that is, making their own garments, also at housework, by this we mean training them to be good bread-makers, and as efficient as possible in the laundry. The girls in summer, under supervision, work out of doors planting and weeding the garden, picking strawberries, peas, beans, etc. They also gather apples and perform much light work....One of our restrictions, some work was let on limited contract for machine knitting was that no girl should work more than three consecutive months in the shop." Another interesting school in Massachusetts, the Plummer Farm School, had its thirty boys work at gardening in the summer and chair-seating in the winter, with some domestic work, which are, in the estimation of Supt. Johnson, the "best employments when near a good market for vegetables and small fruits."

From the Minnesota State Reform School Supt. Riheldoffer writes: "We have always conducted our school with sole reference to the reformation of the inmates; preparing them, by education, and the knowledge of some branch of skilled labor, for self-support and citizenship. We do not approve of contracting their labor and have never done so. When even boys get the idea that the state is using them to make money, without reference to their interest, it begets discontent and want of confidence in the charitable intentions of their overseers. Some have avoided all labor that does not afford an opportunity of learning some manly employment. Many of our boys go out skilled mechanics, at once demanding good wages. I have no hesitation in commending our method, in this regard, as the best in use. If our shop only pays expenses we are satisfied." This school had 15 boys employed as tinsmiths, 430 at wood-work, 5 at printing, 10 at seed growing; and [the] rest at domestic work.

In the New Jersey State Reform School, at this date, extensive contract work was being done, but under direct control of the school. The school takes and controls the contract. Supt. Eastman desires "that every boy must be brought to feel not only that the industries, but that the whole institution, is merely a means in the Superintendent's hands, to be used by him, or under his direction, for the reformation of the boy's individual character. . . .Now what of this shirt manufacturing itself (the work taken on contract most extensively) as an education to the boys? I like it for a class. It is clean work and must be critically done, and they can turn their knowledge in it to good account when they leave us. The laundryman and ironer get good wages. But we have too many boys employed in that one department, and the laundry business does not obtain in every part of the state. I would multiply industries without increasing our pay-roll too much. We have an excellent carpenter and blacksmith. Had we a suitable building, a class of boys could be profitably employed, making and ironing wagons, etc. They would meet with ready sale. We could at once open a printing department, teaching the boys to set type for our local newspaper. In our shoeshop, if it were large enough, a class could be taught the use of wax end and awl, in making horse halters, lead and tie straps, etc. Since saddlery, harness, and trunk making are extensive trades industries in most of our large cities, I could doubtless get work for them to do on as favorable terms as shirtmaking. I would have a tin-shop. With no very great outlay at our brick yard we could start a pottery. . . .Our labor is not sold by the day, but rewarded by the dozen or the piece at living prices. The foregoing new industries I would conduct in the same guarded manner."

The Newark City Home had at this time children whose age averaged 12 ½ years. Says Supt. Harrison: "First, and above all else, I think duties pertaining to the farm are best adapted to us in the care and culture of our wards. If I could so arrange it, I would provide labor for all in the fields during the spring, summer and autumn. The winter months should be employed in teaching skill in manipulation. Any branch of light labor, which affords a chance for advancement in skill, neatness, and dispatch answers the purpose of reformatory teaching. We use the brush industry and compel painstaking. (Five hours a day are devoted to the several employments). Our object is teaching, not profit. Habituation is one of our aims. . . .We must cultivate pride of person, self-reliance, rouse the moral faculties to activity, cultivate every sense—all which are sometimes lost sight of, in the practice of those industries in which competition is fierce."

Supt. Carpenter of the New York Juvenile Asylum writes: "In an institution like this, I think all children of suitable age to work, can be most profitably employed in making the clothing including the shoes of the children, mending the same, doing the house work, etc. That is most profitable to the children themselves and probably quite as profitable to the institution." He objects to the contract system because "it is antagonistic to the reformation of the boys."

The following is the opinion of the Managers of the Catholic Protectory of New York: "We consider that the most desirable method of employing children in institutions similar to that under our charge is by some trade or occupation by which they will be able to support themselves after leaving the institution. Where that is impossible on account of the uncertainty of the time when they will leave the institution, it is desirable that they should be engaged at some occupation which would accustom them to labor and teach them habits of industry. These should not be of such a nature, however, as to interfere with their physical or mental, growth or development; and for that reason the system of hiring out their labor by the day to contractors has never been permitted by the Protectory. The limiting of the hours of labor would rather aggravate, than remedy, the evil, by causing contractors to exact a greater amount of work from the children."

Supt. Douglass, of the Ohio Reform School says: The juveniles "should be taught some trade, whereby they can earn a living when away from the institution." Supt. MacDonald of the Toledo House of Refuge finds that "as a rule, boys committed to Reform Schools are from a low order of parentage. I never knew a case where a boy was committed who had been a regular attendant at the public schools. They will not readily make skilled tradesmen."

Supt. Laverty of the Philadelphia House of Refuge thinks that the contract system under certain restrictions "is the best for the class of children that we have in the House of Refuge. The great object is to teach them habits of industry, as an important auxiliary to their moral and mental training."

Supt. Fairbanks, of the Vermont Reform School writes: "As to the time of work, I would grade it according to the age and strength of the child. The work should be, if possible, practical and remunerative. By practical, I mean such as will fit them to earn a livelihood when they leave school. We work most of the boys in the shop at caning chairs. This work educates them in the habit of industry, teaches them to apply themselves to the work in hand. So far, so good, but it would be far better, especially for the older boys, if the work was such as they could engage in with profit when leaving the school. For this reason we propose entering more largely into gardening, that more boys may be employed thereat. I have also urged for some time the making of the frames we cane, since they could be made with profit and little outlay for machinery. The larger boys with a turn for mechanics, could make the frames, thus gaining a knowledge of the machinery, etc., by which they could be fitted to enter most of the woodworking shops in the country. . . . I think little of an industry that simply employs—teaching merely application and industry—and does not educate for practical life. . . . The locality of the school will have much to do with determining the kind of employment and the means available for such ends may have still more influence."

The Girls Industrial School of Wisconsin at this date taught the girls mostly domestic work, but did extensive custom laundry and sewing of many varieties. Mrs. Cobb, the Superintendent writes: (The various varieties of domestic work) "are taught by instructors as well educated and as well paid as the literary teachers, and the classes are changed quarterly, so that within two years all girls above twelve years old may learn all the parts of housekeeping and needle work well. We use the best text-books on household economy, and require intelligent training, not only in cookery, but in domestic science, care of the sick, etc. Our custom work comes from the best families and is required to be done with the utmost nicety. . . .Having learned as much as we can teach them our girls can, if they must, afterwards turn to the manufacture of cheap clothing on sewing machines in shops, or to the large laundries; but the chances are against such a necessity in their future, as they will be fitted for higher work."

3. PRESENT DAY INDUSTRIAL EDUCATION OF GIRLS

The problem of industrial education as it confronts the Girls' School is simplified by the fact that much of the institutional work—cooking, sewing, domestic work of all sorts—is of a kind which the girls are most apt to follow on leaving the school; and it is further simplified in that any and all of the staff can easily be more or less expert in domestic work. On the other hand it is made difficult by the fact that in a large institution much of the domestic work must assume a wholesale character which is not productive of either personal interest or the artistic excellence which is desirable in home-keeping. A more fundamental difficulty is that the home training and parental oversight of the girls usually committed to these institutions has been so slight or of such an injudicious character as to result in a more or less complete absence of habits and interests in domestic work. In most cases the industrial training of the fourteen- or fifteen-year-old girl must be begun at the lowest point of the scale and be gradually built up.

The testimony of most of the Girls' Schools is that their inmates are peculiarly susceptible to personal influences, and therefore much of the success of the educational work depends upon the tact, sympathy, and strong motherly qualities of the women of the staff. Under one type of housemother the girls may work rebelliously, perfunctorily, and with growing distaste for their employments. Under another, with a different personality, they may learn to work with earnestness and pleasure, and with a growing disposition to find in their daily tasks inspiration for a subsequent career of wholesome industry. Trained teachers for work of this character are usually unobtainable; and the best results seem to be reached by the selection of women who possess in large measure a combination of tact, sympathy, and firmness, such as one would find in a woman of good common sense and a wide knowledge of human nature.

Few of the girls' schools seem to have been obliged to utilize the labor of the inmates unduly in the direction of contributing to self-support. In all of the schools the teaching of dressmaking and some allied occupations has given the opportunity so much desired in the Boys' Schools—of providing work which should be educative and which would at the same time provide a source of individual interest and enjoyment of the product. It will be realized that very little opportunity is afforded in boys' schools to have children do things whose fruits are theirs to enjoy; while the girl who in the course of her education makes for herself an article of apparel is provided with a strong personal motive for interest and individual effort. Very much, however, of the domestic work of girls in institutions must lack this individual character; and here again, as in the case of the teacher's personal qualities, a slight difference of adjustment may produce a wide difference in the educational outcome. In some cases the work is so carried on that many girls come to dislike it and to resolve to do anything but domestic work on leaving; in others, the girls learn to take a positive interest and to develop skill in the work with a conscious view to its application.

Nearly all girls in Juvenile Reform Schools must expect to be self-supporting when paroled or discharged. Ultimately, of course, many of them become housewives; but there is a considerable intervening period for which the educative work of the institution must provide the basis of support. In respect to available trades which may be taught in such schools there is frequent complaint of their scarcity. Apart from domestic occupations, there are few callings for which girls can be specifically prepared. The teaching profession is out of the question for these girls. An occasional institution has made some sporadic efforts at typewriting and stenography, but apparently with no great results. In the manufacturing states many girls go to factories, but for this work the school can give little but the most general preparation. Many of the girls of the Oak Lawn School in Rhode Island declare their intention of going into factories rather than into housework, because in the former they can have holidays, Sundays, and evenings free—reasons which seem to animate many other girls than those in reform schools.

A considerable variety of garden work, floriculture, and fancy domestic work, besides music have been developed in many girls schools; but these find their justification in their contributions in a general way to taste and refinement and development rather in opening the way to vocation. Many of the schools find in fancy-work, millinery, bead-work, and music their best aids in discipline.

Unfortunately for a complete discussion of this subject there is not obtainable material for an exact statement of the work usually attempted or accomplished in Juvenile Reform Schools for Girls. We can only say that, as a rule, the girls are divided up according to the arrangement of the institution, their own ages and capacities, and the needs in various divisions of work. Where feasible girls are given opportunities or are required to practice at various forms of employment, seldom are records kept of numbers any one kind of work. Some condensed accounts, taken from the reports of various typical schools, will furnish the most available review of the contemporary ideals and methods of these institutions.

The Chicago Refuge for Girls has department training in "sewing, cooking, embroidering, laundry work, and all general housework, giving every member of the family an opportunity to prove her efficiency and worth in each branch. The latest achievement in our industrial department has been the making of baskets of all sizes from the large, firm baskets, to the tiniest sewing baskets. And, too, the girls have added to their crafts the useful and clever art of caning chairs." The Industrial Teacher reports an income of $710.25 in her department on work sold, the average number of inmates being 124. It is noted that the girls do a large share of the caning of chairs, painting of furniture, etc., for the institution. A well-equipped cooking school has been in operation in this school for eleven years, with a special teacher of the subject. "Every girl is required to spend two hours a week under this teacher's instruction."

In addition to the customary lines of domestic work, the girls of the New Jersey State Home "have done considerable outdoor work, caring for the lawns, and assisting the men, who are thoroughly trustworthy, on the farm collecting the vegetables and fruits." The superintendent "hopes that by the next year they may have entire charge of the chickens." Part of each evening is taken up by fancy work which is regarded as a useful adjunct to discipline.

An extensive line of kitchen and sewing products is noted in the Report of The Missouri State Industrial School for Girls. "Could people step into our families any morning hour and see the children busily and happily cooking, setting tables, cleaning rooms or sewing they would not think it different from any well-ordered home, except for the numbers. . . .But this steady training and busy, happy life tells in the well-equipped girl who goes into the active world a useful woman with a desire for good living and clean surroundings. Every girl is obliged to take training in all branches of domestic work and be a good housekeeper when she leaves."

Of the few girls' schools which try to contribute to their own support we have an example in the Baltimore City Industrial School for Colored Girls which with an average attendance of over 80 reports an income from "Sewing Room"of $1,537. And this amount of work "Owing to the high price and therefore the scarcity, of cotton (for the Contract Room) has been far below the average." "Our sewing room plant is fully equipped with modern machines and adequate power. . .and in the very near future we shall have an up-to-date laundry; our kitchens are models with steel ranges and all necessary culinary appliances." "A great deal of patient teaching is required in the contract room, as each year the competition grows greater and the manufacturers more exacting." But as a purely educative measure the Superintendent hopes to establish individual gardens for the girls.

Girls come to the Maine Industrial School "from homes where the comforts of life are few. The beauty, usefulness, and possibilities of life are new to them and it is interesting to watch their development along their new lines. With a few exceptions the girls take a great interest in their work and books, and a marked improvement is soon noticed. The girls are the assistant cooks, housemaids, laundresses, and dressmakers in a large family where the purpose of all is to learn habits of industry and those things which fit one for useful life. No small importance is attached to giving the girls a pride in their surroundings and in making them neat and thorough in their work. The girls make flower gardens in the spring and care for them through the summer, watering them daily and gathering the flowers to decorate the dining-room and other parts of the house."

Sewing and dressmaking are specially directed pursuits in the Connecticut Girls School and also in the Oak Lawn School in Rhode Island. In the latter "all new girls begin in the sewing-room and others come in if discharged for incompetency or misconduct in other places. (But) from this department girls are drafted off to fill vacancies all about the house; as a consequence of which only the smaller girls stay the four months' term designed for instruction in this branch." This school has lately introduced raffia [weaving baskets and hats] work and basket making, under charge of a special teacher, ten girls getting instruction for one and a half hours per week. Five girls at a time learn cooking, doing this work for both inmates and teachers. Nine girls are detailed to the laundry work and changed every four months. It is asserted of the laundry work that it does not seem particularly inviting to the girls.

Some of the schools find that the routine work of cooking for the institution does not furnish enough in the way of education for the girls who look forward to employment in domestic work. The Indiana school notes the establishment of a model kitchen built by a special appropriation $700 from the legislature "accommodating ten girls (at a time). The class is in the hands of a trained teacher; all class work is done under direct supervision and the girls have the actual experience of cooking and serving the article of food on which the lesson is given." The work is declared to be thoroughly practical, and to find application in the culinary department of the institution. The Ohio Home and that of Wisconsin also notes especial attention to domestic science. In Michigan "since my last report 140 girls have taken the course of instruction in cooking, 61 of whom graduated with honors. Our examinations are rigid, and a girl must be a good cook before she can graduate. The object of our cooking school is to teach our girls a better and simpler way of living. It is to relieve women of the monotony of the kitchen and to plead for pure, wholesome food devoid of grease and digestible. Another object is to teach the proper combinations of food, more artistic table arrangement, to know how to make the kitchen attractive, rather than to destroy love for the work."

In contrast to the domestic work with its practical character reference should again be made to the increasing interest in out-of-door work. Michigan reports a greenhouse directed by a special instructor. "This branch of industry has proved a blessing to the institution in many ways. All plants for the farm and garden as well as for bedding have been grown here and transplanted by the girls. We have as a consequence been furnished with an abundance of vegetables fresh from the garden. The flower beds have brought love and happiness to all hearts and cheered many a poor sin-sick girl, and by their silent messages have awakened new aspirations in her life." The Iowa Home reports that many girls are employed in summer on the lawns with the flower beds, in gathering vegetables, and in garden work generally. "This gives them a light and very healthful exercise, besides plenty of fresh air and sunshine. This works wonders in each case where the physically weak, nervous and debilitated girl comes to us." In the Massachusetts School the long two months' vacation from studies is passed largely in outdoor work. Lawn-mowing, weeding, and gathering vegetables serve to fill the hours of the girls "that may not be left idle." It may be noted in passing that this school also requires sloyd [wood carving] and gymnastics for all the girls. These industrial features, however, cannot yet be said to be typical; many of the girls' schools still retain some features such as constricted quarters, a more or less repressive discipline, and belief in the potency of hard labor which prevent any developments of the outdoor type of work.

Typewriting is reported as one of the subjects taught in the Girls House of Refuge, Philadelphia. In the Iowa Home "a recent addition has been made by the Board in the rental of four typewriting machines for the purpose of giving those who have talent and desire, a thorough business course in connection with their higher school studies, comprising bookkeeping, typewriting, and stenography. Already we have met with good success with the two machines we have had in the institution. We think this can be done even better than in the average business college because of the healthy conditions and environment conducive to good study and work." In the Wisconsin Home a "new industry has been introduced in the shape of carpet and rug weaving, and a loom has been placed in our new building." In that home, also, "the arts and crafts are practiced in the making of baskets, lace-work, bead-work; and many varieties of fancy-work, which, besides teaching the girls to be skillful, has yielded an income of over $500 in the last two years. In the Michigan Home "the craze for fancy-work has not abated and, besides Mexican drawn-work, lace-work, embroidery, and crocheting, we have begun the making of 'Abnakee' rugs and Indian basketry."

But, from the standpoint of vocation, the superintendents seem to agree with the report of the Massachusetts School that housework is the one kind of labor for which there is always a demand and in which a girl is comparatively shielded from temptation. But it seems hard to develop an abiding interest in it and some of the schools are studying possibilities in other directions. In the Massachusetts home, because "most young women prefer other kinds of work to housework it is attempted to start them at something else before they pass out of the care of the school."

This fragmentary sketch can only give an impression of the work actually being done in the field of the industrial education of girls in juvenile reform schools. It is probable that the schools most frequently referred to are doing, on the whole, the best work in this direction, partly because they have more abundant support from the state or from philanthropy; and partly because they represent a more alert attitude on the part of their officers in keeping "up with the times." But the work will vary greatly in qualities which admit of no categorical analysis. Some of the homes are given over to the bugbear of cleanliness and the inmates are kept everlastingly scrubbing on the much overworked floors and furniture. This has had its justification in a now obsolete pedagogy which held to the notion that "cleanliness," "thoroughness," and other matters of habit and mental attitude could be produced in the individual by a sufficient prolongation of specific exercises. As we shall have occasion to note again when discussing the industrial training of boys, there is a subtle difference between work which educates and that which, done perfunctorily, may produce habits and a certain skill, but with accompanying distaste and mental determination not to follow it up when once the school is left behind. Booker T. Washington has popularized a distinction here which may be very near the psychological truth: "Under slavery, the black man was worked; under the educative conditions of Tuskegee he works."Apparently the girl who "is worked" in an institution does not promise well for the future, while the girl who "works" and who is therefore receiving true industrial education will, ere long, lead an independent and worthy life.

It is of interest to note, too, that the schools for girls encounter the same social difficulties as develop outside in the transitional matters of our economic life. Bread-making and laundry work, for example, are arts and capable of extended teaching did the conditions which formerly prevailed still survive. But these arts have largely come under the sway of manufacture and division of labor and have become the occupations of men aided by machinery. Many of the girls, on leaving the schools, will go into factory work; but so specialized is this that the school can give only the most general preparation for it, preparation, indeed, which hardly causes the girl to believe that she is receiving any vocational education. Again, domestic work in these institutions is subject to considerable measure to the unpopularity which afflicts it among young women not in the schools; and this, even when it is taught most successfully.

From the foregoing sketch it is evident that, however far from realizing their own ideals the institutions may be, the best of them have fairly definite goals towards which they are working. Among these may be enumerated: (a) The industrial work of the schools should not primarily be organized to bring money into the school. A few schools report small incomes of a few hundred dollars from custom sewing, cane seating, custom laundrying, and from the sale of crochet and various kinds of fancy-work; but the amount so realized is only a small fraction of the necessary expense of the institution. (b) On the other hand, a large part of the necessary work of the institution is done by the inmates, this ranging from wall painting and papering and the repair of furniture to cooking, sewing, and housekeeping generally. As already indicated the range of educational possibilities in domestic work is very great according to the type of institution and director of the work. But there is discernible a strong tendency to individualize the work, to remove from it the uneducative features of "gang labor" and in other ways to render it attractive to the girls. And when the girls are paroled to service, increasing efforts are being made to locate them where mistresses will evoke the girl's interest in work rather than make her a domestic drudge. (c) With the building of schools in the country, the disappearance of prison walls, and more advanced notions of wholesome life, an increasing premium is being put on garden work, the cultivation of flowers, vegetables and fruits, and on sloyd and other forms of manual training. The vocational value of this work may not be apparent, but, in the minds of the directors of the education of these girls, its sedative and moralizing influence is ample justification for the time and expense required. The schools fully realize that they have not yet solved the problem of industrial education so far as girls are concerned; but educators know that juvenile reform schools for girls are by no means the only schools that find themselves facing very great difficulties in this direction.

4. INDUSTRIAL EDUCATION OF BOYS

Remembering that schools for juvenile offenders were at first regarded merely as prisons in which the children could be segregated from the more hardened offenders, we can easily understand at least one of the motives which developed the early systems of labor in these schools. The child as an offender against the social order should be made to pay back as far as possible to the state the expense of keeping him in confinement. There were, of course, other reasons. Where philanthropy established these schools an enormous work was found which had to be done and the means where with to do it were scanty. Recourse was naturally had to work which could be done by children without obvious injury and which would contribute to the necessary support of the institution. Where carefully managed, this work, while frequently not educative in the sense that was urged, was, nevertheless, not injurious and it seems highly probable that at no time did the children, except in individual schools where abuses had entered, suffer development and character as much as do today the thousands employed in glass factories, textile mills and coal mines.

But in the early seventies the pressure of a different ideal was felt by the schools and thenceforward a new development is distinctly traceable in the boys' schools. This was, at first, in the direction of teaching trades which would be of considerable profit to the inmate, morally and vocationally, on his leaving the school. It had to be confessed that the industries which had proven feasible and financially profitable in the institutions were not such as to lead to industrial efficiency outside. Contract sewing and tailoring, cigar-making, brush-making, glove-making, knitting, shirt-making and cane-seating of chairs were factory industries which did not lead to economic independence, nor were they educative.

Under varying conditions, then, the schools began to look for lines of work which could be carried on within the institution, which would meet the educational ideal of efficiency, and which would be, at least, as inexpensive as possible; for it did not take long to discover that there are many trades which require for their teaching an elaborate equipment. Naturally, attempts were made to utilize the plant and necessities of the institution itself as educational opportunities; and as the schools have, one by one, removed or founded in large farm spaces the country, this has been increasingly possible.

Apart from the purely domestic industries of the institutions, which will be discussed later, there gradually grew up a variety of occupations connected with farming and gardening and the care of stock. The buildings provided opportunities for carpentering, blacksmithing, plumbing, painting, masonry, tinning, brickmaking, furniture making, and a variety of repairing, all of which might, under competent direction provide educative work for a few boys, while contributing, indirectly, to the reduction of the expenses of the institution. Where circumstances permitted it was found that telegraphy, shorthand, and printing were trades which could be successfully dealt with by institutions. It has also been found that band music provides a line of work which combines the various desirable qualities of contributing to the morale of the institution, of producing distinct educative results, and providing a possible occupation for the paroled or discharged boy. Leather work, basketry, venetian iron-work, and floriculture in greenhouses are the other trades which have been developed, in occasional institutions.

Finally, came the manual-training movement. Financially, this form of industrial training has severely taxed the schools, for it is highly expensive in plant, material, and instructing force, while its return in the way of saleable product is practically nothing. The justification of manual training, however, is that it possesses a more highly educative value along all industrial lines than does any other vocational work which can be given to children. Giving special skill in no trade, it is supposed to give the pupil training and concrete experience with the materials and manipulations which lie, in greater or less degree, at the bottom of all trades. It is believed to stand to industrial education in somewhat the same relationship that arithmetic does to the varieties of business practice, or reading to the study of the arts and sciences which come to us in books. Many of the schools have taken up the manual training movement vigorously and, under the sloyd or some other system, have organized regular courses.

As we find the schools at the present time, it is possible to study the work done in them in the way of industrial education under four main divisions. There is, first, the work which is retained largely for productive purposes. The Connecticut School for Boys has six shops in which the cane-seating of chairs is the special work; in the New Jersey State home, brush-making is carried on, though in diminishing amount; the Baltimore House of Refuge, and St. Mary's Industrial School of Baltimore do extensive work in custom tailoring; St. Mary's also has brush-making shops which employ 123 boys; the House of Reformation for Colored Boys of Maryland has a cane-seating shop which employs 83 boys; the Louisville Industrial School does extensive cane-seating; and harness-making is done in the Boys Industrial School of Kansas.

In the second place, a large number of boys are kept constantly employed, in all the institutions, in various forms of domestic work which range from the unskilled labor of sweeping and weeding to the more difficult callings of table-serving and baking. Under this head also belongs much of the farm work done by the institutions. Frequently the least skilled and least promising boys are

101

assigned to work of this character, partly because discipline and oversight are more practicable. It is not too much to say that from one-third to one-half the boys in most of the schools follow this general work, usually for half of each day.

Shoemaking, tailoring, mending, gardening, working with stock, teaming, carpentry work and blacksmithing, tinning, and a number of other occupations constitute a third group of industries; these are remunerative to the institution, though only in reducing running expenses, and it is possible to give an interest and degree of proficiency which will lead the boy to follow one of them permanently. Usually some boy with natural talent is selected for this work, and one who has proven himself trustworthy. Limited as many of the schools are in opportunities for these trades, and in teaching force, only a small number of boys can follow them; but in the better schools these boys seem to follow them with much profit and likelihood of finding therein a permanent career.

In the fourth group of occupations we find those which are not in any way to be regarded as remunerative, although in individual cases, as printing, they may occasionally prove so, but are maintained primarily for their educative value. Outside of sloyd and printing, these are few and poorly developed; in fact, as in other fields of education, there is at present considerable doubt as to where such subjects may be found, and how they may be handled when found. The mechanic arts work of the Rhode Island Boys School is said to take the place, very successfully, of a period of apprenticeship for those who enter machine-shop work which is, of course, an ever-present employment in that state.

Now, of course, the four lines of work outlined above vary much in their educational possibilities; but it cannot be assumed that any of them is without great service industrial education. It seems to be a fact that many of the boys who enter juvenile reform schools are incapable of learning what might strictly be called a trade. They lack the intelligence, the application, and possibly the physical development. And it is of course equally true that very many of them, when received, have had little or no habituation to work of any kind. In fact, owing usually to the neglected and vagrant lives they have led, they are usually prejudiced and habituated strongly against steady employment of all sorts. Some of these boys seem to be so constituted that they will work only under constant external pressure; others seem to be devoid of initiative and can only accomplish results in the field of wholly routine labor. Many seem permanently destined to fill the ranks of unskilled labor whose only capital is muscular strength.

Owing to the varied and sometimes indefinite character of the records kept and published by many schools it has not been feasible to present in statistical form a survey of the industrial work actually carried on. It may indeed be doubted whether it is possible to preserve such records in a way that will make them very serviceable, in all schools, for there must be frequent shifting and rearrangement of the inmates according to the necessities and opportunities of the work. Farm and garden work, for example, must vary in its demands, with the season. Domestic work is fairly constant in quantity but it is desirable for many reasons that boys be frequently shifted about from one phase to another in it. Again, unlike the practice of schools of other characters, juvenile reformatories cannot receive and dismiss their classes at stated seasons of the work. Boys are being committed at all times, and for the new arrivals work must be found at once somewhere; and boys are being no less constantly released on parole and each one thus allowed to go creates a vacancy in shop or home which must be at once filled. On these grounds the somewhat indefinite character of the statistics presented finds its chief excuse. Some schools, however, present suggestive statements of division of labor and extent to which trades are followed. The varying forms of classification used make it necessary that the work of the schools should be described individually. It is believed that, taken together, these schools present fair types of conditions generally prevailing.

The Connecticut School for Boys is an unusual example of a school which combines productive industries on the one hand with a highly developed system of modern manual training on the other. It has six chair-caning shops which returned the institution $7,624 in 1904-5. Printing, the manufacture of clothing, and the farm seem also to have been slightly productive industries. But during the same year the Manual Training School had an attendance of 216 in the departments of sloyd and bench work, wood-turning, and forge-work. Besides these lines an average of 14 boys were employed in the tailor-shop making clothing and mending for the institution; 18 to 20 in the printing office; 30 on the farm in summer; and a smaller number look after stock in winter; while from 6 to 10 have regular employment in the various classes required for laundry, dining-room, kitchen, sleeping-rooms, etc.

With an average enrollment of 823 during the fiscal year 1903 the Ohio Boys Industrial School shows the following distribution of occupations. A considerable number of boys committed for truancy do not take up industrial work, but attend school all day.

Tailoring.	64	Employed at store-room	3
Teamsters.	18	Carpentering.	8
Assistants to cottage matrons.	80	Street construction	5
Printing	32	Shoe shop	20
Street and lawn department.	22	Blacksmithing.	4
Steam laundering.	28	Farm and general work.	80
Brick making.	32	Cooking	30
Tin shop.	4	Baking	9
Floriculture	8	Painting and glazing	6
Electrical department.	10	Gardening	24
Engineering.	7	Dairy	8
School of phonography	10	Plumbing.	8
Band.	24	School of telegraphy	20
Butchering.	4	Table waiters.	37
Hospital steward	1	Mending-room	32
Office boys.	5	Horticulture	6

It will be noticed that practically none of these industries are remunerative in the sense of bringing in money; though very many of them are distinctly profitable in supplying the labor, repairing, and products needed by the institution. The report of the Superintendent for 1903 urges upon the legislature the need of an equipment for varied manual training and of money wherewith to pay teachers in these lines. In estimating the amount of efficiency acquired in various lines of industrial work, it must be remembered that the boys attend school half of each day; and that the duration of their stay in the institution varies from 14 months to 2 ½ years.

Each Department of the Ohio Boys School keeps careful account of the labor done. The Report of the State Board of Charities notes that much of the work of erecting new buildings has been done by the various trades classes and that of the 1210 acres occupied by the institution, 250 are under regular cultivation, besides 200 in fruit.

St. Mary's Industrial School of Baltimore had, during 1904, a total attendance of 876. The school receives a part of its support from the State of Maryland and from Baltimore, but is obliged to supplement these sources of income with donations and the productive labor of the boys. The distribution of boys among the various lines of work was as follows on November 30, 1904:

Department — Bakery	5	Engine-rooms	5
" Brush (3 floors)	123	Greenhouses	4
" Carpentry	3	Farm and Garden	5
" Hosiery (house)	6	Halls and dormitories	12
" Printing	22	Kitchen and dining-rooms	18
" Shoe	6	Laundry	6
" Tailor (city)	163	Painters and glaziers	3
" (house)	38	Mattress-making	4

The productive character of much of this work may be judged from the Treasurer's report which shows that for the year ending at the above date, the income had been $14,128 from the shops (printing, brush, and city tailoring), and from the farm and greenhouse $14,216, much of the latter, of course, being used for the support of the inmates directly. All the boys attend school from seven to ten each morning. This school believes that its work in printing and floriculture is peculiarly successful in that it combines productiveness for the institution and a fairly thorough vocational education which the boy is likely to profit from when released.

The Maryland House of Reformation for Colored Boys gives the following statistics of its occupations: Total number employed, 182. In cane shop, 83; farm, 30; shoe shop, 6; laundry, 11; domestic cleaning etc., 30; tailor shop, 8; blacksmithing and painting, 2 each; carpenter shop, boiler house, hospital, 1 each; and a few sick, unemployed, or miscellaneous. The Superintendent finds that the chair-caning no longer pays and as it has little educative value, something else should be substituted. As the boys are not old (median age slightly over 13) it is difficult to find suitable industries for them, but he thinks more should be employed on the farm.

Another Maryland School which receives part of its support from the State and the City of Baltimore is the House of Refuge. Out of the 220 boys in this school 93 were employed at contract work (city tailoring apparently), 33 at domestic tailoring and sewing, 10 in farm, greenhouse, or yards; 8 in boiler house or making repairs; and the rest, with the exception of 29 juniors who were in school full time, at various forms of domestic labor. But in addition to the above, the school has a well-equipped manual-training school which employed 51 boys during year ending December 31, 1905 at such work as forge, machine, sheet metal or venetian iron, and drawing-work. There are also printing and wood-turning departments where systematic instruction is given, but the relative numbers taking this work are not stated.

As noted before, the Rhode Island Boys School attempts instruction in certain trades to the end that the boys may go directly into the shops of Rhode Island. With a total attendance of 660 for year ending January 1, 1905 there were in the various trades departments the following numbers: printing, 15; blacksmithing, 17; machine, 24; carpenter, 15; mason, 25; shoe, 20; engineering, 14; tailoring, 34. Extensive farming was done by the larger boys, and the smaller ones are recorded to have raised poultry to the value of $633.

One of the best equipped schools for industrial work is the Philadelphia House of Refuge, Boys Department. With an average attendance of nearly 800 and with over 1000 boys receiving instruction for some time during the year, the school has part of its population distributed throughout its various shops as follows (not all of the boys, of course, having been employed during the entire year): masonry, 27; shoe, 23; printing, 54; blacksmithing, 16; tailor, 72; sewing and repairing clothes, 64; carpentry, 47; painting and frescoing, 29; engineering (machine work, electricity, plumbing, etc. 42;) bakery, 14; laundry, 92; and a large but unspecified number working on farm, at domestic work, and miscellaneous occupations. The trades classes have been utilized to erect buildings, to build walls and culverts on the grounds, and in making furniture for some of the cottages. Farming and dairying work sufficient to meet the needs of the institution is carried on, but it does not appear that any products are sold. It should also be noted that all of the work results in some valuable output—that is, none of the trades work is taken solely for practice, but a definite product is sought and expected.

The following table is given by the Michigan Industrial School for Boys as showing the distribution of inmates in trades during the years 1902-3 and 1903-4:

	1902-3	1903-4		1902-3	1903-4
Printing-office	60	60	Boys' dining-room	20	25
Tailor-shop	70	70	Mending-room	45	45
Shoe-shop	35	35	Dormitory and cleaning	60	60
Carpenter-shop	50	40	Officers' kitchen	10	12
Engine-room	12	12	Office-boys	2	2
Paint-shop	20	20	Hospital-boys	2	2
Bakery	14	14	Dairy	30	25
Laundry	15	16	Farm and grounds	227	240
Boys' kitchen	20	25	Sloyd department	---	16
			Total	688	714

This school has also a sloyd department which has recently been started; and it asks for an appropriation wherewith to start a department of telegraphy and stenography, believing that these would provide a considerable opportunity for boys looking for good vocations.

A good manual training school is part of the equipment of the Wisconsin Industrial School for Boys. The following table shows the labor distribution among the occupations June 30, 1904:

Bakery	18	Sewing-room	10
Carpenter-shop	4	Shoe-shop	15
Engine-room	8	Sloyd	80
Garden	45	Stock farm	10
General farm-work	16	Tailor shop	25
General service	55	Teamsters	9
Laundry	13	Yard	9
Office	2	Paint and blacksmith shop	8
		Total	327

From the standpoint of industrial education in general it is impossible for us to give more than a tentative interpretation of the above tables. All of these schools are working experimentally in greater or less degree, and of none of them can it be said that they have either the equipment or trained teachers in all respects that they would wish. It must be remembered that a considerable number of the children are below the age at which children are supposed to work systematically; but the necessities of discipline in these institutions are such that the boys must be kept employed much of the time. Hence some of the domestic or contract work may partake of the nature of "busy work" such as primary teachers frequently resort to. There is no evidence that the work, in any of its forms, becomes physically oppressive to the child, when the short hours and mild control are taken into consideration.

The changed spirit in the work of the juvenile reform schools can be most satisfactorily exhibited by their own reports of their work and ideals. Naturally, these tend sometimes to be optimistic and perhaps somewhat overstate the actual conditions of affairs, since all of these schools are obliged, in the present state of public sentiment, to constantly demonstrate their right to existence and support. Frequently those connected with the schools are enthusiasts and believe greatly in the importance of the work they are doing. While, therefore, the accounts given below, which are digested from the reports, are by no means a full and exact statement of conditions, they do serve to indicate the schools' at their best and to show what are the ideals and standards that now obtain.

Berkshire Industrial Farm is a privately managed institution in New York State, with an extensive tract (800 acres) of land and some eighty boys. The work is largely farming and the blacksmithing and carpentry work that go with farming. "To keep the boys busy is the main reforming agency we have, with the goal before them that industry and good conduct will bring them good marks, and those will advance their grade, and enable them to gain an honorable discharge. They are all working to go out into the world, as they fancy, of independence, but no sooner are they out than they appreciate the happy life of the farm and without exception want to come back and make visits." A carpenter now directs their manual training classes of six boys each, each boy ten hours a week in the shop. In the summer these boys work out-of-doors in building construction and other carpentry work. There are other special instructors for glass-setting, painting and repairing; for forge work and blacksmithing; and for printing, the school publishing a monthly paper. Farming and stock-raising are carried on quite extensively, and steam-fitting and shoe making are industries practiced as far as facilities will allow. This school has attempted to realize the conditions which surround a boy on a normal home farm, and much attention appears to be given to recreation, games and free play generally.

The Illinois Manual Training Farm School does not receive the worst delinquents, but rather those bordering on that stage. So successful do they believe their division of work between school and farm and shops to be that the President of the Board, Mr. Butler, expresses himself thus: "The work in the school is now made almost as interesting as the work in the shops. Possibly some day the Public Schools of Chicago will divide their school hours as we now divide ours at Glenwood, one half of the time being given to books and the other half to work in the shops." Again, speaking of the material with which they have to deal: "The boy in the city whose mechanical genius makes it possible for him to teach his fellows how to pick a lock, is just the material needed for our manual training school. After he has worked for a week in the machine shop of this building he will look upon something beneath his notice. . .This boy is not bad. He is just a boy, and because he is a boy he must have something to do. The sidewalks and the streets offered but little opportunity for play, and he and his friends naturally took up other matters. That is why he learned to pick locks." And again: "It is safe to say that 300 of the 365 boys at the school today are born leaders. They are naturally captains, and are going to be captains throughout their lives. Each of these boys will control, perhaps, ten others." Farming, printing, manual-training and machine-shop work, and miscellaneous work at moments in making novelties as colored bead chains, purses, burnt wood, etc., are the industries noted. A considerable number of boys served as caddies on an adjacent golf-links, and the money so earned has been used in making improvements (swimming pool and instruments for the band) in which the boys themselves were greatly interested.

Some statistics of the various lines of work in the Baltimore House of Refuge have already been given. This school is on the eve of moving into the country where it may have ample territory and develop the cottage system. Among the advantages expected, "The plan affords an opportunity for teaching the boys farming in all its branches, inducing masonry, building of cottages and other structures, repair work of varied kinds, horticulture and agriculture, in addition to the Manual Training which has been a marked success in our present quarters. . . .Another important factor is the relief of urban congestion and the dignifying of rural pursuits in the minds of the boys. Most of us must do that which is ordinarily termed commonplace work. To teach the boys that there is a commendable dignity about everything that is to be done, and that all work that is honestly and well done deserves and will receive commensurate reward, is something that is sure to be helpful to the boy and the State."

"The Trade Schools of the Philadelphia House of Refuge have reached the point of affording for the larger boys useful and skillful labor which enables them to readily get mechanical employment after they leave the house, at satisfactory wages; their knowledge of the use of tools makes them independent, and they perform most of the mechanical work about the buildings. They are now engaged in constructing additions to the School House which are in every way equal to the work on the main building." It is noted farther on in the Report that of the large number of boys employed on the farm, most of them are from the country districts, and that the majority of these obtain "a knowledge of agriculture under proper instruction" such as will open up useful employment to them on their return home. Some of the cottages have developed family gardens which have furnished liberal supplies of flowers and vegetables and which serve to enlist much interest on the part of the boys.

The above schools are under private or corporate management and supported largely by philanthropy. It is characteristic of these schools that they may, especially at the outset, embark in more experimental work than is possible in state institutions. But it is also true that they are often handicapped for the large funds necessary to carry on the modern forms of industrial training. There is a strong probability that many of these homes are able to develop the "home" atmosphere more fully than the state schools and that, in consequence work which might ordinarily partake of the character of drudgery of factory work may assume an individual and interesting character. The Berkshire Farm Schools, the George Junior Republic, the Illinois Manual Training Farm School, the Thompson's Island Farm School of Massachusetts, and many others might be cited as possible examples. One cannot say that this is necessarily so; in fact there is good evidence that some of the privately controlled and perhaps privately supported schools make least of an appeal to the individuality and educative possibilities of the children. Sometimes such schools are little more than the old type of house of refuge with industries developed as fully as possible to contribute to the support of the institution. Nevertheless, it is to the privately controlled schools that we must look for many interesting variations in industrial development. Men and women of philanthropic intentions and experimental turn of mind, with more or less insight into boy nature, will, in the smaller private schools, give the fullest test of theories in this field.

Passing mention only can be to the work in a type of school which has developed under the auspices of certain cities or counties. These schools partake of the nature of parental schools, though sometimes only court cases are received. Such a school as this is the Newark City Home, New Jersey. Its Superintendent believes that it should, however, become truly the parental school of Newark, receiving children before they have necessarily crossed the borderland of criminality. It has developed manual-training extensively. "There is not a child in the Home who does not receive some sort of manual-instruction. The shops, the kitchen, the sewing room, the field, the sloyd or wood-working schools, etc., all offer an excellent opportunity for the development of self-activity and the advancement of manual skill. Occupations here are as follows: Sloyd and basketry, 25 to 30 boys daily; printing department 15 to 20 daily, and shop proves quite remunerative; shoemaking 8 boys; tailoring 12 boys; engineering, laundry, bakery, kitchen, farm and considerable general building. Many of the boys who learned printing while in the establishment are holding now well paid positions." The Trustees assert that "in detailing boys to work, their natural endowment, their mental and physical qualifications, and their rank in the class room are principally considered." And again: "In case of equal qualification for a certain trade, those children who have to support themselves are given the preference. But no matter whether the boys are occupied in school or whether they are kept busy in the shop or field, the educational element is never lost sight of. Important as the acquirement of knowledge undoubtedly is, their future career depends upon tile formation of character, the strengthening of the will power, and development of self-activity, all of which are of vital consequence."

Several counties in Massachusetts maintain Truant Schools are practically farm schools. "The boys are employed at farm work and in the care of live stock," says the report of the Essex County Truant School: "In winter the boys have carpentry, printing, and caning chairs." The average age of boys committed is only 11 ½ years.

Out-of-door work is practically impossible in the large John Worthy School (the Parental School of Chicago), owing to lack of room. Hence much is made of manual-training and bench and lathe work of all sorts. The smaller boys work at card-board, paper, raffia, decoration, drawing, sketching, coloring and pyrography [wood burning] work, while telegraphy and typewriting are features that are well developed for the older boys, as is also printing. One notes with some interest in the last report (1904) that "the class room methods were changed during the year and now none of the classes in the first, second and third grades are taught manual-training in the work shop, but their entire day of six hours is devoted to class room studies and in teaching the essentials on which an education is based." When we recall that a large number of the first, second and third grade boys. . .are from twelve to sixteen years old, one wonders what was the pedagogical reason for the change.

A City Home which is striving to obtain a country environment is the Cincinnati House of Refuge. With an average number of inmates of nearly 450 this institution is still confined to the indoor industries. Sloyd, carpentry, printing, tailoring, shoemaking, baking, engineering (as assistants to institution work), greenhouse floriculture, and the band are the lines developed in addition to the usual domestic work. In the sloyd work 48 boys have received daily instruction in the Swedish sloyd system, which "means the proper use and care of tools, making the hand obedient servant of the brain, training the eye for good form and shape, and teaching neatness and correctness in the execution of their work. Several boys have finished the first course of fifty models, and are now working on the second course of 36 models."

Among the homes supported and controlled by the State, the St. Charles Home for Boys in Illinois is the latest and in many appointments it is thoroughly modern. The Superintendent, who has had the planning of the buildings says that it "is our purpose to plan and construct our farm and industrial building so that each will be adapted to serve a double use. For example, the well-lighted, well-drained and well-ventilated dairy barn will not only serve as a sanitary place in which to stable cows kept for producing milk, but also a place where the boys will daily be given practical knowledge of the principles of hygiene, and practice of the laws which determine the health and comfort of domestic animals and also the fitness or unfitness of animal products for human food. The dairy barn will also be a laboratory in which boys will learn, among other things, how to compound a ration best suited to the characteristic needs of each cow in producing the largest quantity of pure milk at the least cost. The creamery will not only be a place suited to the care of milk and making butter and cheese for daily use, but also a class-room in which the boys will be given such technical training as will qualify them for skilled helpers in farm dairies and creameries. So also in planning and building the breeding and feeding barn, the shops and all industrial buildings, their fitness for giving industrial training is a feature which must be given first consideration, because the demand for lads and young men having technical training and practical experience in husbandry and other industrial lines always exceeds the supply." The educational method designed for this school is an alternation of class-room work with some form of substantial training, "in which the giving of technical instruction is daily associated with learning to do by doing." Again quoting the Superintendent: "I have learned by observation and experience that very few boys fail to become intensely interested in some branch of husbandry or in some of the useful trades." This school, formally opened July 5, 1905, has an equipment of nearly 1000 acres of rich land, $325,000 worth of cottages and an additional sum of $135,000 to be put into further equipment.

Extensive outdoor work characterizes the practice of the Colorado State Industrial School. Industrial work and schoolwork come on alternate days. The wood-working department of the manual-training shops seems to especially attract attention. Having over one hundred and twenty acres, the school carries on agricultural operations to supply the needs of the school and it is noted that a coal mine, worked by the school, the digging of a deep well, and the erecting of additional buildings are among the local industries. The legislature is asked to provide the funds to develop a conservatory partly to aid in gardening and for ten typewriters so that boys who desire to fit themselves for office work may have the opportunity. Printing is also a local industry. The authorities believe that with the pressure on the institution of new cases boys are frequently paroled before they have accomplished as much industrially as should be the case. Hence the provision of appropriations for more cottages is made.

The State of California has two large reform schools. The older, the Whittier State School, has 120 of its 160 acre tract devoted to farm, vegetable garden, and orchard. A large variety of fruit trees are found on the place, besides a fairly extensive equipment of cows, horses, hogs, chickens, etc. "The farm work is mostly done by the boys. General farming is taught to such boys as wish to learn; also horticulture, gardening, and floriculture. The place has a greenhouse in charge of a florist as instructor, and flowers are grown in great profusion." A central three-story building has shops for the various industries as laundry, tailorshop, shoeshop, printing-office, carpenter' shop, electric lighting plant, power plant, etc. "Some boys are instructed in all these departments." The Preston School of Industry, occupying 570 acres of land in the middle part of the State of California has also extensive provision for farming and is seeking to develop trades schools.

In the State of Washington the Board of Control of State Institutions has sought to develop systematic productive labor in all the institutions with the result, so far as the State Reform School is concerned, that "in the shoe department we have continued the manufacture of shoes for the Insane Asylums and Soldiers' Home. The tailoring department, in charge of a competent tailor, is turning out large quantities of clothing for the Hospitals besides making all the clothing required for the boys at the School." But this manufacturing is not the sole industrial work of the boys of the Washington Reform School. "Besides tending the farm, the boys have cleared a large tract of land during the present term, which is now being broken and will greatly increase the tillable acreage of the institution. The carpentry department has been employed the greater portion of the time in making general repairs about the buildings, in painting, in building a shed 16 by 70 at the cow barn, building a greenhouse, and other work along these lines." This institution has about 140 boys whose median age is slightly under 13 years at commitment.

The Missouri Training School for Boys has 358 acres of land but finds this insufficient. Many of its buildings have been erected by the boys, the State supplying only the lumber, heating apparatus and other manufactured articles.

"The bricks were made by the boys and all the work upon the buildings was done by them under the supervision of the officers of the school. . . .The boys while doing this work received practical instruction in brick-making, brick-laying, carpentering, plastering, painting, plumbing, and other useful trades, so that there was a two-fold benefit to the State." The superintendent notes in his report that the equipment for teaching printing is too small and recommends increased facilities in this trade.

A carefully graded course in manual training or wood-working is one of the features of the Kansas Boys Industrial School. A variety of articles made by the pupil gives the familiarity with tools which makes much more possible the teaching of the trades which follows. Besides the manual training, this school notes as its trades carpentry, harness-making, shoemaking, cooking, engineering, bricklaying, laundry, farming, gardening, dairying, and baking. Some of the boys who work at harness-making become excellent workmen "and by the time they leave us they are fully qualified to conduct shops of their own." The industrial problem of this school, especially when it comes to paroling the boys to homes, is said to be complicated by the fact that about one-third of the boys are colored. The school has no shop for the printing trade and urges an appropriation therefore, the superintendent believing that "the printer's trade is one that appeals strongly to many boys, and with a knowledge of typesetting many of them could leave school fairly well equipped for making a living."

In the Iowa Boys' Industrial School the Superintendent also asks that appropriation be made for the establishment of a printing office. Telegraphy is now being taught and it is hoped to enlarge this department of work. Extensive farm work is carried on and the Superintendent points out that, with the large average attendance which is slightly over 500 more land could be utilized. But he thinks that possibly farm-work is not the best form of industrial training. "I am inclined to the opinion that so far as bettering the condition of the boys who come under the care of this institution is concerned, that an extension of the shop work and trades would be better than a larger farm, for the reason that very few of them will follow farming after they pass out of the school. Ninety per cent of the boys come from towns and cities and they will go to their homes and follow some trade or avocation which will permit them to live in a town or city. They do not take as kindly to farming while in school as they do to the shops."

As previously noted the Wisconsin Industrial School for boys has a large class in manual-training and sloyd. Carpenters and other wood-workers train the boys in the use of various machine and hand tools and the boys "learn to make the classes of joints, besides articles of use such as tables, chairs, desks, etc., and do various kinds of repair work." "About eighty of the smaller boys who are too young (out of 333 boys committed during the biennial period 1902-4, 104 were from ten to twelve years of age) and not strong enough physically for work in the field or in the shop do sloyd work two hours daily during a good portion of the year." These smaller boys in summer do light field work, as weeding, picking berries, etc. There is noted bench work, carving, basketry, rug-weaving, pulp work, plaster-paris molding and chiseling, drawing, water-color painting, and colored crayon work. It is interesting to find the superintendent of this school also expressing his opinion on the question of what employment the boy is apt to follow. "Most of them (i.e. the six hundred and more boys in the school and on parole) are doing well, particularly those placed in good homes in the country. Most of them, however, are city boys, with no desire or aptitude for country life. For them employment must be obtained in the cities. City employers of labor are earnestly requested to think of these boys, and whenever possible to give them a chance to make men of themselves."

The Michigan Industrial School for Boys has already a fully developed line of industries of the usual type but the Superintendent wishes to add a large department of typewriting and stenography. "In looking out for employment for boys, which I am constantly doing, I find, after careful investigation, that a department of stenography and typewriting would be a valuable acquisition for this school. In two of the rooms stenography is being taught, but to be of real benefit to the boy, typewriting should be taught at the same time and should be taught in a room for that purpose, as the teacher cannot give the class in stenography special attention when she has fifty or sixty boys in other studies. We could turn out some fine operators if we only had the equipment. It would cost about $2000 to fit up a room and equip it with twenty good typewriters and about $600 per year to hire a competent teacher. It makes a great difference to a good brainy boy whether he leaves this school at seventeen with or without a means of earning his living. Boys, as a rule, are not lazy. They like to work, if by working they can accomplish something. What a boy dislikes most of all is to work just for the sake of keeping himself busy."

To the list of trades now become familiar, the Indiana Boys' School adds gas-making, plastering, brick-making and bricklaying. Great stress is laid on the practical and educative character of the work done in the trades. "No polytechnic or technical school keeps industrial education more prominently in view than does this school. Realizing that all boys cannot enter the "Trades' Schools" extensive manual-training schools have been established. The wood-shop contains 48 work benches, well equipped with tools. Here two classes are taught each day. The course of instruction is the same as the best sloyd schools in Sweden. The blacksmithing and ironworking shop is equipped with the latest improved forges, and here 22 boys can be taught all kinds of iron work, including horse-shoeing." Of this school the Board of Control says: "In the present unstable and turbulent condition of the industrial world, the Indiana Boys' School is one of the very few places in the state at which a Hoosier boy, by birthright inheritor of equality of opportunity with anyone anywhere is able as a right to learn certain useful trades at which men can make their living."

"In assigning boys to a department, natural inclination is taken into consideration as far as possible," says the Superintendent of the Ohio Boys' Industrial School, "so that a boy can learn a trade for which he has a natural bent, and which he will probably follow when he leaves the institution. There

113

are some boys, however, who have not the ability to take up a trade or receive technical training. These boys are assigned to ordinary labor, or work which they can perform." Of 482 boys committed to this school during the year 1904, 103 were twelve years of age or younger. The Superintendent feels that manual training for the smaller boys should be established. "This should be along the sloyd system, and then extended into a more simple form of drafting and wood-working. A system of this kind could be established without great expense and would be of great value in teaching the boy how to skillfully use his hands." Telegraphy is one of the strong features of this school. "We have very little trouble in securing positions for boys going out from this department, and, as a rule, the boys are doing well."

The New Jersey State Home adds to a full list of usual institutional industries telegraphy and stenography; and a well-developed sloyd department under special instructor. Here "in addition to the usual knife and bench work and wood carving usually found in a department of manual-training, we have made a specialty of pyrographic work. This brings out the regular principles of construction and also free-hand drawing, burning, and the application of color. We do not claim any particular advantage in the act of burning, but the fact that a pupil must make a good free hand design before he will be allowed to burn it on wood, which he is always anxious to do, makes it a strong lever in favor of drawing. We have modeling in paper pulp for younger pupils, from which they get a knowledge of form work, which cannot be had by other means. We expect to take up basketry later." This school is one of the very few state schools that manufacture articles for sale. It still retains a brush-making shop, but appears to attach less importance to this work.

The Maine State School for Boys also receives a slight income from manufactured articles (cane-seating of chairs), but it is looking forward to the development of other trades. Hitherto farming has been their chief reliance, and the rudimentary carpentry and blacksmithing which go along with farming. Of their inmates "more than one-third come from the country, and will probably return to the country after leaving school. These boys often prefer farming to mechanical or business pursuits, and they gladly avail themselves of the opportunities they have here of learning more about farm work. . . .They get a practical acquaintance with the arts of agriculture, horticulture, and dairying.

But there are other boys to whom the country life does not appeal. They are the boys who will probably live in the city, and many of them have a liking for some mechanical pursuit. We have an excellent mechanical school where the rudiments of carpentry are taught and where boys can acquire skill in the use of wood-working tools, but I believe we ought to extend our industrial and manual training into new fields, so that we may be able to better equip such boys for the activities of life. In some of our reformatory schools bricklaying, painting, printing, blacksmithing, etc., are taught the boys and I trust that we may later be able to give the boys increased opportunities of learning trades which shall make them able to earn 'a respectable living' when they leave school."

The Massachusetts School for Boys has long had developed extensive lines of farm-work, building occupations, some of the structures now in use having been largely erected by the boys, carpentry and printing. Manual training and sloyd, however, have in recent years received especial attention. With a total enrollment of 554 during 1904 and an average daily attendance in the school of 329 (including the Berlin School for smaller boys) we find that there were 232 pupils in various manual-training classes; 140 in sloyd; 74 in wood-turning; and 18 in carpentry. The Superintendent thinks that the spirit of this work is shown by the following quotation from one of the teachers: "This one point I have tried to keep in view all the year, that if a boy failed to be interested or, to accomplish the thing undertaken, the teacher was at fault, not the pupil." The boys released on probation from this school average about fifteen years of age (15.3 years in 1904) after an average detention (for those released for first time) of 18.4 months. Hence it is not pretended that the boys are taught trades; that is left for the apprenticeship or later period. But "during the past year several applications have been made by the boys near their honor grade to be allowed to stay and learn a trade. This may be a pointer towards the duty of opening the way to teaching trades to certain boys who have stability and purpose enough to hold them steady for the few months necessary to gain the elements of a trade. It would seem reasonable to supply the opportunity to those anxious to learn a trade and willing to defer to a future date their probationary success that the opportunity might be grasped. A few marked cases of success on the part of some thus instructed would seem to indicate that there is a field for usefulness which has not been sufficiently considered. Again: "A serious lack of the school is suitable employment for a considerable number of boys out of school hours. The teaching of trades might in a measure supply this want."

The teaching of agriculture, in contrast with merely working at it under direction, is attempted in the Lyman School. "Practical lessons have been given in the school gardens in preparing the ground, sowing seeds, hoeing, killing destructive insects, and harvesting, during the summer months. Each class-room was given a piece of ground 60 feet by 48 feet, divided into 40 plats, with paths. 32 plats were planted to vegetables, and eight to flowers." In these a variety of vegetables, etc., were grown and careful record kept of the return, and its value. "The great result (of the work) was not the amount of crops raised, but the interest in agricultural work which was kindled in every boy. It is recommended that more ground and more time be given to garden work next year during the summer months, that a piece of ground be given to an ambitious boy where he may spend his leisure time if he desires; that the boy be allowed to have the crops for his own use or be paid for the produce at the price it would receive in the outside markets." It is also noted that the increasing interest in agricultural work has led "to the taking of sixty boys from the lowest grades into the greenhouse for one lesson each week, in mixing soils, potting plants, making cuttings, planting seeds, pricking out and transplanting. The present interest guarantees good results." The report of the Principal of the School Department under whom the above work has been carried on contains some interesting suggestions which bear quoting: "The only hope of developing moral life in a boy is to get him interested in some kind of work. The best way to start this interest is to give the boy an opportunity to learn a trade. This should not be required, for then it would defeat its own end. If it is made elective the larger per cent of our boys will select a trade with some wisdom after six months' experience in the school. The boys should receive first upon entering the school their manual-training work and then be allowed to choose their trade. To get boys interested to learn a trade the work should be conducted for the purpose of teaching the trade and not forgetting a certain amount of work done in the most economical way, and yet most trades could be made partially self-supporting." [This marks the end of this chapter narrative.]

Biographical Sketch

Dr. David Snedden, who was an adjunct professor at Columbia University's Teachers College when he wrote the book from which this chapter is excerpted, was a very important contributor to the literature of correctional education, vocational education, and urban education. In many ways he inspired Austin MacCormick, whose work is the topic of the next chapter.

CHAPTER X

VOCATIONAL EDUCATION

by Austin H. MacCormick
(Excerpted in its entirety from
The Education of Adult Prisoners, 1931, pp. 99-149)

Vocational education is that type of education which gives training designed to assist an individual to earn his living. It includes training for the professions, agricultural education, home economics training, commercial education, and education for the trades and industries. In current educational parlance the old industrial arts and manual training courses are considered a part of general rather than vocational education. The Federally-aided state program operated under the National Vocational Education Act (Smith-Hughes Act) passed in 1917 is confined to agriculture, trades and industries, and vocational home economics, all of less than college grade, and the training of teachers in each of these fields.

The Extent of Vocational Education

In practically every field of human endeavor some provision has been made for vocational training by private or public agencies. The trend in vocational education today is toward rendering more service to adults. One of the most important things accomplished by the passing of the National Vocational Education Act was the inclusion of adults among the group to be served at a time when the idea of adult education was comparatively new. Under the stimulus of this act vocational education has expanded tremendously in America in the last decade. It is estimated that by the end of 1935 there will be a total of more than 3,400,000 persons taking training in public vocational schools of the kind provided in the Act.* For these students more than 72,000 teachers will be required. Of the students more than 1,600,000 will be male and probably more than 1,800,000 female. They will be distributed somewhat as follows: in industrial and trade courses, more than 1,800,000; in agricultural courses, more than 600,000; in home-making courses, more than 1,000,000. Taking into account public vocational schools which are not reimbursed from Federal funds, extension work in agriculture carried on by land grant colleges, the work of private business colleges, the day and evening schools conducted by the Y.M.C.A. and similar associations, the huge enrollment in correspondence schools, corporation schools, and schools operated under the auspices of organized employers and organized labor, it is estimated that before 1936 there will be a total of 7,000,000 people in the United States receiving training for some occupation.

---

* Lee (ed.): Objectives and Problems of Vocational Education, pp. 426-7. McGraw-Hill, 1928.

Absence of Vocational Education in Prisons

In view of this expansion it is a cause for wonder that our prisons, especially those bedeviled by problems of idleness, have not established programs of vocational education. As a matter of fact, in the prison field we must theorize about its possibilities, for no prison in the country has a program of vocational education worthy of the name and in no prison is the industrial and maintenance work definitely organized to provide vocational training. In our prisons training for occupations is given only incidentally in the industries, on the prison farm, or in the various maintenance details. Occasional prisoners are taking vocational courses by correspondence, but almost without exception they choose their courses without guidance, pay for them from their own funds, and study them without assistance from the prison authorities. There are a few exceptions to this general rule of letting prisoners work out their own salvation, but they are found in prisons handicapped by their industrial organization, by lack of funds, and all the other obstacles which balk vocational education.

Reformatories for Men

Reformatories for men, in contrast with the prisons, usually set up fairly elaborate programs of vocational education and make the training of the inmates one of their main objectives. Only a few American reformatories have succeeded in establishing well-balanced and effective vocational training programs. Among the chief causes of the failure of the majority to do so are that they prescribe vocational instruction on the mass-treatment basis rather than on the basis of individual analysis and guidance; that they rely too heavily on unit trade schools and emphasize the skilled trades to the neglect of other occupations; that their trade schools often have meager or out-of-date equipment and teach obsolete or vanishing trades; that their instructors are usually underpaid and often incompetent; that too great emphasis is placed on routine practice drills and too little on participation in practical work; that they are not permitted to establish a variety of productive industries and other enterprises having training value; that those industries which are established are far below the standard of similar industries outside; that insufficient emphasis is placed on the necessity of approximating outside working conditions and the standards of competitive trades and industries as to quality, speed and accuracy; and that, in general, the program is not organized to provide a proper correlation of theoretical instruction and practical application on productive or useful work.

Reformatories for Women

Reformatories for women have a better opportunity than institutions for men to set up successful programs of vocational education because the work of the institution provides training in so many occupations which women can enter after leaving the institution. The training which they offer, however, is too often incidental rather than organized. Their salary schedules ordinarily do not permit them to employ enough trained instructors. They necessarily emphasize home-making occupations to the exclusion of the trades and industries. Their productive industries are usually limited in scope and their trade and industrial education is confined to very few occupations, in many cases to only one: power machine sewing. Largely because of the lack of opportunity to offer practical experience, they are notably weak in their programs of commercial education, in spite of the fact that the proportion of women to men in commercial pursuits is steadily increasing. Notwithstanding their shortcomings, the reformatories for women, speaking generally, are more successful in providing vocational education than either the prisons or reformatories for men.

Its Value for Prisoners

The case for vocational education in penal institutions need not be argued. Laymen and prison officials alike accept the fact that it is needed; their only question is whether or not it can be successfully carried on and whether or not the expense which it involves is justified. If it could be demonstrated that a considerable number of prisoners were turned from crime by being given adequate training for satisfying and lucrative positions on release, the question of expense would be answered. In spite of the conservatism of state legislators and executives a successful program of vocational education would undoubtedly secure public support and approval. The educational slogan most frequently heard from laymen is, "Teach the prisoner how to earn an honest living." People advocate vocational education for prisoners who are not interested in any other type of education, except perhaps the education of illiterates. If a program worthy of the endorsement of reputable leaders in a state is set up in a penal institution, it is probable that appropriations can more easily be secured for it than for any other branch of the penal educational program. The problem is how to get started.

The cause of vocational education for prisoners, especially in reformatories, has suffered because of the exaggerated claims that have been made for it and the unjustified hopes that have been held out for it. It is folly to think that we can make a useful citizen of any harum-scarum boy by teaching him plumbing or electrical wiring, or that the adult drifter who has stuck steadily to nothing except petty crime all his life will immediately become a hard-working and law-abiding man because he has been taught typewriter repairing. We can only hope that the chances of their taking steady employment and leading law-abiding lives will be increased if we give them the means of earning an honest living and perhaps arouse some interest in a useful vocation. Aside from its own value vocational education has marked value as a means of stimulating interest in general education. Many of the fundamental processes, especially of mathematics, which a man needs in his daily life have no interest for him until he sees that they are a necessary part of training for a job. The man who has never felt any regret over his inability to read a newspaper or magazine may take a course in reading in order to be able to follow job instructions.

Difficulties and Essentials

As was pointed out in the chapter on The Student Body [see 1931 edition, pp. 13-27], it is a generally recognized fact that the great majority of prisoners is vocationally untrained. But it will probably be a long time before penal institutions can establish complete programs of vocational education in spite of the economic and social waste that might be prevented. This is especially true of trade and industrial education. The cost of buildings and equipment for trade instruction, the salaries of skilled instructors and directors, and the establishment of industries and training projects represent appropriation items which state legislatures are slow to pass. Many of our institutions are already suffering seriously from the problem of idleness because of conservative state policies. Proposals to increase industrial facilities to meet this condition are concerned less with those industries which have vocational training value than those which will show profits in dollars and cents. One of our most persistent fallacies is that profitable production and vocational training are incompatible.

Another fallacy is that it is sound business policy for a state to operate industries which show large profits because they can utilize large numbers of unskilled workers in the quantity production of one or two products. Examples of such industries are the garment factories to be found in so many of our penal institutions. Let us assume that such an industry shows an annual profit of $100,000, which is a high figure. Ten ex-prisoners who might perhaps have been turned from crime by training in a worthwhile occupation may easily commit depredations in a year totaling over $100,000. One of them may take a human life whose value is immeasurable. The one-industry institutions and those concentrating on get-rich-quick industries may show impressive financial profits, but these are usually more than balanced by the social losses involved in failure to fit men for free life.

For the development of a well-rounded program of vocational education in the penal institution the following things are needed:

1. A diversity of productive industries having vocational training value, organized and operated as nearly as possible in accordance with the standards of outside industries.

2. A complete agricultural program, based on the scientific principles of modern agriculture.

3. Reorganization of the maintenance details and insistence on better methods, skilled supervising personnel and modern equipment so that these details can be used for instruction.

4. A variety of special training projects to supplement industries and maintenance work.

5. A diversity of vocational schools and courses, well organized and staffed with a trained personnel.

6. Provision for instruction in subjects supplemental to and related to vocational training, and in subjects needed as ground work for vocational courses.

7. Provision for individual vocational guidance, correlated with placement and follow-up after release.

8. Complete correlation of theoretical instruction and practical application, with readjustment of the institutional program to permit a proper division of time between instruction and participation in productive or useful work for training.

9. Acceptance of standard methods and objectives.

10. Sufficient funds to make attainment of these objectives possible.

The problem of finances is of paramount importance. Unfortunately, none of the Federal funds available for the promotion of vocational education under the Smith-Hughes Act can be used in "schools and classes designed for the benefit of delinquent, dependent, incorrigible, defective, or otherwise subnormal youths or adults." The foregoing is quoted from a definite ruling of the Federal Board for Vocational Education (Bulletin 17, p. 94). While penal institutions cannot ask their respective states for Smith-Hughes funds, they can benefit indirectly from the Act. In the establishment of a trained personnel, the determination of content and method, and the formulation of desirable standards for an effective program of vocational education, the Federal-state programs have rendered valuable assistance to penal institutions and to all other agencies undertaking vocational education. Every year more and more trained teachers and directors are being produced under the Federally-aided program. They are residents within the states and, although penal institutions do not come within their field, they can be relied on for informal assistance. Some of these trained men can be lured into the penal field. The textual material, expert job analyses, and teaching methods which they employ can be directly transferred to the penal institutions. The types of organization which have become standardized can be used as models.

Trade and Industrial Education

Trade and industrial education, one of the most important of the vocational education fields, need not be defined exactly. The policy of the Federal Board for Vocational Education is to list all occupations not distinctively commercial, agricultural or home-making as trade or industrial pursuits. Practically all the types of organization set up under the Vocational Education Act can be successfully followed in penal institutions, with some modifications necessitated by the fact that the Federally-aided program is concerned for the most part with the younger workers. This fact does not affect the basic plan of organization, which supplies a convenient starting point for adaptation.

Types of Organization

In the Federal-state programs* six types of trade or industrial schools or classes may be organized, as follows: (1) Evening industrial. (2) Part-time trade extension. (3) Part-time trade preparatory. (4) Part-time general continuation. (5) Unit trade (commonly known as day trade). (6) General industrial (in cities under 25,000).

1. *An evening industrial school or class* is designed to give instruction in a particular trade, supplemental to the daily employment, to persons who have entered upon employment in that trade or industrial pursuit. For example, an evening industrial school for employed plumbers and plumbers' apprentices could be established to give these men instruction in plumbing shop practice; in blueprint reading for plumbers; in state and local rules and regulations for plumbing installation; and in other allied subjects, all related to the plumbing trade. The instruction would be given in the workers' leisure time outside the hours which constitute the regular working day.

2. *A part-time trade extension school or class* is designed to give instruction to persons who have entered upon the work of a trade or industrial pursuit, to fit them further for useful employment in the trade or industrial pursuit in which they are employed. The Federal standard requires that instruction must be given for not less than 144 hours per year. In this type of school or class the plumbers or plumbers' apprentices mentioned above might be given the identical instruction set forth for the evening class but this would be considered part-time work if it were given during the hours which constitute the regular working day.

3. *The part-time trade preparatory school or class* is designed to give instruction to persons who have entered upon employment, this instruction to be such as will fit them for useful employment in a trade or industrial pursuit other than the one in which they are employed. Here again the Federal standard requires instruction for not less than 144 hours per year. In this plan of organization the work mentioned above for plumbers might be given within the hours that constitute the working day to a group of men employed as janitors, messengers, manual laborers, farm hands, and in other occupations except plumbing, the instruction being devised to prepare for entrance into the plumbing trade. The work of a part-time trade preparatory class would seldom, if ever, coincide with that of a trade extension class dealing with the same trade. The function of such instruction is to serve as an entering wedge, to be followed later by part-time extension work.

---

* See Bulletin No. 17, Federal Board for Vocational Education. Much of this Bulletin is here quoted almost verbatim.

4. *A part-time general continuation school or class* is one designed to give instruction to persons who have entered upon employment, the instruction being in subjects which enlarge the civic or vocational intelligence of workers. This is the type of organization customarily found in states whose laws compel young workers to continue their education after entering employment. The principal educational objectives are (1) employment adjustment, (2) vocational and educational guidance, and (3) social adjustment.

5. *The unit trade school or class* is one designed to fit persons for useful employment in a particular trade or industrial pursuit through instruction devoting not less than half the time to practical work on a productive or useful basis and extending over not less than nine months (thirty-six weeks) per year and not less than thirty clock hours per week. For instance, when a group of persons not yet employed attend an all-day school or class for the purpose of preparing for entrance into the printing trade, and when the instruction given in both shop and related class work is based solely upon printing trade needs, this constitutes a unit trade school or class.

6. *A general industrial school or class* in the Federal program is one designed to meet the particular needs of cities or towns of less than 25,000 population as an alternative to the establishment of a unit trade school, on the assumption that a community of this size would find it difficult to absorb an entire group after graduation into any one trade. In organization it follows the unit trade school plan, not less than half the time being devoted to practical work on a useful or productive basis. (The penal institution need not concern itself with the inability of any one community to absorb all the graduates of one of its trade schools, inasmuch as they will be widely scattered throughout the state or the whole country after release.)

Objectives

As will be seen above, the Federal-state program embraces three general objectives or functions, as follows: (A) Trade preparatory, preparing for advantageous entrance into a trade or industrial pursuit; (B) Trade extension, giving to persons who are already employed in a trade or industrial pursuit instruction which supplements their daily work in order to enable them to become more proficient in the work in which they are engaged or to prepare them for advancement in the same general line of work. (C) General continuation, the primary objective being the promotion of civic or vocational intelligence.

A. *Trade Preparatory Types of Organization.* To prepare different groups of individuals for advantageous entrance into a trade or industrial pursuit, several types of organization may be set up, as follows:

1. *The day trade school.*

2. *The general industrial school,* similar in objective and organization to the day trade school.

3. *The cooperative course,* in which the students are divided into two equal groups, one of which attends school for a week or for some other fixed period of time while the other group is employed at work in industries or trades, the groups shifting at the end of the fixed period.

4. *The part-time class (discontinuous),* in which attendance is distributed throughout the year for a certain number of hours per week. This organization is designed primarily for workers who are temporarily or unsatisfactorily employed and who wish preparatory training so that eventually they may be able to enter upon a more permanent type of employment or one in which there is a better possibility of advancement and permanency. Such classes ordinarily give instruction covering four to eight hours per week throughout a period of at least nine months per year.

5. *The part-time class (intensive),* designed to prepare for entrance with advanced standing into a trade or industrial pursuit. This type of organization is usually found where the preliminary preparation that the school can give is not sufficient to justify organizing a nine months' day trade course. In certain types of trade, such as telephone operating, power machine stitching in garment trades, tile setting, bricklaying and plumbing, an intensive part-time course is often organized to give instruction for a period of from two to five months in length, following which the students are placed at work in the industries or trades with advanced standing, in many cases to receive further instruction in trade extension courses. Intensive part-time courses usually concentrate on the manipulative and directly related phases of the trade for from six to eight hours per day.

B. *Trade Extension Types of Organization.* Trade extension courses, designed to give instruction which will supplement the worker's knowledge or skill in the job on which he is employed and which will assist in preparing him to advance to eventual promotion, may be given under the following types of organization:

1. *The evening school or class.* Under Federal standards instruction given in such a class must be confined to material which is supplemental to the daily occupations of the class personnel. Without having any school shop equipment, it is possible to give instruction to mechanics in the technical and theoretical sides of the trade, in blueprint or plan reading, shop mathematics, estimating, and the science underlying the practice of the trade. When equipment is available, they may also be given specialized training in phases of manipulative work which they lack or do not have an opportunity to acquire in the jobs on which they are employed.

2. *The part-time class (discontinuous)*, which enrolls workers who will attend for periods usually extending from four to eight hours per week over at least nine months per year. In the majority of such part-time extension courses the four hours per week are not utilized in training for manipulative work but in a study of the related science, mathematics, or drawing of the trade involved.

3. *The part-time course (intensive)*. This is particularly designed for those engaged in occupations which are of a seasonal nature. Short intensive courses are set up during the dull or slack seasons, varying in time arrangement from three weeks of intensive work, eight hours per day, six days per week, to courses extending over two or three months in time, embracing from six to eight hours per day of instruction.

C. *General Continuation Courses*. In the Federal-state program these are set up under but one form of organization, as follows:

The part-time course. Since the instruction given in such part-time courses concerns itself largely with the promotion of civic or vocational intelligence, the general continuation objective is usually not considered directly vocational.

Variety of Training Possible

The above outline of the types of organization sanctioned by the Federal Board for Vocational Education under the provisions of the Smith-Hughes Act indicates how penal institutions may vary their program. It also shows how invalid is the excuse usually given for failure to establish programs of vocational education in these institutions: that they cannot afford to set up expensive trade schools. The full-time trade school, requiring elaborate equipment, is seen to be only one type of effective organization. With some adaptations every type of school or course authorized in the Federal-state program can be set up in the penal institution.

Participation in Productive or Useful Work

The opportunity to perform practical work is an absolute essential of any effective vocational training program. In prisons this is doubly true; the daily life is one of monotonous routine and there is a natural tendency to avoid the unaccustomed routine of study unless its practical implications are constantly in view. The way in which prisoners, especially young ones, respond to a productive enterprise is well known to any institutional officer who has taken listless, malingering prisoners from a bricklaying class and has seen them come suddenly to life on the job of constructing a real brick building. The best arrangement in penal institutions is one under which every prisoner has a regular working assignment as well as a training assignment. It is probable that adult prisoners will advance more rapidly in vocational training courses if they do not attend continuously. The morale of the institution will be better when the institution is considered as a community of employed workers, receiving full opportunity for education, rather than as a community of men attending school.

An Ideal Plan

The ideal training plan is found where the prisoner is being trained on a full-time basis but is devoting at least half his time to a working detail which is coordinated with his training and which affords him an opportunity for direct application of what he learns during the hours spent in the training school or class. In many penal institutions this is possible for only a comparatively few prisoners and in only a limited number of occupations, unless special training projects are set up. This is especially true of institutions having only one or two industries and those whose maintenance shops are meagerly equipped and have little work to perform. A prison whose major industry is a shirt shop will have in this shop several hundred workers who have no idea of following that trade on release from the institution, but who desire vocational training. In this case it is necessary to give training on the part-time basis, allowing some of the men assigned to the shirt shop to attend trade preparatory classes, and others who have a background of skill or experience in some occupation to attend trade extension classes. When, as is rarely the case, the inmate population is so small that no prisoners can be spared from either the industries or the maintenance details during the working day, it is necessary to arrange for instruction in evening classes.*

The Full-time Trade School

The full-time trade school has been found less effective and more expensive than other types of organization. There is, nevertheless, a place for it in any institution. Because of the shortness of sentences it is desirable to assign some prisoners to intensive courses on a full-time basis. If, however, these courses comply with the standard requirement as to participation in practical work the students are in effect holding down working jobs while taking training courses. There are many difficulties in the way of the establishment of full-time trade schools. They are expensive of installation and their equipment needs constantly to be brought up to date. They are not effective unless they are well staffed with competent instructors. They can serve only a limited number of men. At best the number of trades which can be successfully taught is small, for the actual working conditions of probably not more than twenty of the thousands of industrial occupations can be satisfactorily reproduced in trade schools. On the other hand, mastery of some trades can be obtained by intensive application in a good training course covering a period of thirty to ninety weeks. If institutional trade schools avoid the error into which those in the reformatories usually fall, that of spending too much time on routine

---

* See Prosser and Bass: *Adult Education: The Evening Industrial School*. Century, 1930.

exercises and busy work, if the requirement that at least half time be devoted to practical application is lived up to, and if men are selected for training and are not assigned in a wholesale and haphazard manner, the full-time trade school will prove an effective agency.

The trade school, in addition to training full-time students, can serve as a training center for many of those who are being instructed on the part-time plan. The carpenter school, for example, will have a certain number of students who remain in the school for an intensive course in carpentry throughout their sentences, being assigned to productive work about the institution only as a training project. It will have another group of students consisting of those men who have been assigned to the carpenter detail and who report to the school for a number of hours each day or week for instruction. This may take the form of training in special techniques or instruction in such subjects as the mathematics of carpentry or blueprint reading. A third group will be in preparatory training for assignment to the carpenter detail. Some trade schools, such as the school for printers, will be at the same time training courses and productive working projects.

This means utilization to the full of the staff, buildings and equipment of the trade school, but the courses given there should be distinct. We should get as far away as possible from the idea of a general trade school and should think always of vocational schools or courses as training for specific vocations. A number of vocational classes may occupy the same building and may be under the same general direction, but each has its own definite objective and should have its own distinct course of training and its own staff of instructors. Because of the necessity of getting along with inadequate training staffs, we tend in penal institutions to organize catch-all trade schools and to require the same staff to teach or supervise an excessively large number of related trades. We should not plan a school in the building trades but rather schools or classes for house carpenters, bricklayers, plasterers, plumbers, electricians specializing in house wiring, and so on, unless we are trying to train general contractors and building foremen rather than competent artisans in the various building crafts. In brief, objectives must be definite rather than general.

The Part-time Cooperative Plan

An adaptation of the part-time cooperative plan, under which two groups of students alternate between work assignments and vocational school, would undoubtedly prove practicable in penal institutions in spite of the difficulties involved in the arrangement of schedules and a possible curtailment of production in industries affected by the two-shift system. The organization of training on this plan is most easily effected when the institution has so large a population that industries and maintenance details are overmanned and a two-shift system is feasible. It is practicable, however, for a part of the prisoners in even those few institutions which have enough work to keep all their prisoners employed. Incidentally, the adoption of the part-time cooperative plan would help solve the problem of unemployment. Experience has shown that the week-in and week-out system of alternation is the best arrangement. There are few industrial processes which cannot be dropped by one shift on Saturday and picked up by another on Monday with little lost motion. It is unwise to make the alternating periods either too long or too short. Work and instruction are bound to be thrown into confusion if they are put on a half-day-in and half-day-out basis. On the other hand, there is a tendency to become rusty on both work and instruction if the periods are as long as two weeks.

The part-time cooperative plan, as usually organized throughout the country, is designed for younger workers and is based on an arrangement between trade school authorities and industries whereby the workers are allowed to alternate between school and employment. In its application of this idea, the institution is at the same time the educational agency and the employing industrial organization. It is necessary merely to coordinate two parts of the same unitary system. The ideal cooperative plan demands that the employed hours supply practical application of what is learned during the training hours. The idea of alternating employment and training, however, can be applied to the institution even when the working assignment bears no relation whatever to the training course being followed.

The part-time cooperative plan does not necessarily mean that all men assigned to a shoe shop, for example, will spend every second week in a class devoted to teaching the technique of shoe-shop practice or related subjects. The ideal situation, in which the week on the job and the week in training are devoted to the same vocation, cannot be attained with all prisoners or in all occupations. It is not reasonable to assume that every man assigned to a prison industry wishes or intends to make it his life occupation, although proper vocational guidance will see that every industry is manned as far as possible with men who intend to continue in it on release. During the instruction week, one man may be devoting his time to intensive practice on a more difficult process in shoe manufacture than the one he has been performing during his employed week. Another will be taking a "vestibule" or trade preparatory course in house wiring. A third will be taking general education courses or special courses in mathematics and blueprint reading. The advantages of the part-time cooperative plan are so many that it is worth all the effort required to overcome the obstacles which stand in the way of its organization and administration. It is especially well adapted to the needs of men assigned to skilled maintenance details, for their practical work can be made a unitary part of their training. It also meets the needs of such vocations as the building trades, in which it is difficult to give effective training in school shops. That the part-time cooperative plan is the coming thing in vocational education for workers is generally recognized by leaders in the field.

Other Part-time Training

When neither the part-time cooperative plan nor the full-time training plan is practicable, it is necessary to arrange for part-time training of the usual type on either a trade preparatory or trade extension basis. During slack seasons the employed prisoner may be given an opportunity for a part-time intensive course. Throughout the year those whose working assignments do not keep them busy all day may be given part-time discontinuous courses followed for a few hours each day. Any prisoner who has energy enough to take a training course at the end of his day's work may be given a part-time course in an evening school or class.

The Superiority of Full-time Training

The superiority of full-time training under proper conditions to all other types is clear. It must include participation in practical work. Of full-time training, Dr. David Snedden says:

> All kinds of part-time vocational education are probably very uneconomical of the learner's time and public money when contrasted with full-time training which employs full measures of participation in commercially productive work as part of the training process under, of course, technically expert and educationally expert supervision. This judgment applies to evening school instruction, continuation school instruction and training, most forms of correspondence instruction and all other more or less fragmentary offerings, with one basic exception.

> That exception is found where the learner: (a) has substantially learned the major part of the vocation; (b) where he has clearly developed excellent powers of self-education in this field; and (c) where published materials for extension correspondence or other methods of self-education have been made well available. Under these conditions true part-time training may best combine economy and efficiency. (Note that where learners share in commercially productive work under direction of the school or as a basic part of school work, this is full-time, not part-time, administration.)

To prisoners falling in the groups cited above, a certain amount of training can be given very informally by supplying textbooks, correspondence courses and other material which they can utilize intelligently and effectively because of their background of training and practical experience or their capacity for self-direction. This is a safe method with only a limited number of men. The ex-clerk or the experienced salesman can often teach himself if he is supplied with good textual material related to his profession, just as the skilled automobile mechanic can safely be given a correspondence course in aviation motors, but for the great majority organized and directed training is necessary.

The decision as to whether any particular prisoner should be trained on the part-time or the full-time basis depends on a variety of factors: the occupation for which he is being trained, the opportunities for practical application offered by the institution, his previous occupational history and probable occupational future, his present knowledge and skill, his capacity for learning, his ability to carry on study in theory, the length of his sentence, etc. A large number of prisoners in institutions where there are productive industries will probably always perform routine work with very little definite vocational instruction. Others will spend all their time in intensive training courses with practical work as a part of their training. For others instruction will be on a part-time basis, their time being divided between instruction and employment on working details related or unrelated to their training courses.

Opportunities for Practical Training

The Federal-state program assumes that when workers attending trade schools or classes are employed they are in trade or industrial pursuits where standards of competitive production prevail. The training facilities afforded by the industries and maintenance details of the usual penal institution obviously cannot compare with the opportunities offered by the average community. The institution is a community, however, and a large number of occupations are represented in its daily activities.

Training in Industries

Industries can be effectively used for vocational training if we set up those which have training value, house them in good buildings, equip them with adequate modern machinery, install well-trained superintendents, foremen and training supervisors, and manufacture a good product for a real market at as near the usual industrial standard of quality and speed as possible. Among the industries which have potential vocational training value are the following: shoe shops, print shops, textile mills, dye plants, clothing factories making civilian clothing (the ordinary shirt shop or work clothing factory has almost no vocational training value), foundries, brick plants, cement plants, furniture factories, canneries, grist mills, shops manufacturing auto license plates and highway markers, other metal shops, farm machinery plants, and binder twine plants. A greater diversity is plainly needed.

Many of the processes in the ordinary industry are best learned by the pick-up method on the job itself. In any manufacturing plant, however, there are a number of processes requiring special training. This can be given either in the course of the day's work by a skilled foreman or instructor, in a preparatory training course, or in a part-time extension course. Many manufacturing concerns give a preliminary course of training and later, after the employee has gone to work on a full-time job, give him extension training of the special type needed as well as instruction in supplemental and related subjects. The training courses given by the National Cash Register Company, The Dennison Manufacturing Company, the American Rolling Mills Company, and other large manufacturing corporations will serve as valuable guides to institutions planning to train their prisoners in industries.

We must not feel that the man who operates a machine which he masters in a few days is receiving no training of value. If he is kept up to a proper standard as to quantity and quality of production, he is at least fitting himself for a job operating a similar machine outside, even though insufficient transfer of skill takes place to make his training of equal value for another job. The routine worker, moreover, receives moral training which cannot be divorced from vocational training, in that he learns to put in a hard eight hour day of work and finds, often to his surprise, that he can keep it up for months without quitting. This is moral training which many prisoners need badly. It is partly nullified if he is not kept up to the standards of outside industry. One of the disastrous effects of overcrowding our institutions and overmanning their industries is to make industrial snails of men who must be whippets to get by in competition. The importance of pace in training needs continual emphasis. If a man must tend four machines of a certain type in an outside shop and turn out 1000 pieces a day to hold his job it is bad training to allow him for months on end to turn out only 250 pieces and to tend only one machine.

Special Training Projects

It is impossible for penal institutions, because of the limits that are placed on their industrial expansion, to organize enough industries to supply productive work for training in the variety of occupations that can be taught effectively. Where suitable industries are lacking it is necessary to develop artificial industrial training projects, or to select those parts of even the poorest industries which can be utilized for training: for example, the cutting room in a garment factory. A new policy should be considered by penal authorities: attempting to make arrangements with manufacturing or other commercial organizations to install in the institution enterprises performing part or all of a productive process for the sole purpose of providing practical work for vocational students. This should not be difficult for institutions located in or near great manufacturing centers, and it is not impossible for others less advantageously located. For example, a prison which cannot establish a complete shoe shop can contract with a nearby shoe manufacturer to install several departments in the institution. A similar contract can be made with a furniture factory to do the finishing work, or with a foundry to make rough castings.* A contract might be made with a nearby garage to turn over all its valve grinding, brake lining and complete greasing jobs to the prison automobile school.

Training on Maintenance Work

The maintenance details of every penal institution offer opportunities for the teaching of a large number of occupations, although there is little variety

---

* This is written with full appreciation of the possibility that various states may pass restrictive legislation affecting prison-made goods when the Hawes-Cooper Bill becomes operative in 1934.

in the work to be performed by any one shop and it is often necessary to plan artificial training projects. The following are some of the vocations represented in the maintenance details of the average institution: truck driver, chauffeur, automobile mechanic, automobile washer, gardener, greenhouse employee, cobbler, blacksmith, carpenter, painter, plasterer, concrete worker, brick mason, electrician, stationary engineer, fireman, power plant employee, janitor, cleaner and presser, tailor, waiter, hospital orderly, nurse, cook, baker, meat cutter, storekeeper, laundry worker, teacher, librarian, mail clerk, general clerk, typist, shoe-repairer, welder, and telephone operator.

As has been indicated, the part-time cooperative plan of instruction is particularly well adapted to the training of men in the maintenance details. Another practicable way is to assign extra men to every working detail. This means no departure from ordinary institutional practice, for maintenance details are characteristically overmanned. Of the men assigned to any detail, the larger number should be considered as being in training. They correspond to apprentices working as helpers to journeymen. In every detail there will be prisoners who were skilled in the trade before they entered the institution or have received sufficient training there so that they may be classed as journeymen. Training for these men consists of improving their technical skill and increasing their knowledge of related theory. Their presence on the detail assures the work of the institution being carried on. Under proper direction they can serve as foremen-instructors for the "apprentices." Some of this group can safely be given correspondence courses, texts and other study material to use with little assistance from instructors.

Instruction in connection with maintenance details can be given in all the standard forms: preparatory courses for those who wish to prepare for entrance into specific occupations represented among the details, and trade extension courses for those who have experience in the trades represented among the details or are acquiring that experience on a maintenance assignment. Both preparatory and extension courses may be on either a part-time or a full-time basis. In either case the maintenance work is utilized to provide the required practice. The cleaners, messengers, manual laborers and other catch-all details will always contain a large number of men with no vocational interest or aptitude but there will be others in these details who are waiting for their opportunity to secure assignment to a position requiring skill and offering training. The latter group may be excellent training material. They can be tested by brief try-out courses and, if they show promise, can be given preparatory courses pending their assignment to the desired detail.

We must not expect a man to learn a skilled trade by merely participating in the work of that trade on a maintenance detail without organized training. Maintenance work can be utilized to supply the practical part of the training process but it is not the whole process. Few prisoners have enough experience in a skilled trade to follow their own noses. The most effective use can probably be made of maintenance work for training in the trades by supplying short-unit preparatory courses and then assigning the beginner to a working detail as an apprentice or helper. As soon as he is assigned trade extension instruction should be provided on the cooperative plan or during a part of the working day or during the evening hours. When assignment to a full-time trade school is prescribed the training course will necessarily involve participation in practical work on a working detail.

Fields to Avoid. Penal institutions tend to offer instruction in obsolete trades or those which are rapidly becoming so (some of the woodworking crafts, for example), and also to concentrate on trades which are well unionized,* have rigid apprenticeship systems, and are reluctant to accept other types of training as substitutes. The latter group includes, to be sure, some of the trades most worth teaching: the building trades, the electrical and printing trades, etc. In teaching these trades current requirements and restrictions should be taken into account.

The Trade of Automobile Mechanic

Institutions are slow to provide training in one field which is not unionized, has no apprenticeship requirements, and offers well-paid employment to thousands of new men every year. This is the automobile repair trade. More prisoners apply for instruction in it than in any other single trade. They are often refused for fear that it will encourage them to become automobile thieves. The fact is that automobile thieves are not often recruited from the ranks of mechanics.

The fascination which the trade of automobile mechanic has for male prisoners should be capitalized. It is wasteful to permit every man who wishes to take a course in automobile repairing to do so, but even under a rigid system of selection there will be in any prison a large number of men who can properly take a course for automobile mechanics and garage workers. These will include some men who have already had experience in the trade and others who are entering it without experience. Facilities, equipment, and methods of instruction will differ for the two groups. Experienced automobile mechanics can be instructed effectively by the use of charts, models, and other laboratory equipment. A new or special type of lubrication system can be demonstrated with charts and a cut-away motor. Laboratory equipment of this type is needed for the inexperienced group also, but the green man cannot be instructed by use of this material alone. He must learn the working correlation of all parts of the car and must acquire skill in manipulative work before his attention can profitably be turned to specialized equipment and operation.

A few institutions, most of them reformatories, have established schools or courses for automobile mechanics and in all institutions the men assigned to the institution garage have an opportunity to learn something by the pick-up

---

* In a number of states the unions are liberal and cooperative in their attitude toward ex-prisoners.

method in the care of official cars and trucks and in occasional work on cars belonging to officers. No institution in the country, however, has an effective training course. Equipment is incomplete and in many cases obsolete, and instruction of high quality is lacking. The chief weakness is the lack of enough practical work to give the student practice under outside garage and repair shop standards. The city trade school is permitted to do commercial work, but a conservative official and state policy prohibits this in penal institutions. Effective preparatory courses for beginners and extension courses for men who already have some experience can be conducted even under this handicap, but a complete course, which takes the beginner through to the point where he can hope to get a position as a mechanic or helper, is difficult to set up unless the school has a large number of cars representing a wide variety of makes on which to work. Commercial work should be permitted to make this possible.

Information of value regarding proper equipment, standards, and methods of instruction for schools in automobile repairing can be obtained from the Federal Board for Vocational Education, from state directors of vocational education, and from large city trade schools. A useful booklet is the Board's Bulletin No. 109: *Layouts and Equipment for Automobile School Shops. Bruce's Shop Annual*, cited in the Appendix [of the 1931 edition], contains much valuable information and standard shop layouts.

The Vocational Teaching Staff

No institution should hope to set up an effective program of vocational education without the services of at least one expert vocational director. In institutions where ingenuity will have to be exercised by the staff in utilizing poorly equipped and inefficiently operated industries and maintenance details as training projects and in planning artificial projects, there should be at least one trained vocational coordinator whose duty it is to devise effective methods of carrying out this essential part of the program. Every instructor should be expected to work out his own detailed problems of coordination, but so many problems affecting the whole routine of the institution are involved that coordination must be centered under the direction of one man. This is a difficult task, involving thorough knowledge of the technique of job analysis and of training methods. The staff should also include as many trained instructors, representing as wide a variety of vocations, as the budget will permit. The success of a vocational training program, especially in a penal institution, depends largely on the teacher.

Qualifications

The more important characteristics which a candidate for a teaching position in a trade or industrial school should possess and some practical suggestions as to how the possession of these characteristics may be determined are given in Bulletin 17 of the Federal Board for Vocational Education . . . [a summary of which is shown below].

Qualifications	Suggestions as to how the possession of these qualifications may be determined
1. Trade mastery or occupational competency.	1. (a) Employment record, (b) statements by employers and supervisors under whom the man has worked, and (c) practical performance test conducted by a qualified committee.
2. Occupational prestige and standing in trade.	2. Supporting evidence secured from employers, supervisors, and fellow workers.
3. Pride in his trade.	3. Personal interview by qualified representative committee.
4. Self-confidence.	4. Personal interview by qualified representative committee.
5. Ability to get along with associates.	5. Employment record, evidence procured from former employers and supervisors.
6. Ability to work harmoniously with official superiors.	6. Employment record, evidence procured from former employers and supervisors.
7. Ability to get a job done under difficulties.	7. Employment record, evidence procured from former employers and supervisors.
8. The habit of regarding himself as a success in his field.	8. Personal interview by qualified representative committee.
9. Habit of meeting responsibilities.	9. Employment record, evidence secured from former supervisors.
10. Ability to express himself clearly and briefly, both orally and in writing.	10. Interview in which the man is encouraged to do considerable talking himself in replying to questions, supplemented by a suitable written statement on some topic with which the man is thoroughly familiar.
11. Good character.	11. Evidence secured from associates and persons of known standing with whom the man has had business dealings or persons with whom he has associated in fields unrelated to his work.
12. Suitable age.	12. Birth certificate or affidavit.

At the present time it is recognized in every state plan (Bulletin 17 is here paraphrased freely) that the teacher must possess trade mastery or occupational competency. The instructor must know his job and there is no satisfactory substitute for this qualification on the part of a trade or industrial teacher. No amount of general education or technical training will enable a man to teach a trade if he lacks the all-important qualification of being a master workman in that trade. In some states a total of eight years experience in the trade, including the period of apprenticeship, is required. Other states accept men with less experience, and the minimum which the Federal Board has approved in any state plan is one year of journeyman experience in addition to the completion of apprenticeship or its equivalent.

The other qualifications are self-explanatory, with the exception of age. In most state plans twenty-five years of age is set as a minimum because, in most cases, a man will not have secured satisfactory experience before he is twenty-five years of age. The practice of setting up a maximum age is not so general. Maturity and wide experience are decided assets, although they are sometimes balanced in the older man by less desirable qualifications.

The objectives which have been set up in training programs for teachers of trade and industrial work of the vocational type also indicate what may be expected of a good teacher. These training objectives are the following:

(1) Ability to teach the manipulative, technical, and informational branches of the trade.

(2) Ability to plan instructional work.

(3) Ability to use good methods of personnel management in dealing with individuals or groups of individuals under instructional conditions.

(4) Ability to keep the necessary records and make such reports as may be called for.

(5) Ability to analyze a job or series of jobs in the trade taught.

(6) Ability to use an analysis for setting up a course of study and organizing related technical content.

(7) Ability to discriminate between the importance of the mechanics of organization in the school and the function of instructional work.

(8) Ability to appreciate the difficulties and problems of a learner in the trade.

(9) An intelligent appreciation of the importance of vocational education and the relationship of the program to other fields of education.

(10) An understanding of accepted standards for trade and industrial education.

It will not be possible for some penal institutions to finance adequate staffs. These institutions should do the best they can by employing as industrial and maintenance foremen men who not only know their trades but also have or can acquire teaching skill. Much can be done under the lead of a few competent foremen if the advice and assistance obtainable from such sources as the Federal Board of Vocational Education, the Department of Agriculture and other government agencies, the directors of vocational education in the various states, corporation schools, State Departments of Agriculture and Colleges of Agriculture, and the staffs of city trade schools are secured.

Job Analysis

Objectives (5) and (6) cited above are of prime importance. The necessity of scientific job analysis as the basis of training courses is now well recognized. A job analysis is nothing but a scientific method of planning a sequence of lessons leading to the attainment of an objective in skill or knowledge, the objective having first been clearly defined and broken down into its component parts. The analysis determines what is to be taught and in what order the successive steps are to be taught. The job analysis on the [this]. . .page, which covers the first steps in the bricklaying trade, indicates the general method of analysis. It is quoted from Bulletin No. 95 of the Federal Board for Vocational Education, an analysis of the bricklaying trade. Analyses of many other occupations have been made and are available in the bulletins of the Federal Board and from other sources. When shortage of time or lack of facilities makes it impossible to teach complete trades or to follow standard published analyses, the vocational education director and the instructors in an institution will need to make special analyses in some cases with a view to producing boiled-down courses. The condensed vocational courses developed during the World War were based on such analyses.

BRICKLAYING.
Block—BL-I.—Block Base: Jobs Calling for Semifinished Work.
Block objective: Ability to do common brick jobs where finished appearance of the work is not an important issue

Job		Trade technical knowledge			Auxiliary information		Training progres- sion.
Type Job	Objective	Draw- ing	Science	Mathe- matics	Recognition of stock; trade terms	Care of tools; safety	
1. *Type Job specifications—* Backing up with common brick, using running bond against a vertical wall between estab- lished vertical ends not over the length of 6 bricks. Surface appearance not important. Work- ing from inside wall. Mortar ready mixed. Type jobs: *a.* Backing up the face of an 8-inch wall between window jambs. *b.* Backing up as above, between door jambs.	Some ability to spread mortar and place brick cut to length on inside tier of wall, between vertical ends, using running bond. Ability to arrange courses so as to come out even and level with top face tier.	......	Mortar dries out when exposed to air. The larger the surface is exposed the quicker the drying. Dry bricks ab- sorb water from mortar. Water evaporates more on a hot day than on a cold day. Frozen mortar expands and will not set. Frozen mortar will not stick to brick. Salt or calcium chloride in mortar lowers the freez- ing point. Mortar made with hot sand and hot water will often set before freezing. Warm bricks cause mortar to set quicker. Stretch- ing over and under end joints which are weak, make end joints stronger and stretcher courses more rigid.	Eye estimation of length in brick units. Eye estimation of mortar in terms of number of bricks in bed course.	Recognition of stock: Ability to recognize com- mon brick. The recognition of mortar in the right condition. Trade terms: Backing, cutting off, spreading, running bond, header, stretcher, trowel, mortar board, brick hammer, salmon brick, and lime brick, hard burned brick, overburned brick, sill, joists, weather strip, course, bed joint, vertical joint, cross joint and jamb.	Care of tools: Clean- ing trowel at end of job. Safety: Lime in mortar burns the skin. Keep mortar away from trowel handle and ferrule.	*Instruction required: How to pick up mortar, spread mortar, place brick, cut to length for an inside tier of wall between vertical ends, using running bond; how to arrange courses so as to come out level with the top of the face tier.*

137

Guidance

Another essential of a successful training program is vocational guidance, with which placement and follow-up after release should go hand in hand. We cannot hope for satisfactory results if vocational education is given on the mass treatment basis. There is an abundance of printed material on the subject of guidance.* The vocational guidance expert must be familiar with the standard technique of determining individual needs and capabilities and must have intuitive shrewdness in assessing motives. He must be thoroughly familiar with general employment opportunities and requirements and the training necessary to meet them, with current employment conditions and significant trends, and with new developments. He must be especially familiar with the different attitudes displayed toward ex-prisoners by various employing and labor groups. Finally, he must work in close touch with the parole authorities.

Many occupations require a minimum of instruction and can be learned very quickly on the job. For the prisoners who are to enter these occupations the institution can well concentrate on vocational guidance and vocational adjustment. If one helps them to select the semiskilled or unskilled occupations for which they are best fitted and in which they will be best satisfied, and helps them by proper placement to adjust themselves more successfully to the working world, he will have done about all he can.

Aptitude Tests

The person who is inexperienced in vocational guidance is inclined to place too great reliance on mechanical aptitude tests. Many tests of this type have been developed, but it cannot be claimed for them that they have established their validity in indicating what occupation or even what type of occupation the subject tested can best enter. They may safely be used if they are considered as devices for throwing a little additional light on the problem rather than as supplying a definite answer to the questions arising in vocational guidance. It is probable that there are few specific aptitudes that can be determined by formal tests with sufficient certainty to justify basing guidance into specific occupations on tests alone.

Intelligence Tests

General intelligence tests also have limited value in vocational guidance. The results of these tests should be taken into account in all guidance, for some occupations cannot be successfully entered by persons who fall below a certain intelligence level. There is, however, a great variety of occupations which can

---

* See Federal Board for Vocational Education Bulletin No. 66, Bibliography on Vocational Guidance.

be followed by persons on any given intelligence level and a wide range of intelligence levels can be found in any given occupation. Intelligence tests present negative evidence in that they may indicate what vocation the person tested cannot successfully enter, but do not indicate what specific vocation he can successfully enter.

Time Required for Vocational Training

The time required to master any given vocation is dependent on so many factors in a penal institution that ordinarily accepted standards, based on the usual time required in a school or class in a free community, cannot be applied. One reformatory for men gives as its justification for not establishing a program of vocational education the statement that "the period of apprenticeship to all crafts and trades is four years while the average term of our inmates is approximately only eleven months." This is an unwarranted application of standard apprenticeship requirements to the penal institution, which can hope in only a few cases to take a green man and give him a complete apprentice and journeyman training in a skilled trade.

Number of Weeks

Instruction in a skilled trade is only a part of the vocational education program of a penal institution and even in these trades effective training, if it is intensive, can be given in much less than the usual apprenticeship period. Dr. Snedden states that "first class full-time vocational training for probably half the industrial and commercial vocations now followed in America need not take more than eight to twelve weeks of forty-four hours each; twelve to eighteen weeks of full-time training will adequately equip most young women of eighteen to twenty-five years of age for the vocations of home-making; and thirty-six weeks of intensive full-time first class training prepares for agricultural vocations." The war-time education of 1917-18 proved that full-time training of from six to twenty-four weeks, if taken by sufficiently mature persons, will suffice for many of the difficult trades. After one's general education is completed satisfactory results can be obtained by intensive full-time training (with sufficient participation in productive work) for periods of "eight weeks for a juvenile vocation, sixteen to twenty-four weeks for an operative journeyman's vocation, and thirty-six to ninety weeks for a mastership trade." Moreover, as Dr. Snedden points out, by those of not less than median intelligence (100 I.Q.) optimum proficiency may be reached in certain trades—automobile repairing, house carpentry, job printing and others—by thirty to one hundred and twenty weeks of assiduous practice. It is generally recognized that most workers need short-unit intensive courses fitting them quickly for employment rather than longer and more extensive courses. The adult prisoner does better work and maintains his interest more steadily when he comes to a definite point of achievement frequently, even though related short-unit courses may in reality form one consecutive long course.

Number of Hours per Day

During how many hours of the day and week should training be given? This must obviously vary with the course and the student. The Federal program sets up certain standards for trade and industrial education which can be used as a basis, although the requirements are probably too severe to be practicable in most institutions. These standards have already been cited. They are, briefly, (1) that part-time schools or classes must be in session at least one hundred and forty-four hours a year (computed on a basis of four hours a week for thirty-six weeks, the usual school year); and (2) that instruction in the unit trade school or class must extend over not less than nine months (thirty-six weeks) per year, and not less than thirty class hours per week, and that not less than half of the time shall be given to practical work on a productive or useful basis. This means about three hours a day on practical work. The time arrangement of part-time intensive courses on a seasonal basis in the Federal-state program varies from three weeks of six days per week and eight hours per day to two or three months of six to eight hours per day. Other part-time intensive courses on a trade preparatory basis give instruction from two to five months for six to eight hours per day.

Vacations

Most penal institutions in their general education program have a summer vacation of two or more months. This is not sound practice for either general or vocational education. Vacations for the educational staff should be distributed throughout the year in the same way that they are for other members' of the institutional staff. Vocational training should be a continuous process with only such breaks as are desirable at the end of unit courses. This is especially true where the training is coordinated with an industry or maintenance detail whose work is necessarily continuous. "Experience has amply demonstrated that the 50-50 type of cooperative schools can be best operated when the program is continuing to the same degree that the operation of the cooperative plant is continuous. This calls for the operation of the program at least fifty weeks per year. Vacations for students and instructors are arranged in a manner similar to that which prevails in industrial organizations, where everybody can get a vacation without making it necessary to shut down the plant." *

Division of Time

How should time be divided between general and vocational education? The most desirable situation exists when the prisoner has completed his general education before he undertakes vocational education. Because of the shortness of the average sentence and the loss of interest which is likely to result from such an arrangement, it is impossible to insist that the first months or years of

---

* Federal Board for Vocational Education Bulletin No. 17.

a prisoner's sentence be devoted to completing his general education and that he shall not be allowed to proceed with vocational training until his general education is completed. With prisoners the two types of education must proceed together and an effective correlation must be worked out. The prospect of acquiring competence in an occupation is the star to which the prisoner may hitch his wagon of dull, monotonous work in reading, writing and arithmetic. Pursuing the two types of education together does not mean dividing the prisoner's day into two equal parts, as many reformatories do, and requiring him to attend the "school of letters" during half the day and the trade school during the other half. The division of time between the two types should not be arbitrary; it may be on a 50-50 basis or in as lopsided a proportion as 90 to 10. It should be based on individual needs. In actual practice, much of the program of general education is so closely interwoven with vocational training that they are practically one.

In some outside trade schools the day is divided so that half, approximately three and one-half hours, is spent in the shop and the other half is again divided. One quarter is devoted to related trade subjects and to the underlying mathematics and science of the trade. The remaining quarter is devoted to academic instruction of the classroom type, and to such extracurricular activities as athletics, moving pictures, dramatics, club meetings, and publications. In these schools the time that elapses before a student enters on definite training for the trade which he wishes to study depends on what group he falls into. There are those who know what they want and who show aptitude for it, those who have a general idea what they wish (for example, to study one of the building trades), and those who have no notion what they wish to do. Those who are ready for instruction are sent immediately to the appropriate shops. Those who are not sure are placed under a special supervisor and are given tryout courses in single shops or in a general shop where five or more trades are represented. Those who have no notion what they want to do are also sent to the general shop or are shifted around among the other shops for observation and tryout. They are sometimes kept as long as a year under tryout training.

Education for Agricultural Pursuits

One type of vocational education, education for agricultural and allied pursuits, can be carried on successfully by practically every penal institution in the country without a large outlay of money and with a fair likelihood of the educational project proving financially profitable. All but a few institutions have farms, dairy herds, poultry plants, and piggeries. Farm programs in penal institutions are receiving increasing emphasis as institutions grow larger and the difficulty of keeping the prisoners employed increases. The opposition which has tended to retard the development of productive industries has fortunately not extended to farm work, and institutions are often able to obtain appropriations for the expansion of agricultural activities when they cannot secure funds for the establishment of industries.

Its Practicability in Penal Institutions

Education for agricultural work is particularly well suited to the penal institution. There are probably 8,000,000 adult men on the farms of the country today and 200,000 men are annually recruited to agricultural vocations. Large numbers of prisoners come from rural communities and go back to them when released. Some of them are employed on large farms, some operate small farms of their own, and others operate a garden, keep a cow or two, and have a small flock of poultry. For this group agricultural education is a direct avenue to greater earning capacity or more economical living. It has direct practical significance; its method, subject matter and end-results appeal to prisoners in a way that the more theoretical, abstract and formal types of education do not. It is possible on the institution farm to apply the sound principle of vocational education that one learns best on the job. Expert guidance and help are available from a large number of sources; one can draw on experts representing agencies, both state and national, whose function is to disseminate knowledge for the improvement of agricultural methods and to supply advice and instruction wherever it is needed. Simple textual material, practical in nature and designed for the use of persons of limited education, is available from a variety of sources at little or no expense. Finally, the farm is well adapted to educational work in that the prisoners detailed there have greater freedom than those employed inside the institution and suffer less from the handicaps of routine restrictions.

There is almost no limit to the variety of subjects which can be taught. Instruction involving a proper correlation of practice and theory can be given in general farming, market gardening, truck gardening, general animal husbandry, swine husbandry, dairy operations, poultry raising, fruit growing, berry raising, canning and preserving, and greenhouse operation. All of these activities are now being carried on by penal institutions in various parts of the country. Closely related to the agricultural field are such other outdoor occupations as the building and repair of bridges and roads, and forestry. Specialized courses can be given in building repair and other types of carpentry useful on the farm, concrete construction, simple bricklaying, the repair of mechanical equipment customarily found on a farm, and other work which any man operating his own farm or employed on a farm may be called on to perform.

The Necessity of Selective Assignment

A new basis of selecting men for detail to the farm must be established before this branch of vocational education can be developed to its full effectiveness. Prisoners are now customarily selected for the institution farm on these bases: that they know something about farm work, that they are able-bodied, and that they can be trusted to work without guards. Important as the last consideration is from the standpoint of discipline and character training, it would be better to abandon the idea that the farm should be almost exclusively operated by trusties in order that we may detail more men who are capable of profiting by agricultural training and who need it more than they need any other type of education. If the institution authorities do not find it possible or desirable to detail more guards to the farm, it is probable that a more liberal policy of selecting trusties can safely be adopted. There is something about the wholesomeness of outdoor work that seems to give steadiness and reliability to men who at first glance do not appear to be of the trusty type. Education for agricultural vocations suffers from the same handicap that limits education within the prison: overemphasis on the necessity of safeguarding prisoners and lack of emphasis on the necessity of giving opportunities for training which may in the long run prove an effective safeguard against crime.

In selecting men for farm details, attention should first be paid to those who have been engaged in agricultural pursuits or are planning to enter this type of work after release. Of this group, preference should again be given to those who are capable of profiting by instruction and who really wish to learn. Candidates for the farm detail will include those who need general training and those who need to specialize in some one branch: for example, poultry raising or one phase of dairy operation. Some men on release will seek employment on large farms where they may do one special type of work; others will go to small farms where they will be required to do anything and everything. After the original assignment has been made, prisoners under instruction should be moved about freely in order that they may gain general experience and may finally fit into the special niche which they can fill most successfully.

Combining Production and Training

The practical question asked by any institution official operating a farm is "How can I get the necessary work of the farm done and still have time to give more than incidental instruction?" This can be done by adding extra men to every detail. As a matter of fact, institution farm details are usually over-manned. Enough men should be added so that each detail consists of a number of men who have passed through the preliminary period of instruction and are largely engaged in routine work and a number of others who are beginners. The latter will succeed to the top positions as their predecessors finish their terms and leave the institution. As beginners they will devote a great deal of their time to organized instruction, participating in the routine work as a part of their practical training. The men who have passed through the beginner stage will receive decreasing amounts of instruction but will nevertheless be in training until they leave the institution. The "apprentice farmers" will work with the "journeymen farmers" and under their direction. For example, to every poultry house which would normally be cared for by two men a third man, an apprentice, will be added. The apprentice will spend a certain number of hours each day in actual work, but will report to the instructors during the remainder of the day for class and individual instruction.

Organization of Training

Several standard types of organization are practicable. The full-time training plan (routine work being a part of the training) is feasible whenever

143

the prisoner can be assigned to that type of farm work in which he is to receive instruction. When there are not enough of the more desirable assignments to absorb all the student-farmers, even with extra men added to each detail, it is necessary to give training on a part-time basis. For example, assume that the poultry plant has its full complement of beginners and advanced workers, and that a number of men detailed to the farm as general hands, employed in cultivating or haying or fencing, want to learn how to operate an incubator or a complete small poultry plant. A part-time class must then be organized for this group, perhaps in the evening. Agricultural evening schools, as usually organized in free communities, devote their time largely to technical subjects. A full discussion of these schools will be found in Federal Board for Vocational Education Bulletin No. 89, *Agricultural Evening Schools*. Short-unit full-time intensive courses are preferable to part-time classes in most agricultural processes, for they need to be carried on continuously throughout the day as a practical working operation. The short intensive course on a seasonal basis offers an opportunity for instruction of this type. The part-time cooperative plan, with two shifts alternating between work and school, appears less practicable in agricultural education than in trade and industrial education.

Direct training of individuals or classes by competent instructors will prove the most effective method of teaching. Much of the teaching needs to be by demonstration and practice and must be a part of the practical work. The study of texts or of correspondence courses can never be substituted effectively for direct teaching, although they can sometimes be used safely by the man who has an opportunity to apply what he studies, especially if he is also receiving some assistance and guidance directly from a teacher. Good correspondence courses in agricultural subjects can usually be secured from the State Agricultural College, although many of these courses presuppose too much education and scientific knowledge. Those sold by correspondence schools operated on a commercial basis are often too general and discursive. Any agricultural correspondence course, whether obtained from state or private sources, should be examined carefully by an expert before it is purchased.

The Necessity of Specific Training

In all teaching of vocational agriculture to prisoners we should avoid highly technical general courses and concentrate on simple and specific courses. The average prisoner will enroll in a course in animal husbandry, but what he really needs to know is how to take full charge of a small herd and to meet the specific problems that come up in the course of a year. This can best be learned on the farm under instruction which includes relatively little pure theory. Instead of trying to give instruction in soil analysis we may better give each student the address of the state agency to which he should send soils for free analysis. Our aim, in brief, is to promote specific practical knowledge and skill which is directly applicable under working conditions.

The Project Method

Certain special devices and methods will be found particularly useful in this field. The project method has been found one of the most useful in the teaching of farmers. An individual student or a small group of students is given a definite project to carry on under instruction and supervision: the care of a certain number of cows or hens, or taking full charge of the planting, cultivation and harvesting of a crop on a fixed area of ground. Other individuals or groups may have similar projects and the element of competition is introduced. In the usual project students do not carry on narrowly specialized work but carry a complete process through from beginning to end. On the other hand, a student may be given such a highly specialized project as the analysis of the soils on the various sections of a large farm area. The project method is particularly well adapted to the instruction of those who are to be employed on small farms or who are to operate their own farms.

Exhibits and Demonstrations

Special exhibits and demonstrations, which can be arranged with the help of state agricultural authorities, will stimulate interest and will serve to clarify theoretical instruction. Exhibits of different grades of seed, small models of scientifically planned barns, piggeries and poultry plants, and soil maps of different parts of the state can be set up on either a temporary or a permanent basis. Demonstrations must be used constantly as a part of the teaching method. Special demonstrations, given by experts from outside the farm teaching staff, should be arranged from time to time. A few penal institutions already have regular stock-judging contests in which the prisoners participate with eagerness and which are attended by farmers from the whole countryside. A number of other contests, such as cotton grading and grading seed corn, vegetables or fruit, can be used as a means of stimulating interest and as a test of the students.

State Experimental Farms

Every effort should be made to get the state agricultural authorities to establish experimental farms at the penal institutions. This would save money for the state, for prisoners could perform the large amount of manual labor which would be necessary. It would be beneficial to the institution in that instruction under proper conditions and under expert direction would be made possible. If the state cannot establish a complete farm at the penal institution, a model dairy herd, poultry plant, orchard, or other project can be initiated under the auspices of the State Department of Agriculture.

A Jack-of-all-Trades Course

In every institution there should be a brief practical course for men who are going back to small farms where they will have to play the part of the jack-of-all-trades. This course should teach them how to operate and repair agricultural machinery, build small buildings and make repairs on larger ones, and to perform to a limited extent the functions of the automobile mechanic, general mechanic, electrician, plumber, carpenter, plasterer, and all the other skilled tradesmen whom the small farmer cannot afford to call in every time something has to be done about the farm. The student should be taught how to make, install and repair the usual equipment of the small farm. The aim is not to train professional handy men but to give practical farmers in a simple and condensed course the mechanical skill that they need in the daily routine of any small farm.

Teaching and Advisory Staffs

The penal institution can turn to many agencies for help in organizing and directing a program of training for agricultural pursuits, but competent resident instructors are needed. It is less difficult to find satisfactory teachers in this field than in almost any other vocational training activity, but it is seldom true that the institutional farmer has had experience in teaching. The "practical" farmer may know a great deal about his trade but very little about how to teach it to others. Agricultural colleges are turning out every year large numbers of men who have had considerable experience as practical farmers and who know the scientific theory of their profession and how to teach it. This is the type of teacher needed by the penal institution.

The United States Department of Agriculture and the State Departments of Agriculture have thousands of experts who are trained teachers and who are available for advisory work. Scattered throughout the country are county extension agents whose duty it is to assist farmers and farm organizations. A complete directory of these agents can be secured from the United States Department of Agriculture (address Extension Division) or the address of the nearest county agent can be secured by writing the Department. His headquarters are usually at the county seat, where his office is customarily in the Federal Building. These agents and the state agricultural authorities should be called on by the institution for help in planning the training program and for advice and assistance from time to time after it is initiated. Federal authorities can be called on for general advice, guidance in the meeting of special problems, and the excellent informative and instructional material which they continually publish. Practically all of the services of both state and Federal authorities can be obtained without cost.

Commercial Education

Limitations

Programs of commercial education in penal institutions will always be handicapped by the lack of varied opportunities for practical training. In the offices of the institution, where a number of prisoners are customarily employed, facilities for instruction are limited: only a few of the many mechanical office appliances whose operation is now a specialized occupation are available. It is unlikely that the purchase of appliances for training purposes would be sanctioned. One can always teach the old standbys: stenography, typewriting and bookkeeping. To limit the program to these subjects, however, is to duplicate the weaknesses of commercial schools in the world outside and to neglect more than 95 per cent of all commercial occupations. There are today hundreds of specialized occupations in the commercial world into which men go. Stenography especially is becoming almost exclusively a woman's profession and fewer men are studying it every year.

In general, we may as well admit that the opportunities for commercial education in our prisons and reformatories are so limited that it must be a minor educational activity. It is some comfort to know that there is very little effective commercial education being given in the world outside, except in schools teaching a small number of the older occupations and in actual commercial establishments. Commercial work is largely learned by the pick-up method on the job itself. Furthermore, we must recognize the fact that ex-prisoners cannot enter some types of commercial service and that a man with a criminal record has great difficulty in securing a position of trust in an office or elsewhere. Whenever prisoners are not likely to meet insurmountable handicaps, however, they should be given as much training as possible in order that their superior knowledge and skill may compensate in some degree for their records when they apply for positions in competition with other men.

Office Work

In spite of the handicaps and the narrow range of training courses that appear feasible, commercial education of certain types can be given to a number of prisoners. The more important offices of the larger institutions, those of the Warden, Deputy Warden, Chief Clerk, Disbursing Clerk, Steward, Storekeeper, Parole Officer and Record Clerk, afford one opportunity. Men assigned to these offices can supplement theoretical training by a certain amount of practical application in stenography, typewriting, bookkeeping, accounting, filing, etc. They can be instructed in the use of the few mechanical appliances available. The more capable prisoners will usually be assigned to the offices relatively early in their sentences, for there is an immediate demand for the services of any prisoner capable of doing good office work. They can, as soon as assigned, be put on a full-time training basis, their daily work filling the requirement that part of any training course be devoted to practical work. Others, who aspire to positions in the offices, can be given preparatory courses in either a full-time or a part-time training class. If the training class is used as a feeder for the office details, even a green man can receive a training course and complete a substantial period of employment before leaving the institution. Civilian clerks and the more capable inmates will usually have to be utilized as instructors, but arrangements can sometimes be made to secure a number of part-time instructors from the nearest city.

Buying and Selling

Instruction in occupations concerned with buying and selling is possible for only a few men. A number of prisoners have had enough experience in these occupations so they can successfully study correspondence courses. The man who has had experience in advertising or in the retail selling field can derive some benefit from pure theory, but men without experience should be encouraged to take correspondence courses only in fields in which the institution affords opportunities to apply the course material. Selling cannot be learned from either textbooks or correspondence courses alone.

A Special Course

There is one type of position for which penal institutions might well prepare men very definitely. This is the position of clerk in a store in a small community. If an ex-prisoner applying for such a position can show that, in addition to acting as a clerk, he is capable of keeping the books and typing well enough to send out the monthly bills and to write business letters, he will have a much better chance of securing employment.

A Survey Course

Since specific training for only a few commercial occupations can be offered, a course should be organized to give a survey of the field, indicating what opportunities there are, what the basic requirements are for various types of positions, what the wage scale is, what the opportunities and requirements for promotion are, and how one may secure training after leaving the institution. This type of course can be coupled with a special attempt at vocational guidance for men who think that they wish to enter commercial pursuits. In brief, not being able to give complete training, we may at least give guidance and may help to make adjustments.

Conclusion

In conclusion, the following facts appear of primary importance in the establishment of a successful program of vocational education in a penal institution:

1. We should be content with a limited enrollment if those enrolled are being effectively taught. On the other hand, we should recognize the fact that something of value can be taught the worker in even the most simple and least skilled vocation.

2. Limiting instruction to relatively few trades and the teaching of obsolete or passing trades should be avoided.

3. Training should be planned in accordance with individual needs and capabilities, not on a mass-treatment basis.

4. Vocational guidance should be correlated with careful placement and follow-up after release.

5. The subject matter and method of instruction should be based on actual current occupational standards.

6. The instructor must be thoroughly trained in the vocation he teaches; he should have had training in the technique of teaching it; he should be capable of making scientific job analyses.

7. Ample opportunity for participation in practical work on a productive and useful basis is essential; effective training can best be given on a real job; routine training exercises are not a satisfactory substitute.

8. Practically all the standard types of organization found in the vocational training field outside the penal institution are adaptable for use in institutions; the chief needs are for adequate funds and skilled supervision.

Biographical Sketch

Austin MacCormick was an especially important contributor to correctional education throughout the 1915-1979 period. His book *The Education of Adult Prisoners* appeared in 1931; he went on to serve as the first Assistant Director of the Federal Bureau of Prisons (in charge of education and libraries), and then as New York City's Commissioner of Correction; MacCormick also served as warden at a Federal prison in Ohio; he established what has become the Correctional Education Association, and served as the first editor of what is now the *Journal of Correctional Education*. The next chapter offers a summary of his work and an interpretation of how that work can be applied in the 21st century.

CHAPTER XI

PERSONAL REFLECTIONS ON AUSTIN MACCORMICK'S 1931 CORRECTIONAL EDUCATION BOOK:
THE INTEGRATION OF VOCATIONAL, ACADEMIC, AND SOCIAL EDUCATION

by Robert Mattucci

Abstract

The purpose of this chapter is to connect theories Austin MacCormick discussed in his 1931 book *The Education of Adult Prisoners* with examples from modern correctional education practice. The author began teaching an institutional plumbing class in 2000, equipped with an undergraduate degree in elementary education and a master's degree in vocational/adult education, and 22 years of experience as a plumber. I have never had any formal education in correctional education. MacCormick's book was my first exposure to that field; his genius inspired me to write this chapter.

I implemented some of his ideas in actual, working programs for men and women at county jails in New York State and at a Rescue Mission drug rehabilitation program in Syracuse. The results have included high graduation rates and assignment of former students in entry level plumbing jobs. Collected and treated research data on the program began with its inception.

It is my charge as a correctional vocational education teacher to connect Austin MacCormick's theories with the programs I manage. My hope is that through this chapter some interested correctional educators will benefit from a consideration of MacCormick's ideas and an explanation of how they were applied in these 21st century programs. In other words, the chapter contributes to the process of generally updating his theories to modern conditions. I extend special thanks to Elizabeth Curley for clerical support, Cindi Malone Jones for logistical help, Anne Jakowenko for all the useful advice, Thom Gehring for the editorial assistance, and Isabel Hunsinger for the 1997 article she contributed to *The Journal of Correctional Education* to begin the important process of scrutinizing and updating MacCormick's definitive ideas on our field.

Introduction

In writing this chapter, I feel it is important for educators to understand who I am and my perspective concerning correctional education. Essentially, I am familiar with the practice of vocational education, and I seek to learn appropriate theory to inform my daily practice. As MacCormick wrote:

> In all fields of education, theory is in advance of practice (1976/1931, p.xii).

I am a plumber who developed a program to encourage adult men and women to enter the plumbing profession. The program began in a correctional setting by "accident" after it was rejected a number of times by public and vocational schools. I started teaching in a county jail to fulfill my research requirement for my master's degree in vocational/adult education. The first program graduated only 50% of the class of four youths; one adult dropped out after the first session.

Gradually I recognized that most workers need short unit intensive courses fitting them quickly for employment rather than longer more extensive courses. This insight was later confirmed by MacCormick's useful book:

> The adult prisoner does better work and maintains his interest more steadily when he comes to a definite point of achievement (MacCormick, 1976/1931, p. 134).

In her 1997 article on the continuing relevance of MacCormick's book to the daily work of correctional education, Hunsinger wrote:

> The program must be based on honest, realistic standards, and teachers and administrators must be content with small gains that may be made. Selection criteria must be broad enough to accept and teach those who want to learn, and participation ideally is voluntary with compulsory attendance used only in the rarest and most extreme situations. (pp. 160¬-161).

Again, these concepts corresponded with the attributes of the program I developed.

At the encouragement of the adult education director at the jail a second program was established and implemented. This was really the beginning of my education in the field of correctional education. I had never heard of Austin MacCormick, and I had no idea of what correctional education was about. I used the "inside out approach," rather than read about correctional education theory or how it was supposed to work. I just taught each class the content that I knew they needed to get a job as a plumber on the "outside" after release.

However, I noticed the important effect the correctional officers had on each program. After teaching at four separate and very different county jails, I learned how critical it is to program success to work at a pro-education facility where the correctional officers want to foster rehabilitation—where they do not want the inmates to come back to jail. Unfortunately, proactive correctional officers cannot be found at all facilities. They are usually at facilities that have a warden and/or sheriff who emphasize rehabilitation and have programs geared to help adult men and women through positive reinforcement, a positive attitude toward social re-entry, and a general orientation toward helping inmates become useful, productive citizens. Although all this might seem simple, locating the program at the right facility can be a difficult and time consuming task.

Who was Austin MacCormick?

CEA historian Thom Gehring summarized some of the contributions made by Austin MacCormick.

> Austin MacCormick's efforts in the 1930s capstoned all the former efforts in prison education. His work was also the foundation of everything that followed. MacCormick's 1931 book was rooted in the 19th century ideas of New York's Elmira Reformatory Superintendent Zebulon Brockway, and he trained under Sing Sing Prison's reform warden, Thomas Mott Osborne. MacCormick, who lived from 1893 to 1979, was Osborne's logical successor as leader of the prison reform movement. He
>
> 1. Conducted the first national survey of prison education in the U.S. (during 1927-28 he visited 110 of the 114 institutions that existed at that time),
>
> 2. Founded the Correctional Education Association (CEA) which began in 1930 as the American Prison Association's Standing Committee on Education),
>
> 3. Wrote the definitive book on the subject (*The Education of Adult Prisoners*, first published in 1931),
>
> 4. Served in various important assignments: as the first Assistant Director of the Federal Bureau of Prisons (beginning in 1930, in charge of education programs), New York City's Commissioner of Correction (beginning in 1934 under Mayor Fiorella LaGuardia), Warden of Chillicothe Prison (in Ohio—it was a Federal facility then); he was President Roosevelt's prison expert for Asia during World War II, and Chair of the committee that investigated the Attica riot in the early 1970s; MacCormick also
>
> 5. Established *The Journal of Correctional Education* and served as its first editor (starting in 1937).
>
> Throughout his life MacCormick was active teaching, planning, consulting, and writing. His products are so many and of such profound quality that they cannot be discussed adequately here. The first draft of *The Education of Adult Prisoners* appeared in 1929, and the field of correctional education has never been the same since. (Gehring & Rennie, 2008, pp. 112-113).

Of course, when I started teaching in the institutions I did not even know Austin MacCormick's name. Most readers will be familiar with the problem that correctional educators have accessing the literature on correctional education. The first time I read MacCormick's book I felt my work inside was infused with new meaning, new understandings. Especially relevant to my job of teaching plumbing to confined men and women were MacCormick's chapters on "Vocational Education," "Fundamental Academic Education," "Social Education," and "The Education of Women" in prison. The rest of this chapter is intended to introduce readers to aspects of his book, comments that have been made about it in the literature, and to precisely how all those ideas were actually implemented in my program.

Some Selections from MacCormick's Book, with Observations Regarding Current Applications

> It is generally recognized that most workers need short unit intensive courses fitting them quickly for employment rather than longer more extensive courses (MacCormick, 1976/1931, p. 134).

Short programs have great value when students are learning concepts and skills that are new to them. In the past, many education programs were stuck in long curricula that integrated into common core concepts. In these courses, slow students get lost. As a result they become disruptive. The value of short programs is that, if students fall behind, their needs can be identified and they can be helped through tutoring, mentoring, or a different approach to the subject. This procedure can help build a person's self-esteem rather than diminish it, by showing positive growth through short, bite-size chunks. Slow learners will be able to grow in this environment without being stung by failure and disappointment.

The original concept of my plumbing course required 120 instructional hours. In response to MacCormick's advice and my own experience, it was reduced to 16 hours. An evaluation by a correctional educator with 26 years of service also helped to bring about this change. He said, "your program is too long for most inmates in county jails on short sentences." I reformatted the whole program to be more intense, combining theory and hands-on instruction for a more meaningful program.

By that time I had accumulated 25 years as a plumber, of which 15 were in maintenance plumbing as a specialized profession, so I knew what skills maintenance contractors would need from productive workers. Three recurring curricular themes were toilets, kitchen sinks, and plugged drains. The reformatted, shorter course focused on these three themes.

Common sense in plumbing regulated lesson plan content. I had learned that most inmates lacked even the most rudimentary plumbing experience. Though plumbing went back to the time of the Roman Empire, it was not rocket

153

science. When I started teaching in 2000, in a county jail in Central New York, there were 12 inmates in the class, which met from 6:00 to 8:30 P.M. Teaching the course at night was not really suited to the institutional routine, in part because all the students had been awake since 6:30 A.M. This program had two hours of teaching and learning a night, twice a week, for four weeks. In order for it to succeed, I needed the students' undivided attention but, because of the new intensive course format, there were no breaks during class. MacCormick's book offered cues about how to structure the learning environment, regardless of constraints.

> The ideal cooperative plan demands that the employed hours supply practical application of what is learned during the training hours (MacCormick, 1976/1931, p. 116).

Relevance to the subject matter should be central to all education, despite the drastic changes that have been implemented in most programs during the past five years. Furthermore, the subject matter should be directly related to available employment upon release. Inmates wanted to know how the program would help them in the future, when they re-entered the world.

I had to sell these ideas about the program to inmates in order to keep their attention engaged. In part, this was accomplished by teaching for a portion of the time, and having hands-on activities for another part.

The class was conducted in a 20 x 40 foot regular academic classroom with desks, not in a vocational laboratory or shop. Plumbing tools were mandatory to support the hands-on techniques, but the correctional officers (COs) were skeptical. To them, giving inmates hacksaws or screwdrivers did not seem to be a good idea. Further, I taught alone, without CO supervision. In short, I had to trust the inmates. All this was overcome by a vigilant tool security system with inventories before and after each class. Every tool, nut, bolt, and washer had to be accounted for. Shadow boxes helped the inventories go quickly. I limited the program to the most basic tools used for hands-on demonstrations, without any extras. (Throughout 40 programs since that time, not one tool ever came up missing.)

The program was successful, with accountability built into its very fabric. Inmate students knew that their participation was a privilege, not a right. The graduation rate for the night programs was 60%, usually with the other 40% dropping out during the first two nights. There was a pre-test and post-test and a tool identification test. Positive learning gains were documented; "homework" was mandatory. At some facilities the administration would buy the book for students; at others photostatic copies were used to cut cost.

> Complete correlation of theoretical instruction and practical application with readjustment of the institution program [should be implemented] to permit a proper division of time between

instruction and participation in productive or useful work for training (MacCormick, 1976/1931, p. 105).

This quote reflects the approach that was applied at the next two county jails where I taught the plumbing program. One facility was in Long Island and the other in western New York State. Both facilities were administered by pro-education superintendents, but neither had any programs in which inmates could learn trades. The plumbing course was the only such program at these sites.

Many positive changes occurred in the program during this round of implementation. Primary was time of day—during the mornings and afternoons—the times when everyone expected education to take place. Women were participating now at the original site and the two new locations. All these changes helped increase the average completion/graduation rate from 60% to nearly 100%. They proved to be motivational for the men and women in each class.

Working with incarcerated women was new for me. But MacCormick's book had a chapter on The Education of Women Prisoners, which I found helpful. Therein, MacCormick had written that:

Skill and intelligence do not always go exactly hand in hand (1976/1931, p. 299).

Yet this is only the tip of the iceberg about the differences between male and female inmate students. Over the past six years I taught nine women's programs, and every class was different. Group interaction worked well with women students. However, the groupings sometimes got cliquish until I applied a random selection procedure for group membership. With the men, it worked best when students could select their own group members. Gradually, with help from MacCormick's book, I learned more about the different dynamics of correctional education for men and women students.

It is unfortunately very difficult to give adequate training for the trades and industries in women's institutions (McCormick, 1976/1931, p. 297).

The administrators at the two new facilities where I contracted were aware of the needs of women inmates and were pro-active in helping to address them through this and other programs. Again, teaching confined women was vastly different for me. The women appeared more family oriented, and they nurtured each other more than the men. Group work was more effective, even in a short program, when the size of the groups was two or three, even when one student was more advanced. The more advanced person would take the lead and help the other two, slower students. Mentorship was a valued commodity in this environment. Three results were improved: leadership skills, positive attitudes, and growth in self-esteem/self-worth.

My first taste of real success came during one of the women's programs, when an inmate got into the plumbers local union as an apprentice. She was an excellent student, with good math skills and hand-eye coordination.

The women's programs became an integral part of my approach to plumbing program instruction. They have potential for many more real success stories—through the improved self-esteem that accrues from empowerment, and through actual placement in the work force after release. All this was predicted by MacCormick in 1931, though many of his explanations were deliberately general.

> One can but add his knowledge of prison and penal institutions
> to his knowledge of standard education theory in the hope that
> two and two will make four (MacCormick, 1976/1931, p. xii).

The foundation of the plumbing program is consistent with this observation by MacCormick. How do adult men and women learn in a correctional setting? Should it be by rote memorization, or through exchange of ideas? I learned that the latter was the best teaching method. Group interaction is a valuable tool whereby inmates make the program "student driven," and the teacher facilitates and offers help as needed.

Hunsinger commented on other elements of good programs that MacCormick discussed in his book:

> The range and diversity of the program are as great as that
> of the student body. The program is based on the diagnosis,
> prescription and treatment of each prisoner as an individual.
> There are many variables within the population: age, strengths,
> previous education, starting point, etc., and there may be as many
> grades as there are students within a class. The program must be
> flexible enough to allow each student to move forward as rapidly
> as possible. (1997, p. 161).

In this regard the principles of andragogy or adult education should be applied. Andragogy is a learning theory that uses students' past work experiences to open up new doors to knowledge, often in a group setting. Most adults come to jail with a wealth of experience. One of my jobs is to relate what they learned in the past to the new plumbing material they are learning in this course. How can adult men and women teach each other? Just give them a problem to solve.

Brainstorming is an andragogical tool seldom used because people underestimate the intelligence of incarcerated adults. I was always amazed during the hands-on final exams because adults tended to assume responsibility. Somehow teachers often expect adult students to behave as children do, with the entire responsibility for education resting with the instructor. By contrast, I found that adult inmate students were willing to assume part of the responsibility for their own education.

No one can predict in a group setting how general knowledge or specific task competencies will be gained. Handled appropriately, group interaction helps all the adults in a group to learn—establishing a framework in which people help other people. It really does work. The dynamic energy of every group is different but the positive experiences created through this process are motivational. It causes positive growth and feelings of self-worth in participating individuals, precisely fulfilling the true quest of the teacher. It is not that every person in the course will become a plumber, but that each is reborn through awareness of their true personal potential for positive change. In this sense, knowledge really is power. My charge as a plumbing instructor is to make all the students in my class aware of their internal potential for transformation. Gehring provided a context for this, consistent with the principles introduced by MacCormick: "Adults often bring valuable experiential knowledge and community-oriented aspirations to the classroom; they typically seek specific skills" (2000, p. 152).

Another core concept is that adults enjoy listening to other adults who have a skill or knowledge they want to learn, and will learn from them in a group setting. Of course, they all have different aspirations and learning styles. But the group approach, when used thoughtfully, can accommodate their different adult styles, without the external pressure, threat of failure, or ridicule that tended to characterize their experiences in grade school. One andragogical goal is to make learning fun, so students will pursue it energetically. They are sometimes able to learn without actually knowing how they are changing themselves, becoming better community members. Thus the general program goal of positive change is attained—intense growth within a short time period, to help students feel good about themselves.

In her review and update of MacCormick's approach, Hunsinger alluded to the function of teachers and other institutional staff, as role models.

> Involvement in the education program, by virtue of the contact with teachers, staff and other inmates, decreases isolation and increases socialization of the inmate. The institution operates as an inmate community, with the warden and staff taking the role of advisors to the community in handling its affairs. (1997, pp. 164-165).

As we progress further into the 21st century, it is likely that education will normally be configured to provide broad based, "reality-oriented" programming, not in the sense intended in reality TV, but through practical course content. Houses cannot be constructed without hammers, nails, and a ruler. The builder must understand the tools and how to use them.

Many company managers complain that children are not prepared for the world of work because they are insulated from the world. In order to fulfill their roles as community members, children and adults require exposure to various real world environments, so they can learn how they work. This makes learning easier and more relevant. Although this sometimes demands imagination on the part of the teacher, such connections with the real world help inmate-students learn more of the "nuts and bolts" of the subject. This is project-based student learning at its best. Teachers can learn along with the students.

Some students will enjoy this type of learning and some will not, but their exposure to many environments does promote success. Even if they only learn that they do not want to become plumbers, that may be a useful thing; nothing is worse than having a job that one hates. Realistic exposure to the central elements of the profession will hopefully foster knowledge of which jobs might be good for them, and which might be avoided. MacCormick alluded to this element of vocational education in his 1931 book:

> The opportunity to perform practical work is an absolute essential
> of any effective vocational training program (p. 112).

Hands-on teaching is the glue that ties this plumbing course together. The first three programs I taught in 2000 and 2001 did not include what I later learned was a very important component, the hands-on final exam. By the time of the fourth program I had developed a hands-on exam that encompassed all four major points of the class. It was administered in groups of two, three, or four students, depending on the size of the class, with group membership determined by a random drawing of lots. This single course component made the entire program more "real."

In the real world, union work is not always structured so you know with whom you will partner to accomplish a task. Similarly, the hands-on final exam procedure that I applied made all the class participants work together to solve a prescribed problem, regardless of race, ethnicity, age, or any other criteria. The central dynamics of the program were most evident during this final exam. All four course work stations were used at the same time, to mirror how work would proceed on a real construction project, with each group focusing on a particular task, required to complete it in a timely way, just like in the working world.

The course used teamwork, brainstorming, leadership skills, a focus on positive attitudes, and class dialogue—talking and listening. Everyone had to work together to complete the program. Group interaction and cooperation were essential for success. Each group had 20-30 minutes to complete relevant tasks, which I then checked while offering constructive feedback. If a group completed its task early, its members stayed at their station until they were told to move to the next station. Patience and respect for other class members was emphasized as an important part of the program.

Has the world changed much since 1931? Hard work, attention to detail, leadership skills, community-oriented attitudes, and work skills remain of central importance. They are all attributes of successful workers: bankers, plumbers, architects, carpenters, and rocket scientists. These same attributes and skills can be taught in a jail classroom as well as in a public school. In one way, it is all about success—in life, work, or according to some self-determined objective.

One difficult task for me was choosing a textbook. I used several quality textbooks, but did not achieve the results I wanted. I was seeking a book that each person could use comfortably, one that would be a reference for future work. In the end I wrote my own textbook to convey to students the material they would need for success in the outside, working world. It focused on employability skills, so each man or woman who completed the program would understand the whole course. The book was structured so individuals could use it to help guide their work on the outside after release; if they forgot a step in a plumbing process, they could consult the book. A spin-off benefit was that the information in the text helped students gain confidence in themselves, so they could attempt this work in their own house, or on a job, and do it properly.

Nevertheless, there are many skills that contribute to successful employment as a plumber, some of which relate more directly to the cognitive domain than to the psycho-motor. Primary among these was note-taking skills, which were nonexistent to poor in most classes. Memory skills were not much better. So I designed the textbook, in part, as a reference book of a hands-on nature that everyone would feel comfortable using—but with terms to memorize and the expectation that students would take notes in class. My goal was to simplify each part of the program and make the whole course accessible to each person. Many of the adult plumbing students had multiple learning disabilities. The textbook was intended to be "user friendly," and helped overcome these problems with simple language and multiple illustrations. The book applied 20 years of my plumbing experience and five years of education for my masters degree; it could be used by all students, men and women. It was written on a 5th grade level with pictures and a logical progression of steps to complete each defined task. The text included trouble shooting techniques used for each plumbing fixture I had taught them to install, and explained many "tricks of the trade" to help solve problems that are encountered frequently in the field.

Theory and the hands-on approach go together, as MacCormick proposed in the first quote from his book that appeared in this chapter. My purpose was not to overwhelm inmate-students with theory, but to incorporate it into the course—the theory should "drive" their hands-on activities. One real test of all this came in 2004 when I introduced the textbook. Happily, the students successfully used the text I developed to help them in the hands-on final exam. My purpose was thus achieved: they understood that the textbook was not just a dust collector, but a learning tool that could help them complete their project and the course.

MacCormick commented extensively about the scope of what should be learned, and the way vocational education content could be motivational for confined male and female learners.

> These prospective industrial workers should. . .be given instruction in safety and health, training in their proper relation to their fellow workers. . .(1976/1931, p. 299).

> On the assumption that women need or care very little of this type of education they are not given enough. The exact knowledge of reading, writing and arithmetic necessary as a supplement to specific vocational education skills is not carefully worked out and systematically given. . . (p. 302).

For MacCormick, and for most correctional educators, education connects a series of necessary parts. From a plumber's perspective some of these parts are math, safety, and understanding the duties and benefits associated with being a tradesperson. In doing a specific task, for example plumbing or computer repairs, a complex repertoire of interactive skills is required for the individual to be successful. Therefore all students should be exposed to the requirements for success in many different jobs.

Basic elements of successful job searches could probably be introduced as early as second grade. Why so young? Because people change, and the children's perspectives change quickly. Education is a growth process that takes a lifetime. Through exposure to different jobs, students have opportunities to experience required competencies. This can help them make informed decisions by matching their skills and interests with those needed for particular jobs. Students could also learn of the educational paths necessary to obtain certain types of employment. By the time they enter high school, students should already have thought seriously about many such issues.

These two insights by MacCormick, about the need for related theory and especially for appropriate vocational education for female inmates, were integrated into the new format for the plumbing program that I developed in 2003. The content now goes beyond plumbing maintenance. For example, I developed a construction math program, with pre- and post-tests, that includes reading a ruler and working with fractions. I also went back to school to become a safety instructor, certified to teach in line with the requirements of the Occupational Safety and Health Act (OSHA). These are mandated safety programs that serve as important tools for preservice and inservice employment purposes. As of January, 2006 all workers on state and Federally funded construction projects had to have a card that indicates completion of the OSHA program. Toward that end, I graduated 125 men and women from county jails with this card.

The new, comprehensive program is 36 hours long and encompasses math skills, an OSHA 10 hour construction component, and the revised 16 hour plumbing maintenance course. It is now an accredited college course, offered through a community college in west central New York State, where I am an adjunct professor. Students who complete the program earn 3.6 semester hours toward their vocational education degree. The new course took two years to assemble and the program graduation rate has been 90% or more, with normal class sizes of 12-15 adult inmates. As introduced earlier, homework is mandatory in all my courses, but secondary completion is not required for entry. Approximately 20% of each class is comprised of adults who have not completed high school or earned their GED. They all graduate, usually with good grades in all three of the subjects (math, OSHA, and plumbing maintenance).

Of course, the program is still developing. My dream is to complete the research on which I have been working since 2000 and publish the results on the overall success of the program. This was one of my objectives for 2006. I want all of the 400 plus graduates of the program to demonstrate their success in various ways, mostly by not coming back to the institution. Hunsinger's 1997 remarks helped me put many of the program attributes into perspective.

> MacCormick held no illusions that all the ills of crime and criminals would be eradicated in a single exposure to his program. He did however believe in human beings as worthy and capable of development and change. He was content with small gains and willing to admit that not all inmates could be reached. Through his writing, he has offered us the prescription for the education of the adult prisoner, which is still relevant [today]. . .in the hope we can be successful. (p. 165).

Summing Up through the Big Picture: Ideas from Austin MacCormick's Book Remain Relevant

In researching MacCormick's work and its relevance to the 21st century, I was drawn to two points of reference that show the benefit of a trades program in a county jail and its alignment to real employability potential after release:

First, in the U.S. during 1928, 1,600,000 men and 1,800,000 women were vocational education students (MacCormick, 1976/1931, p. 100), for a combined total of 3,400,000. They needed some 74,000 vocational education teachers. At the time most forecasters predicted that by 1936 fully 7,000,000 adults would be vocational education students (MacCormick, 1976/1931, pp. 99-100).

Second, recent figures can be obtained from MacGillis' 2001 article, which appeared in the *Baltimore Sun* newspaper. MacGillis got his data from the United Association (UA), the International Plumbers and Steamfitters Union.

> As of Sept 2001 the UA has 33,000 apprentices in its 5 year training program. That needs to increase to 50,000 apprentices so that the UA can graduate 10,000 apprentices a year. . . .This

union is not alone in its shortage of skilled labor—electrical, sheet metal workers and carpenters are facing the same shortage. . .The demand for plumbers and pipe fitters is growing. The US Bureau of Labor Statistics estimates there will be 76,000 unfilled openings for plumbers and steamfitters by 2008. . .'You used to have a lot of vocational training schools and schools would put a lot of money into training. Now it's "Johnny is bad so put him in shop class." [High school] counselors are pushing people at us who have no skills.' (MacGillis, p. 1A).

Yet despite all the demonstrated needs, vocational adult education in corrections is still an adventure because our field is still emerging, still awaiting the recognition it deserves.

Of some types of education work advocated in these pages it is impossible to say that experience shows they will succeed for they have not been tried in any penal institution (MacCormick, 1976/1931, p. xii).

Still, the descriptive and curriculum literature on these programs is growing in scope and quality. One relevant study accrued from the program described herein.

Study of Recidivism and Other Program Attributes, Conducted in a County Jail

I started collecting data from my first programs at a county jail in West Central New York State in 2003. The study included age, ethnic origin, sex, and program group. I used data analysis to correlate variables related to 114 adult program graduates. These were 93 men and 21 women who completed nine institutional programs that were implemented over two years. Human interaction is always difficult to measure, yet each program had the same basic parameters: pre- and post-tests, curriculum content, 16 hour length of class, and so forth. There were many dependant variables, and the independent variables were presented in association with each different class and the institutional requirements.

Facility staff ran the plumbing program students' identification numbers through their data base to check how many recidivated—how many came back to jail, for either the same offense, a different offense, or for violating probation. The length of time studied was six to 18 months after release. The results suggested that the skills and attitudes gained through the plumbing program were a great help to the ex-felons' effort to re-enter society after release. Recidivism was significantly reduced and employment opportunities were more readily accessible. A few graduates even joined the International Plumbers and Steamfitters Union. The purpose of this chapter was to focus on curricular components of a 21st century program and their relation to the program MacCormick advocated 75 years ago. Details of the recidivism study will be presented in a subsequent article.

Biographical Sketch

Bob Mattucci has been a correctional educator since July, 2000. He has taught at four county jails, a Rescue mission, and a youth program. Prior to his educational career he was a plumber for 22 years and a laborer for 13 years. Bob holds a B.S. in Elementary Education and a Masters degree in Vocational Education. His plumbing program began as a result of a curriculum development course he took and has evolved yearly to relate to the target population. He is working on a project with the Rochester Institute of Technology Criminal Justice Department with plumbing program graduates to validate the benefits of the program and follow up on graduates' success.

CHAPTER XII

PRISON X

by Mark Dearing

Abstract

The U.S. has approximately 5% of the world's population yet it now incarcerates 23.4% of the world's prisoners (Wikipedia, 2010, 28th paragraph). For every 100,000 Americans, 754 are locked up in correctional facilities across the U.S. (Wikipedia, 2010, 3rd paragraph). California leads the country with a record of 169,153 men and women incarcerated (CDCR, 2010, chart). It is estimated that 70% of all California inmates who leave prison (parole), will return (recidivate) within three years (Office of the Governor, 2010, fact sheet).

Statistics from The Bureau of Justice Statistics present a variation on this theme, with a ratio of 456 in every 100,000 throughout the nation as a whole (Petersilia, 2005, p. 6). Society has historically failed to prepare for those returning to our communities and our workforce. The overriding question most would ask is how and why are so many of our citizens ending up in prison? Reactive accusations do not lead to proactive solutions. What can correctional educators do about all this?

Introduction

To change the world one has to first be willing to change one's self. The willingness to challenge personal paradigms that conflict with your "highest good" principle is a necessary component to learning and growing in any environment. You have to find out who you are and what exactly you want to change. To accurately conceive the magnitude of this issue in a prison setting, multiply that concern times the number of individual prison yards and the personalities comprised within those yards, and then multiply that number times the number of prisons.

The men and women who voluntarily participated in the Orange County (California) Department of Education Offender Employability Continuum Program workshops witnessed firsthand the importance of summoning strength and humility to accept and apply lessons that the workshop or class facilitators presented. Seven dynamic correctional educators facilitated character based literacy and employability objectives in prisons. The six hour day class left many students feeling as if they had been awarded a secret and very rare learning experience, a spiritual and physical escape.

"Sucker free Mr. D, sucker free." I looked hard into Crash's eyes and saw the serious edge had been replaced with a fiery resolve that contradicted his normal, jovial, and self-deprecating manner. A heartfelt smile spread across my face as I considered the forty-year-old, reformed White-supremacy advocate who in his earlier years earned his colors and his moniker putting in time. Now, as I listened to his quiet affirmation about how to remove negative influences, I felt a connection with a man who was looking forward to reuniting with his fifteen-year-old daughter. This same man the day of the graduation, in front of his peers, hugged me without fear of reprisal or shame!

"I've gotten rid of my girlfriend. She just brings me down and is only interested in herself. I'm going to go into business with my brother when he gets off the Four Yard."

Crash was a custom auto detailer. He painted cars that were featured in Hot Rod Magazine, and from what I had heard on the yard he had unbelievable talent.

"Are we talking better than Boyd?" He smiled as he replied, "Better than Boyd by Burnett and James, too." A sudden thunderous yell of "Come on Country," signaled the arrival of Thor, my class leader and leader of the Lakeside Gangsters.

"Sorry Mr. D, I told Country to get the fuck off the handball court. But he wouldn't listen."

Country walked in behind Thor appearing to be visibly upset. "Fuck you, Thor. You said you wanted some coffee so I went back to get you some. . ."

"It's all about personal accountability, Country. Isn't that right, Mr. D?" I smiled at the role playing between the two of them. Thor and Country had known each other for nearly twenty years and had "done time" together for nearly half of those years.

"That's all right, Country. Don't let him grind you. Just cut off his next package," I said.

The two faced off mere inches from each other. Thor reached over and roughly patted Country on the back.

Country replied, "Ya fucker. Remember what I told you earlier?"

Thor knew the answer answered for him. "Deal off huh, Country."

Country answered, "Ya deal is gone!"

Both Thor and I laughed as we watched Country take a big gulp of the prison-made coffee. The remaining members of Class Nine arrived in good order, casually talking about a horseshoe game planned for later that afternoon.

"All right gentlemen, and I use that term very loosely. It's time to get started."

The personal conversations stopped now as I had the collective attention of ten men, all older than me. I looked at them and said nothing as my mind faded back to the first day, to our first meeting, when I stood in the same spot and introduced myself. A burst of laughter brought me back as The Professor and Tin Can were at it again. The two men were constantly at odds, generally about religion, history, science—you name it. Now the two were in one of their normal disagreements when their peers decided to egg them on. With two days left until graduation I knew I was going to miss this Class more than a little.

The idea of a prisoner reentry program is not new to California or the country at large. Thirty-three prisons in the Golden State alone struggle to contain an ever-expanding population that is presently 150% of capacity. Twenty one percent of California inmates successfully complete parole; of those two out of three return for parole violations. This suggests that the concept of "rehabilitation" is not working (Petersilia, 2005, p. 2).

My road to prison started after spending fifteen years working with at-risk youths as both a special education intern and regular education teacher in English, Science and History. Additionally, I coached wrestling, self-defense, and flag football. Two years as an in-school counselor provided a modest backdrop for my pending prison term. Five of those years were well earned at a comprehensive special education site; learning from the ground up—among other things—curriculum design/implementation, behavior modification, and classroom management, as an Instructional Behavior Technician. I brought these skills to prison along with a passion for students and a sincere belief in second chances. The learning curve was steep as I became aware of prison politics in California correctional facilities.

My impressions thus far are that there is tremendous potential behind the walls of prisons waiting to be heard, recognized, and inspired. Therefore, the value of this pre-release program is obvious. I have been reminded daily that the issue of the color line of which W.E.B. Dubois wrote in *The Souls of Black Folks* takes on an entirely different meaning in a prison environment.

The seven correctional educators in the Offender Employability Continuum, sponsored by the Orange County Department of Education, routinely individualized an established character-based curriculum that can be utilized by a wide range of academic backgrounds. We created for each student an opportunity at self-discovery, thus maximizing that person's opportunities for gainful employment. The curriculum design provided a foundation from

166

which we applied strategies for introspective examination and inter-personal dialogues. Ideally, this promoted positive, comprehensive change. To merely provide information, resources, or guest speakers would do very little to motivate adult men and women to reform.

Change

I stood quietly at the front door of my classroom as I watched a few students walk in. They looked as though they had just been put on death row. A few others walked in with purpose and resolve, determined to get their sentences commuted. After I assured those students that the "govenator" would not be making any last minute phone calls, I encouraged them to hear me out. My eyes locked on to a few who appeared to have accepted their three week fate in my class, and were open to positive change. I walked up to a man I will identify as Ozzie. He had played baseball (short stop) in high school. Ozzie told me that he was looking forward to what the class had to offer. I took his humble affirmation and sent it 410 feet over the center field wall as motivation to find and "create" more Ozzies. Then several inmates walked in with little white pieces of paper in their hands as if they were messengers on a most desperate mission. I acknowledged their presence while extending my hand for a shake.

"How are you? I am Mr. D. How can I help you?" They each paused for a moment then extended their hands in response.

"Mr. D, we already had a pre-release class, and we all have jobs waiting on the outside for us." I looked into their eyes as I considered the merits of the statement.

"You have never had my class before, have you?"

"No, but they're all the same . . ." I smiled as I looked at all of them once more.

"My class is only meaningful if what you've already been doing isn't working? However, if you ask around, you will hear positive comments about the workshop. Despite the fact you already have jobs waiting for you, what you learn in here could prove very useful on the outside. Why don't you give it a couple days and see what you think?" Although these gentlemen decided not to stay, most inmates that I personally recruit stay for the class and end up graduating. Those like the few I just mentioned were arbitrarily assigned (ducated) to my class.

It is imperative to establish trust with students in my class in order to effectively assist them with intrapersonal paradigm shifting. According to Carl Rogers, "The person-centered approach rests on a basic trust in human beings' tendency to realize their full potential" (in Corey and Corey, 1997, p. 277). This occurs in the group setting if acceptance and trust are present.

I have to identify their current values as I remind them of ones forgotten or not yet internalized. I need to do this in an exciting, fresh and innovative manner that can be applied on various educational levels in a three week class. Moreover, I have to do all this while operating within California Department of Corrections and Rehabilitation procedures and protocols that are punctuated by security lockdowns, administrative visits, in-service training, and inside medical ducats (appointments).

I target three key therapeutic conditions for growth in my approach to teaching with my workshop participants:

1. Congruence (genuineness) of the facilitator within the group dynamic.

2. Unconditional positive regard (acceptance). "When group facilitators display a positive, nonjudgmental, accepting attitude toward their clients, therapeutic change is more likely."

3. Empathetic understanding (empathy) of the group members' internal and subjective paradigm.

Additionally, Rogers placed significance on the facilitator's ability to communicate this understanding to group members. (Rogers, 1986, p. 278).

As a correctional educator, the value of focusing your teaching style to embrace genuineness, acceptance, and empathy is that it will foster greater holistic gains for both the incarcerated client and the educator. These three core concepts (genuineness, acceptance, and empathy) have enabled me to effectively address my students' multicultural backgrounds, varying personalities, and addictions, in a manner that maximizes employability objectives and character based curriculum goals. By the completion of the fifteen day workshop fifteen individual process patterns are discernible within the collective that are inherent if the group is functioning properly.

My first impression driving up to Prison X was of its barren terrain. Inmate rock crews covertly greeted me with scanning stares, immediately registering my vehicle and arrival time, which would be methodically stored as potentially valuable intelligence for a later date. My week-long, initial orientation allowed me time to acclimate to my new surroundings, at least in terms of the administrative piece of the puzzle. During one of these moments I casually glanced out the window and noticed a group of inmates loitering on a slanted platform I would later know as "the ramp." That entire week, whenever I had free moments, I would analyze their movements and read their lips, trying discern their conversations, and eventually complete a circle of which I was now a part. That circle started in high school tutoring emotionally disturbed students, climbed through all the grade levels in public school, and come to rest in prison.

The week-long orientation concluded, and I prepared to start my own class. I watched a class graduate from another teacher, and was excited at the sense of accomplishment and reward on their faces as they walked up to receive their graduation certificates. Many of them were grown men who had never received any type of accolade for personal achievement, let alone a high school diploma or G.E.D. certificate. I was eager to start my own class and graduate my own students.

I learned very quickly that safety and security trumps all cards in a prison setting, and I was informed that I no longer had a classroom in which to teach. My work space had been moved to accommodate correctional officers going through C.P.R training. I was directed to use work change (a place to physically inspect inmates). Feeling like I had caught a lucky break, I silently congratulated myself that the correctional gods would not hear me convene my very first class. My students had odd looks on their faces as I began to quote poetry to them. It was Langston Hughes' poem Harlem [2]: "What Happens to a Dream Deferred?"

I wondered if they were smiling at me because I was so green. I knew that, as in any new job, I would have to earn their respect in order for them to trust me and follow my lead. So I began reading. "Does it dry up like a raisin in the sun?" The sound of a key turning caught my attention as I turned and saw a correctional officer walk in, followed by a group of inmates. I was not sure who they were; maybe they were additional students who had just been added. I continued to read to my class, "Or fester like a sore—And then run?" Now the recently arrived inmates were pulling their pants down and spreading their respective cheeks and coughing. Now all my students shared a broad and mischievous, collective smile. I returned their smile and continued, "Does it stink like rotten meat? Or crust and sugar over—like a syrupy sweet?" The procession of inmates now pulled their pants back up and walked past with the same smile my students had on their faces. "Maybe it just sags like a heavy load. Or does it just explode?" With that I dismissed the class to see if I would be having any other "late arrivals." I finished the week and actually made significant progress, despite teaching in work change, toilets flushing, and body cavity inspections.

The last and most important memory I have of my first week is of a young man I will call Mr. Clean. He was about 5'9" and 190 pounds, cut up like the television ad version of the cleaning guy. This inmate had been down (locked up) since 1998, and one day he pulled me to the side and asked if I would help him with his communication skills, specifically speaking in front of others. I was eager to help Mr. Clean, who had not walked the streets as a free man in nine years. I made him my teaching assistant on the spot and developed a lesson on writing business letters that he would later present to the class as part of its public speaking/employability objectives exercise.

Mr. Clean did a fantastic job and at the end of that class everyone gave him a round of applause. The look in his eyes and his firm handshake confirmed for me that it was no small deed. Along with the rest of the 1st Cohort Committee he thanked me for the class when they became my first graduated workshop. I later was informed that Mr. Clean was the black shot caller for the entire yard. Shot callers are the individuals who control all aspects of inmate life. This includes drug distribution, sanctioned violence and everything in between.

It takes a great deal of courage and resolve to change your direction on a path in which few people will move out of the way or help you pass by. Every person who sits through one of my workshops, or one of my fellow workshop facilitators' classes, is attempting to do just that—to change direction. The energy we expend in the workshops, and tools that we bring to bear to inspire these men and women are often met with student resistance and cynicism.

It is easy to criticize those who feel rehabilitation will never work. In fact, I was one of those people. However, the difference that continues to this day for me is that I always treat people with respect. I always put the person in front of the title or offense; people first! To glimpse a future snap shot of society you have but to look at our present prison systems and the philosophy that drives the machine. In science, the undiscovered frontier is our oceans and the fact that in the 21st century so many material mysteries still exist. In society, our undiscovered resource is those men and women preparing to be released from prison. Do our collective attitudes and intentions support and promote this population as a viable workforce and civic resource?

Perception versus Reality

The concept of perception versus reality extends far beyond the electrified fences of Prison X. It transcends borders, crossing over daily lines of communication where it becomes imbedded in diverse cultures. One of my favorite exercises is a poetry lesson emphasizing transferable skills that include reading, writing, analytical reasoning, group collaboration, and active listening. The lesson's objective is to expose preexisting paradigms while interpreting five different poems by anonymous authors. I ask each student to make inferences about the poems. Additionally, I ask them to make assumptions regarding the gender, race, occupation and background of each poem's author.

One student in particular comes to mind for this exercise. I'll call him Mr. Elliot like the actor from Road House. Mr. Elliot, it turns out, grew up in the same small town as I did. He even knew my grandma. Off to a good start, I gave Mr. Elliot a lot of latitude as he recounted stories of the glory days of I.B. (I.B. up). That was until we came to the perception versus reality exercise. When I asked for his feedback on the poem "Lavender Proposal," he responded, "It was probably written by a gay bartender." Everyone started cracking up so I repeated the response.

"You think it was written by a gay bartender?" Again, the laughs came even harder this time.

"No, actually Mr. D, I think it was written by a gay, cross-dressing bartender." Absolute pandemonium erupted as dry eyes blurred with deep, heart-felt laughter.

I asked if there were any more responses but my question was drowned out in the laughter. I continued through the activity and upon completion everyone was dying to know the identity of the authors of the poems we all read and evaluated each for meaning. (a) "First Son's Legacy," (b) "Fragile Chord," (c) "Lavender Proposal," (d) "The Reality of War," and (e) "Warrior's Legacy." The crescendo built and I dragged it out until count. I released them to return to their housing units amid a chorus of complaints and pleas, "just tell us."

After count cleared (a count occurs three times a day on our prison yard to ensure no inmates escape), they all returned promptly to our class and were eager to hear the identity of each author. As I looked into their eyes I saw their curiosity—so far subdued—about to break free, so I told them. As I wrote "Mr. D" next to each poem the looks on their faces were priceless; especially that of Mr. Elliot.

"Mr. D, I didn't mean anything by what I said earlier." I kept a straight face while he was speaking to me.

"What part Mr. Elliot, the fact that I'm a gay bartender or the possibility that I might be a gay cross-dressing bartender?" Now the entire class, myself included, was cracking up. The lesson in every class I give yields very similar results. It is one of many that my students now enjoy. It teaches why assumptions based on perceptions can be at the best comedic, and at the worst deadly.

In the three years I have spent as a correctional educator observing and listening, I have learned a great many important things. First and foremost is the importance of care and compassion. Throughout my life I have attempted to practice courteous manners and respect toward all with whom I have come in contact. My grandma made it one of her top priorities as well as hard work and the desire to learn. When I first arrived at Prison X it was therefore natural for me to extend respect at all times. Walking by and seeing different emotions on inmates' faces, I simply said, "Hi, how are you doing, sir?" A correctional officer told me, "Mr. D, if you treat every inmate like you would want them to treat your mother, sister or family member once they parole you are going to do just fine in here."

Communication

I believe that, for our entire existence, the two most significant aspects of being human (besides our ability to love) are our desire to give in to greed and our inability to communicate effectively. These two factors have repeatedly plagued our world, stimulating war, famine, hate, and general unhappiness. The most disturbing aspect of this reality is that the majority of us are capable of moderating greed as well as communicating effectively, both personally and professionally. To this end I have been fortunate enough to experience a wide array of jobs and short careers that afforded me opportunities to witness various levels of communication and the personalities behind the words.

As a correctional educator the single most important tool at my disposal is my ability to communicate effectively with inmates in a diverse population. I have graduated 200 students from 21 workshops. It is not such a significant number; my peers have been on the job longer and graduated far more. What is significant, and changed me forever, is the collection of memories experienced and shared between the students and myself. In that respect, I feel strongly that if, through the power of a story, I can create and inspire within them the will to hope and the desire to change, then perhaps the process of transcendent improvement can self-actualize.

Another critical lesson I give my students is a communication breakdown exercise. One day I had begun writing down various communication filters that affect how we communicated when a parole officer walked into my classroom. I acknowledged his presence with a slight head nod and continued teaching as if he did not exist. My students have endured a litany of interruptions, so on this occasion I really appreciated the manner in which the parole officer respectfully took a seat in the back of the room and listened quietly. I explained that environment, culture, gender, personality and emotions are key factors that impact the way we communicate (Insel & Roth, 2002, pp. 97-99).

I explained that nonverbal cues are often sent and received without our realizing it. By this time I had set the stage to give them a personality assessment. Constantly surrounded by diverse personalities, they enjoy this activity. When I finished discussing communication styles and the roles we play as individuals and in groups, the parole officer stood up and asked to address the class.

I watched as he encouraged them to, "listen carefully and take in this stuff, it's college level material you're learning." I quickly noticed that they did not really care that I was teaching them college level work but rather that I cared enough to make them more aware of themselves and to think outside the box.

One example of lack of communication that comes to mind was centered in a basic disrespect and lack of compassion. I sat quietly during lunch one day and observed an inmate walk into the program office after knocking first. He explained that the floor officer in his housing unit had sent him to retrieve toilet paper. The officer told the inmate, "We don't have what you need, and did you talk to your floor officer first?" I heard the inmate explain that the floor officer in his housing unit had sent him, so he repeated his message. Then two more correctional officers entered into the conversation. It truly became a scene from the story of Babel. Needless to say, the inmate was sent away with a parting comment of, "If you don't like it don't come to prison. . ."

There are various barriers to effective communication. One barrier that exists is gender roles. This begins within our families and cultures, and is passed on and down with the numerous traditions we cherish and live. Women, for example, use language (conversations) to connect and establish meaningful friendships. Men, on the other hand, usually use language as a tool for dominance or control over others. In short, the best communication skills cannot overcome personality differences; however, when utilized effectively they can facilitate a deeper understanding of the people with whom we professionally and personally interact (Insel & Roth, 2002, pp. 97-98).

In order to manage our relationships we must first gain a basic working comprehension of their functioning parts. We must be aware of our own personal filters and those of the people with whom we associate. As human beings, our personalities shape our daily interactions as clearly as our fingerprints identify us. Instead of the loops and swirls of a suspect's fingerprints at a crime scene, our daily interactions leave lasting impressions.

These social filters essentially act as "gate keepers" to our moral consciences, which in turn operate a two way valve that controls the flow of feelings and emotions we experience, all through the process of receiving and sending communications. Additionally, it is important to understand that one's social thumb print is a combination of one's inherited traits and learned behavior (characteristics). It is obvious what we must do, at least for those of us who want to live happier and healthier lives. In order to appreciate our fullest potential as human beings we need first to acknowledge that we are inherently social creatures. As such, it is imperative that we begin putting people first.

With communication occurring nonverbally 55% or more of the time, depending on what expert you ask, it is extremely critical in a prison environment that we are aware of the signals we are sending. Instructional strategies are a fundamental part of the workshop. I generally spend the first few days of a new class assessing my students' academic levels. The facilitators in my program use voluntary, shared reading practices because of the lower grade levels of most students. I initially start with explicit teaching, presenting concepts aligned with our core reading book. One early example of this explicit teaching is a scenario I provide that requires them to apply their own set of values and principles to a known outcome. I usually begin this as a large group, then break it up into two smaller groups. Once the exercise is finished, the two groups debate their opinions and outcomes. I continue along the same lines when I present the preface of the book, with related activities. Students start to track the lesson objectives and anticipate my expectations. They begin to take ownership of each new chapter and the activities that follow.

I also use indirect instruction and experiential learning. My role shifts from that of lecturer/director in explicit instruction to a more supportive approach for facilitation. I use these approaches with problems as varied as problem solving, reflective discussion, and reading for meaning. Indirect instruction allows my colleagues and I to create the learning environment while students engage in learning. Experiential learning complements the therapeutic approach to group work very well. The emphasis in experiential learning is on the process of learning, which includes five key phases:

1. Experiencing,

2. Sharing,

3. Analyzing,

4. Inferring, and

5. Applying.

Some activities I utilize with experiential learning are narratives, storytelling, games, and role-playing. One role-playing exercise in particular is a favorite of practically every student who graduates from my class (see below).

Lesson Plan: Survival

Anticipatory Set:

Begin lesson with a story of a group of passengers who crashed in the wilderness fifty miles northeast of Vancouver, British Columbia. Encourage class discussion of other accounts of similar events.

Workshop Facilitator Objective:

1. To identify and promote the importance of transferable skills.

2. To facilitate the effective use of communication skills (speaking, listening and nonverbal communication), organization, teamwork, collaboration, consensus building, group dynamics, and of course survival.

Student Objective:

Students will role play the scenario mentioned in the anticipatory set. Survivors are tasked with evaluating twelve survival items. Once these items have been carefully scrutinized, the group is only allowed to keep ten of the original twelve items. Survival items include the following:

1. Cigarette lighter (without fluid),

2. Ball of Steel Wool,

3. Extra Shirt,

4. Can of Crisco shortening,

5. A 20x20 foot piece of canvas,

6. Small ax,

7. Family size chocolate bars (one per person),

8. Newspapers (one per person),

9. Loaded .45 caliber pistol,

10. Quart of 100 proof whiskey,

11. Compass, and

12. Sectional plastic air map.

Direct Instruction/Experiential Learning:

After verbal and written instructions are given, the facilitator dismisses workshop participants to group together as survivors and begins to monitor facilitator/participant objectives. The group then has thirty minutes to complete the exercise. Facilitator has a variety of ways to bring students to the standard/ objective.

Option A—Provide students with no support other than knowledge of facilitator and student learning objectives, and allow students to succeed or fail as a group.

Option B—Facilitator provides students with learning objectives and strategies for greater chance of survival, i.e., indicating specific jobs among surviving members based on each member's personal background, etc.

Option C—A combination of Options A and B.

Discussion/Reflection:

Once the time limit is up reconvene the group and call upon all survivors to reflect back on the entire process, focusing on their learning objectives. The exercise and energy generated from it will take on a life of its own. Once everyone has concluded the discussion, they should indicate the best selection of items and behaviors that they would have needed to survive.

Facing conflicts and facilitating their resolutions are a natural part of being human. The presence of conflict in a relationship is not a red flag. But the way in which we choose to handle disagreements is extremely important.

Human development and growth is an ongoing, fluid process. This dynamic becomes even more intricate when juxtaposed within an intimate or personal relationship. A major goal in the workshop that I continuously repeat, besides overcoming addiction, is the ability to process anger and understand its cause (Insel & Roth, 2002, p. 97).

It is necessary first to understand that the anger is a symptom of an issue that needs attention. What many of my students have modeled, prior to participating in my class, was to suppress their anger. Some have ignored it as naturally as you or I eat or drink water. They have ignored anger, and in turn it has manifested itself as hostility or resentment; like energy, it is not lost, just transferred. Many of my students have felt safe and encouraged enough to share their experiences of anger. However, other students have reacted in an opposite fashion, projecting their own issues as ego-defense mechanisms. Almost all of their personal anecdotes have similar and recurring themes. Fear, distrust and keeping their distance have been the norm, with varying frequency. Moreover, some have reported how they have acted with little or no forethought, and how that has resulted in violence. Below are six basic strategies I teach as tools for them to put in their communication tool belt for coming to terms with conflict resolution (Insel & Roth, 2002, p. 98):

1. Identify the issue,

2. Determine the desired outcome of both parties,

3. Negotiate acceptable compromises that all stakeholders will support,

4. Write out the final agreement-contract (very important),

5. Define realistic time tables that allow for adjustments as needed for success, and

6. Periodically solicit feedback related to the participant's role in the group.

In addition to effective conflict resolution strategies, I provide my students opportunities to develop and fine tune one of the most important aspects of communication, listening. It has been my personal experience that most people engaged in a conversation are not listening effectively. People generally hear less than 10% of what they are being told. According to Stephen Covey we need to "Seek first to understand, then to be understood" (1989, p. 237).

When a dialogue is being played out, participants outwardly send signs of listening; however, often they are internally processing what their next point is going to be, and how they are going to say it to gain maximum effect. Listening is not only a lost art but a true discipline. Covey went on to define principles of empathic communication as they relate to how we, as individuals, listen to each other. There are five different levels of listening; the first four are ignoring, pretending, selective listening, and attentive listening. The fifth level he defined as empathic listening. Below are additional strategies I teach my students to use when having a conversation.

1. Provide nonverbal feedback: eye contact, nodding, smiling etc.

2. Do not interrupt: my students are good at this; to them it is all about respect.

3. Become a reflective listener (disengage your filters, do not judge, analyze, or evaluate). Just listen.

4. Be aware that your opinion, if given, could cause resentment and anger.

5. Summarize what you feel you heard and repeat it back for clarification, to prevent miscommunication.

6. Connect with the speaker's feelings, not just with the words.

7. Validate the speaker's feelings, timing and words; let the speaker know that you care.

If we truly want recidivism rates to drop and rehabilitation policies to work then we must persuade inmate populations to listen to us. We most definitely need to be concerned with the messages we are sending as we communicate. Nothing we do is accomplished within a closed circuit. Everything we do and say creates a lasting legacy that far too often precedes our physical arrival.

On more than one occasion my classes have shown me the truth of these words. In one of his movies Clint Eastwood said, "A man's got to know his limitations." I have thought more and more about these wise words as I have grown older. In prison I learned to appreciate this in the form of the service I provide. Some personal stories shared by my students have touched my heart, while others have chilled my blood. One statement I heard made by a correctional officer to an inmate was, "You will be back because this is how I make my mortgage payment each month." The inmates tell me about all types of statements made to them. My response is always the same. "Do not empower others to control you anymore. Take back your power now that you have a second chance, and do not come back." Many of those who graduate from my class will remember, and take to heart, the sentiments of those who anticipate their return.

People

Unlike my students, I get to go home every day. However, like my students my memories of this place and the people I have met will be carried with me the rest of my life. What I will cherish most is the enormous responsibility with which I have been entrusted. To stand up and deliver hope and inspiration to a population in which many are desperate for a second, third, or fourth chance is of utmost importance. The fulfillment that my colleagues and I receive is priceless when students thank us over and over in the same day and throughout the workshop! To stand shoulder to shoulder and remind them that tomorrow is full of possibilities is of the greatest importance. There is life after prison.

When I think about all the personalities I have encountered, four quickly come to mind. The number four is interesting since Carl Jung defined four classifications of personality. He delved deeply into these four basic personality types. Moreover, his work provided incisive analysis of individual approaches that vary, based on value systems and personal experiences. Although all my students are impressive and I make it a point to remember three things about each of them, there are four students who stand out. I will outline these four personalities using the criteria established in Ritberger's book: *Managing People: What's Personality Got to Do with It* (2007).

If you remember back from when I was attempting to instruct class and was reciting Langston Hughes' poem "A Dream Deferred," I was placed in work change, an area where correctional officers conduct physical inspections. One student who took an immediate liking to me was Mr. Mack Truck. He was a fiery twenty-four year old of Cuban/Puerto Rican heritage. Mr. Truck had a reputation as a fantastic tattoo artist whose beef (crime) was car jacking drug dealers and taking their money and drugs.

Mr. Truck and I quickly found common ground in the classroom setting, as we discussed world events, the breakdown of family structures and of course prison politics. One day we were reflecting on the role his father had played in his life. We discussed his regret of having caused his mother pain with his frequent trips to prison, and how she would soon be facing serious leg surgery. He made a statement, the first in prison that touched my heart, by saying, "You have a friend in me Mr. D." I will never forget, as I walked to turn the lights off at the end of my day, how I turned around to see the heartfelt conviction and sincerity reflected in his eyes. In teaching we have a term called "teachable moments." These moments reveal themselves to dedicated teachers who—against what at times feel like insurmountable odds—overcome all challenges and hurdle the tallest obstacles to reach students' hearts and minds. When this happens the unmistakable light of discovery turns on, validating all our collective fears and insecurities, providing rays of hope to drive us forward, harder and more determined than ever before

In war, the warrior fights for a code. American servicemen and women fight for the brother or sister next to them. For those who never served in the military, or fought a fire, or walked a beat, that may seem difficult to understand. In combat, whether the battlefield is in the Middle East, or on a street controlled by violent gang members, the reason is the same. We fight for the man or woman next to us. In teaching, we fight for the student who cannot yet fight for himself, nor fully grasp the significance of his actions; these reverberations leave a lasting legacy for all of society.

According to Ritberger, Mr. Truck would be a red personality (2007, p. 51-77). Some aspects of the red type are predictable. They tend to be:

1. Stubborn,

2. Systematic,

3. Controlling,

4. Realistic,

5. Hardworking,

6. Passionate, and

7. Loyal (once their loyalty is earned).

Additionally, reds almost always have to buy in to an idea based on their own values and how they relate to what someone else is saying or selling before they will soldier for you. Reds are detail oriented and need structure to operate effectively. They are naturally competitive, which makes deadlines and objective-based tasks their specialty. The military is full of reds who are kept in check, for the most part, by long standing codes of conduct, etiquette, and rank structure.

When it comes to communication style, reds are not effective, team-oriented communicators unless they first get their values satisfied. If they agree with what you are selling, they will move heaven and earth to support your mission. If not, stand fast; there will be dissension among the ranks.

Another personality type is orange. There are many oranges in health care, teaching and social work. Oranges generally shy away from conflict as this puts them at odds with their fundamental goals: peace and harmony. A former student I will call Stallion demonstrated the transformation of an orange personality in a prison environment.

Stallion was a member of my thirteenth workshop. When I first met him I asked, "Why do they call you Stallion?" He smiled at me and looked around the room before answering. He dropped one hand low to one knee in a cupped gesture and responded, "Because I'm hung like a horse!" After laughing so hard my eyes began to tear I nodded as a sign that I was willing to co-sign his bullshit and thus began a relationship that continued until his release.

Stallion's best friend joined the class I will discuss next and the laughs continued. Stallion told several stories while in the program.

"Mr. D, you want to know what my beef is." I said, "Not really, that is none of my business." "Yea," he responded, "but I trust you. I will tell you anyways. I know you are writing a book so I don't mind if you share it." "O.K. Stallion, I'll bite. What gives?" I asked. "Well, I use to traffic drugs, specifically ecstasy, across state lines all over the country. I would wear two knee braces and put up to 1,000 pills in each brace." "They never caught you at the airport?" I asked. "Nope, walked on through every time, and the scanner never picked up on it. One trip in particular I remember meeting this fucking hot ass chick who was giving me play. The flight was to Las Vegas. So of course we started talking about the weekend's coming attractions."

"By the time we landed we both had a few drinks in us. I had mentioned I was in town to do business. So she inquired what type. Although I never said the smile on my face said it all." I said, "Like when you told me the origins of your nickname." "Exactly, so she recommended I meet her bosses, who might be in the market for what I was selling. I got a good vibe so I said why not. We grabbed a taxi and headed for her club. When we got there she took me through the strip joint past some rather large bodyguards to meet the 'man.' I introduced myself and told him what I was trying to unload. He quoted me a figure twice as much as I was looking for. We concluded business, and he offered me a suite for the night at a top casino on the strip. I accepted and was about to leave when it suddenly occurred to me that we would have never met each other if not for the girl on the plane."

I reiterated the point that she actually was the reason that the business deal went down. He recounted that "Her personal business savvy and instincts should be worth something. The boss agreed and gave her $5,000. Moreover, he gave her the weekend off and suggested she escort me for that time. Then we left. She was so pleased with my thoughtfulness that we spent the whole weekend getting to know each other better." I feigned ignorance as I asked him the obvious, "What does that mean? What happens in Vegas . . .?"

From that day forward I watched the Stallion in action. I do that with all my students. Actually, I do that the entire time I am in prison. Unlike in a regular classroom, the implications for not being aware can have dire consequences.

Mr. Stallion is the resident shot caller for the Whites. In prison every race is expected to follow the rules set down by their race first and foremost. To use my students' language, "He has the keys (juice) that drives the car (White population), and the basic goal is to operate wherein the Whites are able to smuggle drugs, use drugs and coexist with various other races. If the natural order of life is disturbed he is responsible for re-establishing order one way or another." Each race has its shot caller. These rules/laws are well-known and followed. Some are written down by some races and some are not. Needless to say, all inmates are aware of the "prison politics" as soon as they get to a prison. I emphasize this point not to glorify the system but rather to point out who really runs the prisons, at least in California. Correctional officers, non-custody and free staff who have crossed these lines have been "touched up and even killed." Again, I do not condone the actions of inmate violence and retaliation any more than the practice of "green justice," or the code of blue (law enforcement enforcing laws as they see fit). What matters right now is that it does go on, and we as a society need to join together to affect positive change. Ritberger (2007, p. 79-107), wrote that oranges are (1) experts in conflict resolution and (2) consensus building who are also

3. Adaptive,

4. Social,

5. Caring,

6. Guilty (though this is often self-imposed), and

7. Tolerant (of individuals).

In terms of communication, oranges are great listeners and expect the same from others. Oranges do not take well to having their feelings and words casually dismissed. Oranges tend to use communication to build relationships and maintain a sense of security. They are masters at getting everyone involved, for better or worse. As the shot caller, Stallion had to adapt his base personality characteristics to adhere to prison politics. This is a dangerous reality, not only for himself but for all inmates. The moment our values become situational or we allow our ethics to be subordinated to the will of the general mass, we cease to operate as fully functioning, healthy beings, and the greater the likelihood that self deception will become our master.

My next personality case study is a yellow. He is smart and intelligent— there is a difference. He is well read and traveled. He once corrected a mistake I made in a polite manner and accepted my apology the following day with even more grace. This man is humble, yet confident, with a leader's touch. His goal is to open a State licensed marijuana shop for "medicinal purposes," and of course to discharge parole. For the purposes of this study let's call him Jim. He is a classic yellow. The first phrases I would associate with Jim are well-rounded and charismatic. Like most yellows he is a natural leader. He solves problems in his mind before he helps others to take action.

I do not have a fantastic story about Jim as I did about his good friend Stallion. I can tell you that I attended a staying clean program one night after my class was finished. I sat in a chair as half a dozen inmates stood up and walked to the center of a room filled with sixty of their peers. I listened as men stood tall and proclaimed what it takes to stay clean and sober. As silence fell, I penetrated the gaze of one behemoth-sized man with a questioning stare of my own before scanning the room.

The speaker for the evening was a Viking-looking man who discussed that he had been in and out of prisons over thirty times, with ten different commitment numbers going back to the late 1970s. I watched intently as Jim stood up to give a positive affirmation about the speaker, as was the custom when someone was preparing to parole. Jim walked up to this warrior; no small man himself, and said, "Give yourself a chance." Too quietly for anyone to hear unless sitting in the very front, Jim repeated the words, "Give yourself a chance." As he did he extended his own hand and shook the man's hand vigorously. I saw the intensity that burned in Jim's eyes. Then I saw for the first time a flicker of hope take hold in the speaker's eyes.

Jim sat down without fanfare, probably unnoticed by the vast majority, save those in the front row. He then cleverly disguised an invitation in the form of a traffic report and invited me to stay until "traffic died down." I played along and sat mesmerized as he deftly executed a discussion about the formation of an orientation group and the dynamics behind group participation. All manner of topics arose as questions were asked and answered. Here, in the stay clean group, he spoke more or less the same as in my class, but in class he gave me my place as the instructor. Here, in his arena, I saw first hand the measure of his character and life experience as he skillfully answered questions. Jim wielded authority with civility. Ritberger (2007, p. 109-134) reported that yellows are:

1. Ethical.

2. Extremely independent,

3. Tenacious,

4. Self-confident,

5. Cerebral,

6. Nonconformist, and

7. Skeptical.

Yellows' communication styles are very clear. They do not like small talk or superficial debates. Yellows prefer to be group leaders rather than to follow leaders. When they have to follow, it will generally be temporary, until they can assume the lead position.

The final personality case study is that of my most unique student. This individual was by far my most fascinating discovery while teaching in prison.

He is the intellectual equal of a great philosopher with the wisdom of an ancient African owl. I say African because Mr. Owl was born and raised in Zimbabwe, the African country formerly known as Southern Rhodesia. I met him one day while walking the hamster trail. That is what we call the crudely shaped, oval track the inmates walk, run and generally loiter around every day, seven days a week, 365 days a year. It faces my classroom and provides me the perfect vantage point for viewing the yard.

Mr. Owl walked up to me and introduced himself as he asked exactly what I taught. I listened to his strong African accent and attempted to discern from what country he hailed. I smiled and extended my hand as I responded, "Life. My class teaches how to be successful in life." He smiled as he contemplated my atypical response. I asked him what country in Africa was he from. He immediately answered Rhodesia, and I saw a slight sparkle of mischievousness dancing in his oval-shaped eyes. Unlike most responses I'm sure he has received mine did not pretend to know the specific country. My eyes reflected this fact and were quickly supported by a sincere apology for my obvious ignorance. "I'm sorry, Mr. Owl, forgive me but where?" Before I could finish he responded, "Present-day Zimbabwe." We both smiled as I acknowledged his ace had trumped my king. So began a brief but powerful and continuously reciprocal teacher/student relationship.

Mr. Owl was part of class 10. He was an extremely reserved yet observant man who carried an overwhelming presence with him any time he entered a room or spoke. I cannot say that I have met too many people who carried a similar presence. The few that I have met were Tony Dorsett, Richard Marcinko, Jesse Ventura, and Carey-Hiroyuki Tagawa; they were each unforgettable. Mr. Owl's persona was most akin to the Tagawa, the Japanese movie star and martial arts practitioner. These two men exude a graceful confidence and timeless patience.

One day I gave the fifty-something wise old owl the task of assigning to each student a virtue from a list of ten essential values developed by Tom Lickona, Director of an organization called the Center for the 4th and 5th Rs. Having already read the value-oriented character exercise, I thought it would be interesting to observe how Mr. Owl related to each of his peers. Additionally, I was curious to see how they would receive his evaluations of them. I went over to him on the day of the lecture and took his seat as is my practice any time one of my students teaches. As I sat back and strapped myself in (figuratively), I immediately noticed a quiet reverence settle over the class. A new teacher had entered the room and the quintessential lesson for all time was about to be woven. My mind was pulled into the greater collective as Mr. Owl quietly walked to each student handing him a piece of paper with a single virtue written on it. Once everyone in the room, myself included, had a piece of paper in front of him, Mr. Owl proceeded to systematically analyze each student, based on his silent observations over the past two weeks.

The first student to whom he spoke sat mesmerized as did we all while Mr. Owl meticulously recounted personal statements that student had made. Mr. Owl recited curriculum taught and emphasized key points as he highlighted the real world life lessons. The room was dead silent as we were all completely taken off our feet by this man's insightfulness and memory. As he walked around the room we waited like small children shackled unmercifully to those last remaining hours of Christmas morning. At one point a student held up a letter his wife had just written him, describing him with the same virtue as Mr. Owl had. His expression conveyed what we all knew: he had just recently opened the letter, and had not shared it with anyone.

When my time arrived I too sat like the child I was in his presence. I eagerly awaited my positive affirmation in the hope that he would unlock any number of doors that remained closed to me. The virtue he honored me with was humility. Most educators I have met speak to students, or at students. I have met very few indeed who invoke internal conversations that whisper of their own success and humanity from the deepest alcoves of their character. We all were speechless at first as we struggled to hold onto and recount what we had just witnessed. Ever the philosopher, traveler and servant leader, Mr. Owl just quietly sat down. We all applauded his rare gift and selfishly replayed the scenario over and over again in our discussion so that we might not forget our shared experience. We all wanted to take that memory with us forever. I will forever remember Mr. Owl as the diminutive man with observant eyes who became my teacher for fifteen days.

Mr. Owl is a green personality type (Ritberger, 2007, pp.135-162). The first word I would associate with him is intuitive. He is a people person, although from a distance.

Needless to say, Mr. Owl gave a final presentation first in his tribal language of Shona and then in English. His ability to form positive relationships is based on communication. Greens are the communication masters. Their ability is derived from their strong desire to interact with others. I suspect that Mr. Owl's relocation to America only intensified this desire. His beef was with the bottle, drinking and driving. I wish this Ph.D. candidate all the best in overcoming and living with his addiction.

Conclusion

What are we all looking for? For some of us is it the winning lottery number or the fastest sports car? Perhaps you are more altruistic than that; happiness then. I think, for the vast majority of us, our desires can be broken down unto Maslow's hierarchy of needs pyramid. His original model portrayed human needs, starting at physiological needs (air, food, water, sex, sleep, etc.), and continuing through safety, love/belonging, esteem, and self-actualization. Consider applying that pyramid to a prison setting. What basic need factors can stand the test of prison politics on an intensive security yard? Might Maslow have constructed a second pyramid to account for the sociological realities of prison life?

How would dear old Sigi (Sigmund Freud) have been received on a minimum security yard in California today? His early experiments with "coca" would most certainly yield him an attentive crowd, at least until he started to probe the inmates' past with psychoanalysis and statements about their mothers.

I think Carl Rogers would have done the best. The significance he placed on the "here and now," coupled with his sincere desire to be accessible to his clients, reflect how my colleagues and I approach our students' holistic needs. Our passion energizes the students' souls. They feed off our enthusiasm, which inspires us to raise the bar even higher! America, the whole world for that matter, needs correctional educators, legislators, governors and most importantly citizens who care about the welfare of their incarcerated peers. Children and teenagers deserve and require their fathers, mothers and/or guardians to be present.

Prison populations across America and the world need correctional educators who care about them on a personal level. They need legislators crafting policies that are responsible, comprehensive and focused on systemic improvements. Inmates need to know and believe that once they have served their time, they will be openly welcomed back to reintegrate within society. And society's expectations for them, to become fully functioning citizens, should be supported by their right to vote. I for one fail to see the rationale behind laws that mandate levels of citizenship in a society that promotes equality and justice. A Spartan compliance response greets all those who face minor possession of narcotics charges, or parole violations; the disproportionate nature of subsequent sentences is evident to everyone. It is a short term solution to a long term social problem. Just try to explain the social influence model or human 401(k) plan that can persuade 25% of the world's incarcerated population that the American dream still exists—just not for parolees. What we as a society proclaim outside prison walls reverberates exponentially within all the country's prison yards.

Biographical Sketch

Mark Dearing can be reached at poseidondearing33@yahoo.com. In the early 1990s Mark worked several special assignments for the San Diego Police Department, including Beach Enforcement, Gang Suppression, and Southeastern patrol. He worked with at-risk children for the San Diego Parks and Recreation Department, and as a behavior specialist for the San Diego School District. Before coming to work at the State of California's Donovan State Correctional Facility, in the assignment he discussed in this chapter, he worked as an eighth grade English and Science teacher for special education students, and as a school counselor. Mark earned his Bachelor's degree with an emphasis in Literature in 2000 and his Master's degree in Educational Counseling with a Pupil Personnel Services credential. His first book, *The X Factor*, is a compilation of historical events mixed with personal experiences and inventions. Mark enjoys Brazilian Jiu-jitsu.

CHAPTER XIII

THE HIDDEN STORY OF VOCATIONAL EDUCATION IN CORRECTIONS

by Judy L. Porter

Vocational programs, academic programs, and work programs are the foundation of the rehabilitation efforts in the correctional system (Stephan, 1997; Wilson et al., 2000). While academic programs are the most numerous in correctional facilities, vocational education is a close second (Lawrence et al., 2002). Harlow (2003) found that nine out of 10 state prisons in the United States provided educational programs for their inmates. Vocational education is important also because such programs have been found to instill in participants many of the desired outcomes of any learning program. These include responsible decision making, maintenance of a work schedule, good interpersonal communication skills, and a reduction of conflict with others in general (Wilson et al., 2000).

Vocational programs are not usually evaluated in a methodologically rigorous manner separately from other programs. In many studies vocational programs' effects are difficult to ascertain given that they are subsumed under academic programs, other educational programs, or correctional industry work programs. This is understandable to some degree, given that many incarcerated individuals have little education and it is necessary to elevate their academic level in order for them to more effectively participate in a vocational program.

Vocational education programs are generally defined as programs that train participants for a job upon release. Such programs were reported to be in place in about 56% of state prisons (Harlow, 2003; Stephan, 1997), 94% of Federal prisons, 44% of private prisons, and 7% of local jails. Many vocational programs offer training and certification in fields such as construction, plumbing, printing, electrician, heating and air conditioning, and other areas. Vocational education in jails and prisons provides incarcerated individuals opportunities to learn skills that can be marketed upon release and is a means to gainful employment, especially if the individual is trained in a vocation that is in demand (Bushway & Reuter, 1997; Tracy & Johnson, 1994; Wilson et al., 2000).

Overall, about a third of state and Federal inmates had taken some vocational training while incarcerated. A little more than a third of African American inmates took vocational education (34%) and a little less than a third of White inmates (32%) took vocational education, while 29% of Hispanic inmates took vocational education in a state correctional facility. Only about 5% of jail inmates took vocational classes while incarcerated but this low number may be a result of the transitory nature of being in jail. Citizens of the United States who were incarcerated in state correctional facilities were more likely than non-citizens to take vocational education with nearly 33% of citizens participating and 27% of non-citizens participating (James, 2004).

Lack of education has long been linked to unemployment and criminal behavior (Bouffard et al., 2000). Harlow (2003) found that the lack of a high school diploma or a GED was a common factor among those inmates in state facilities who had a prior sentence, while those with a diploma or some college were less likely to have had a prior sentence. Prison inmates typically have less educational attainment than the general population (Andrews & Bonta, 1994) and inmates with less education were more likely to have a juvenile record. One study asserts that while higher education is the most beneficial undertaking for offenders, vocational education is also very effective.

Some studies have found that any amount of education or training, even participating in a correctional industry, has an effect on reducing recidivism. There are several avenues for offenders to enhance their skills and reduce their risk of returning to crime. Offenders who desire an advanced degree certainly should be able to pursue that. Restrictions such as the ban on Pell Grants for offenders place harmful barriers to success for these individuals. Studies in general are supportive of higher education as a means to reduce criminal activity.

Similarly, those individuals who desire to pursue a vocation should be able to do so. Those offenders who obtain a skill and even certification in a field have a better chance of finding work. Some programs work with employers to ascertain their needs and offer vocational training accordingly for a win-win situation (Batiuk et al., 2005). Bushway and Reuter (1997) refer to this practice as supply-side programs that are geared toward making offenders more attractive to employers. Demand-side programs, however, help employers reduce the cost of hiring an offender by such means as assisting with bonding the employee and via wage supplements. Demand-side programs also attempt to influence businesses to locate in lower socio-economic communities through incentive programs. A new business in a community plagued by poverty and high crime should benefit the community by providing jobs and capital which in turn will hopefully reduce crime in the community. Thus, vocational education for offenders may well have benefits beyond the individual.

Bushway and Reuter (1997) argue that neighborhoods with high crime need help attracting businesses for obvious reasons. The creation of employment opportunities for young adults in such areas is important to improve the community and reduce crime. Jobs that pay above poverty level wages, and that offer both a chance for advancement and job satisfaction are very important in reducing crime (Bushway & Reuter, 1997, Crutchfield & Pitchford, 1997). Given that there is a large influx of ex-offenders into poorer communities it would be beneficial to have vocational education provided to offenders prior to their release (Seiter & Kadela, 2003).

Lawrence et al. (2002) found a wide range of vocational programs throughout the nation's correctional facilities including auto body/detailing, horticulture, printing, and welding among many others. Many programs offer certificates to those who complete. Some vocational programs are certified through local educational systems or agencies. For example, Wisconsin's correctional facilities have 23 vocational programs—all certified by the local college system. Wisconsin's STEP program provides vocational education both during and after incarceration (Bouffard et al., 2000). Most vocational programs attempt to provide inmates with the skills they will need to secure employment upon release. There are criticisms that vocational programs could be more effective if they were in touch with local industry's employment needs. Inmates who are trained in those occupations that are classified as areas in need of workers by the local employment office are more attractive to employers (Lawrence et al., 2002).

Evaluation of Vocational Programs

A good evaluation of a vocational program helps in understanding if a particular program is beneficial in assisting offenders to gain employment, is more or less beneficial for offenders with certain characteristics, and what may need to be changed in a particular program to improve services to the offender and the community. Evaluation is an important component of any program and should be considered in the beginning stages of program design, but failing that, evaluation should begin as soon as possible. A meaningful evaluation is much more than a process description of how a program was instituted.

The Maryland Scale of Scientific Methods (MSSM) is the method many meta-analyses used to rate program evaluations as to rigorousness of methodology on a scale of 1 to 5. Sherman et al. (1998) developed this scale for the National Institute of Justice to help in identifying those programs that work to prevent crime. The rating is based on three factors: (1) control of other variables that may have been the cause of any observed effect, (2) measurement error that resulted from attrition or low response rates, and (3) statistical power that is adequate to detect effects. Sherman et al. (1998) used the MSSM and divided their meta-analysis into three categories: what works, what doesn't, and what's promising. They found 15 programs in the "what works" category. The most important offender characteristic in this category was age. They found that vocational education for older male ex-offenders works best. In the "what doesn't work" category there were 23 programs, and in the "promising programs" category there were 30 programs. If the promising programs could be evaluated with a more rigorous methodology more could be added to the "what works" category. Similarly, the "what doesn't work" category might be corrected and made to be more effective.

Using the MSSM, Wilson et al. (2000) conducted a meta-analysis of 33 evaluations of vocational, academic, and work programs in correctional institutions and found that most of the studies had methodological problems that made it difficult to assess the effectiveness of the actual program on recidivism. They suggest that in future evaluators incorporate "theoretical links between the program activities and future criminal involvement" and that studies should control for the possibility of effects of self-selection bias (p. 347).

Of the 33 studies included in Wilson et al.'s (2000) study, 17 were vocational programs. Although Wilson et al. (2000) cite many problems with the studies included in their meta-analysis, they state with caution that the recidivism rate for those inmates who participated in vocational education was lower than for those who had participated in adult basic education and GED programs and for those who had been in correctional work industry programs. Those inmates who had been in a postsecondary educational component, however, were two points lower in recidivism than those who were in vocational education. Vocational programs, "showed a positive and significant effect on employment" (p. 360) and they found that despite the methodological problems associated with nearly 90% of the studies "the evidence is encouraging" (p. 36) that vocational programs work to reduce crime.

Two other studies that used the MSSM found vocational programs did reduce recidivism. Bouffard et al. (2000) elucidate problems with program evaluation in their meta-analysis of 13 vocational education programs, five correctional industry programs, and seven community employment evaluations.

Many evaluations link academic and vocational programs together which makes it difficult to determine the impact of vocational programs alone. The status of the offender upon release might affect the likelihood an offender would recidivate. Some offenders serve their entire sentence and are released unconditionally, others are on parole, and some might be in a specialized program such as intensive supervision. The type of parole officer may have an impact on success as well. Officers may be more or less lenient in their styles with some more likely to revoke parole on a less serious technical violation and others more likely to work with an offender in the community (Seiter & Kadela, 2003).

Adams et al. (1994) found 90 methodologically rigorous studies that had randomization or matching assignment of participants into the program group or a control group, used statistical controls and found significant effects. The follow-up period for program participants varied from 14 to 36 months due to variation in release dates. Interestingly, Adams et al. (1994) found that those inmates who had the least educational attainment who participated in academic programs had lower recidivism rates. Their data suggested that a reduction in recidivism rates of as much as 33% can be achieved.

Given the importance of vocational education to individuals, their families and communities, the need for evaluation of vocational programs is important in order to effectively monitor the progress of the program and its effectiveness in relation to desired outcomes. When planning and implementing a vocational education program it would be well worth the effort to put together as rigorous a design as possible in order to provide an in-depth evaluation. While there are plenty of books and articles to assist in evaluation efforts, the MSSM provides a detailed outline of what is desired in an evaluation methodology which could be helpful to program planners.

Vocational education has the capability to assist individuals to obtain gainful employment whether they are in prison, in jail, on parole or probation, released from prison or jail, or in at-risk populations such as younger individuals without job skills. Vocational education can help participants raise their skills, improve their self-esteem, improve interpersonal skills; it is also a motivator for at-risk individuals to be less likely to engage in criminal behavior. Communities benefit as crime rates are lessened, valuable members are kept in the community, and social capital is improved. Businesses benefit as they are able to obtain employees who are skilled in areas that are in need by any particular industry. Vocational education for offenders, ex-offenders, and at-risk groups is a beneficial program for individuals, families, and communities.

Biographical Sketch

Judy Porter is an Assistant Professor of Criminal Justice, Rochester Institute of Technology, where she has been a faculty member since 2004. She is also a senior associate with the Center for Public Safety Initiatives in Rochester, New York. She received her Master's degree in Sociology at New Mexico State University and Ph. D. in Criminal Justice at the University of Nebraska-Omaha. Her research interests include corrections, program evaluation, public housing, communities, and violence. Dr. Porter's e-mail address is jlpgcj@rit.edu.

Chapter XIV

The Battleground in Correctional Treatment is Self-Image

by Richard J. Dackow

For as he thinketh in his heart, so is he (*Holy Bible*, KJV, Proverbs 23:7).

The battleground in correctional treatment is self-image. Correctional education programs provide numerous opportunities to change an individual's self-image: from loser to winner, from inmate to student, from dropout to graduate, from failure to success, from ignorant to literate, from handicapped to handyman, from idle to employed, from drain on society to contributor to society, from foolish mind to wise mind.

Reasoner (2007) states "There is a direct relationship between the perception of social success and self-esteem. This success may include confidence in appearance, academic ability, athletic ability, or social relationships" (25th paragraph). In a comprehensive review of the literature on self-esteem, Reasoner provides considerable research that low levels of self-esteem correlate with high levels of academic failure, alcohol and drug abuse, criminal activity, violence, eating disorders, interpersonal relationship problems, teenage pregnancy, depression, and suicide (2007).

A careful reader will discern that I have used the term self-image, not self-esteem, in the title of this chapter. My choice of the word self-image is deliberate. Even psychopathic personalities will refer to themselves and their associates as "good people." My personal experience working with people in correctional facilities is that there is a subculture for which Reasoner's definition of self-esteem is inverted. Like Jonathan Swift's Dr. Gulliver, we find ourselves in a strange world where all the rules of what we know are molded into grotesque caricature. In this world the tier boss, grievance committee rep, food server, and outside mopper are people of high status within the inmate perception. Thuggery and intimidation earn "respect" that extends beyond the length that one can throw a punch. The true antisocial and narcissistic personalities see only themselves and perhaps a small inner group as having any value. All other people are merely objects to be used and discarded. In their own minds they see themselves as romantic, swashbuckling pirates of the Caribbean, or medieval knights true to their own antisocial code of chivalry. The gang leader is their king. Loyalty to that group is their only value. Their "street cred" and "propers" are their measure of esteem and worth. The correctional educator, like corrections officers, caseworkers, and medical and mental health staff, enters this strange world. The behavioral sciences can offer some guidance in understanding the mind of the criminal, and can help to establish methods and goals of correctional treatment of which correctional education is a part.

Yochelson and Samenow (1977) described how the primary goal of correctional treatment is to correct errors in thinking. Cognitive behavioral therapy is based on the idea that how we think (cognition), how we feel (emotion), and how we act (behavior) all interact together. Specifically, our thoughts influence our feelings and our behavior. Therefore, negative and unrealistic thoughts can cause us distress and result in problems. Ross and Fabiano (1985) were in the forefront in applying cognitive behavioral therapy concepts to correctional treatment. They described the primary goal of correctional treatment as cognitive restructuring to reduce irrational beliefs. In Narcotics Anonymous and Alcoholics Anonymous groups they call the same self-sabotaging thought processes "stinking thinking."

Nowhere is this erroneous, irrational stinking thinking more devastating to the human spirit than when they it concerns a person's self-image core beliefs. Correctional education provides numerous subtle and not-so-subtle ways to help change students' core beliefs about their own self images. After making a mistake, someone who has a negative self image core belief thinks: "I'm useless and can't do anything right." The person continues, "I'll never do anything right," and "I shouldn't even try." This belief impacts negatively on that person's feeling, mood, and affect. The problem is therefore worsened. For example, the student who was unsuccessful in previous school experiences will opt out of educational programs when incarcerated. Inmates who believe they cannot learn react by avoiding educational activities while incarcerated. As a result, a successful experience becomes more unlikely, which reinforces the original thought of being "useless." This becomes a self-fulfilling prophecy or "problem cycle." The efforts of the correctional professional are therefore directed at working to help change this negative core belief. It is done by addressing the way students think about themselves and by structuring tasks to assure some small successes in response to similar situations. Also the correctional professional can help the inmate/student develop more flexible ways to think and respond. This includes reducing the avoidance of activities that would challenge negative core beliefs about self image. As a result, the student escapes the negative behavior and thought patterns which lead to a cycle of failure. In turn the student can become more active, succeed more often, improve core self image and reduce feelings of depression.

Correctional educators often find their greatest challenge is to motivate their students. Prochaska and Di Clemente's (1982) "stages of change" is a developmental model that can help correctional educators in this challenge. Their model is derived from drug abuse treatment, and is a keystone of dialectic behavior therapy (DBT) (Linehan, 1993). In Prochaska and Di Clemente's model the correctional educator cannot simply accept the fact that the student is not motivated for treatment. The correction treatment profession has the responsibility to understand the stages that a person can go through on the path to change, in order to help motivate the student. The corrections professional helps the student/inmate to assess at which stage the person is currently and to help the inmate/student move toward the next higher stage. The model helps to counter the expectation that the situation is hopeless and beyond personal control, to break the cycle of failure. The educator can help students progress by challenging the underlying assumptions that keep them stuck at a lower level, and can help students if they set realistic, achievable educational objectives. Prochaska and Di Clemente (1982) suggested five developmental levels for the change process:

Pre-Contemplation: Client is not thinking at all about changing his or her behavior.

Stage 1—Contemplation: Here the client can see some benefits in changing, but has not started to change and is in a stage of indecision.

Stage 2—Decision: The client makes a decision to change.

Stage 3—Action: The client now begins to act.

Stage 4—Maintenance: If things are going well, then the client maintains his or her progress.

The correctional educator who recognizes a student's stage of motivation can provide appropriate support and suggestions to motivate the student to move to the next stage. Some things the correctional educator can do include encouraging students by challenging their underlying self defeating assumptions, reflecting on different actions for change and the probable effect of those actions, or helping them to consider what small steps they could begin to take in a positive direction—steps which they see as both reasonable and achievable. Showing practical applications is an especially useful motivation technique for vocational educators. A student who believes that he cannot do math might be motivated to learn how to make change, balance a bank book, figure out how much seed he needs to plant a 40 foot by 100 foot lawn, calculate the diameter of plumbing pipe, or the determine the compression ratio of an engine.

For correctional educators lessons can be learned from the recent advances in behavioral therapies that are used in correctional facilities. These lessons can help to frame the way correctional educators view their work, and give them new skills to carry out that work.

Choice theory is the latest refinement of William Glasser's reality therapy. Glaser emphasizes the relationship between thinking and actions and in turn their effect on feelings and physiology. This helps people to understand themselves in terms of their needs, how they think about those needs, and what they do in order to meet their needs. When clients experience psychological distress or emotional pain, it is often because their thoughts and actions are not working in relation to their needs. Reality therapy helps them make more effective choices and thereby impact their feelings and physiology in a positive manner. It is an empowering model which helps clients regain control over their lives, make confident decisions for themselves, and experience a higher level of happiness and piece of mind. It also helps people form positive self-images and build and sustain effective relationships.

Attributes of Dialectic Behavioral Therapy

Dialectic behavioral therapy (DBT) is a comprehensive program which includes a focus on skills training. Developed by Linehan (1993), DBT is now acknowledged as the "best practice" approach to borderline personality disorders. Borderlines include some of the most difficult inmates in terms of acting out and demanding behaviors. DBT principles are being increasingly applied to other groups. Like reality therapy, DBT has a strong emphasis on change, especially in terms of increased self-control over ways of thinking and choices of action, particularly in the face of challenging situations. Through training toward a disciplined focus on thinking and actions, volatile feelings (extreme anger and anxiety) are slowly brought under the client's control. Relationships are improved and the client is able to function effectively in the community. Dialectics is a principle of balancing opposite positions. The therapist acting as a skills trainer helps the client through a series of skill development modules that are taught in both group and individual sessions. The therapist implements the principle of validation of the student's current behaviors in a non-judgmental manner. The principle of validation means that the therapist sees the most annoying, maladaptive behaviors as being the person's "best attempt" to manage his or her life situations—but these attempts are simply not working. As a skills educator the therapist recognizes a need for the student to change to more effective thinking and behavior. The dialectic helps with the need to balance acceptance with requisite change. Skills taught include:

(1) core mindfulness (learning to focus inwardly in a considered way),

(2) interpersonal effectiveness (learning to forge and maintain effective relationships),

(3) emotion regulation skills (learning self-control over volatile emotions), and

(4) distress tolerance (learning to cope with stress and adversity).

Dr. Allister Webster, a psychologist at Nova Institution for Women in Truro, Nova Scotia and Canadian national clinical advisor for DBT states, "DBT is a psychological treatment designed to assist individuals to develop adaptive skills and strategies targeting problematic behaviors that interfere with effectively coping in one's environment and that prevent an individual from feeling she has a 'life worth living'" (2007, p. 2). According to Dr. Webster, "It is particularly suitable for those suffering from high levels of distress, suicidal behavior, low self-image and cognitive distortion (p. 2).

Let me give just one of many examples that stand out in my memory as to how a correctional educator was able to change a woman's self-image in a positive way. In the mid-1970s I was director of Classification in the Correctional Institution for Women on Rikers Island. I remember assigning a young woman to a typing class. She vigorously opposed this; she had planned on spending her sentence reading and doing work assignments to earn a little money for Commissary. I explained that she was not going to be assigned a job unless she attended the typing program, so she grudgingly accepted the assignment. The teacher was not a tolerant woman; she would not tolerate the use of non-business language when students practiced answering the phone on their mock telephone. She would not tolerate sloppiness or lack of effort. But she was exceptionally patient with those students who were really trying but were painfully slow to gain skills. To this demanding environment the young subject of our story came. The teacher explained that she expected nothing less than quality effort from all the students. This was not what our young subject expected from her jail sentence. But after a period of adjustment she found the number of typing errors went down, and her words per minute increased. Soon she was retyping materials for a lawyer concerning her case. She became so proficient at this that upon her release the lawyer hired her as a typist. The law firm provided educational benefits to employees, which the subject of our story used to complete a paralegal course. Combining some earlier college credits earned in prison prior to her criminal involvement, she was able to obtain her bachelors degree. I know this not because she returned to prison, but because one day when registering for a dissertation seminar at Fordham University Lincoln Center Campus I heard someone calling to me in the cafeteria that we shared with Fordham Law School. It was my reluctant typing student. She sat behind a pile of books which she had just purchased to start her second year at Fordham Law. Having survived the first and most difficult year at Fordham Law it was almost certain that she would complete her degree and be admitted to the bar. The Rikers Island typing teacher who had worked with her was teaching business skills, business etiquette, and typing skills. She was changing the way a young woman viewed herself, and reminding her of her forgotten dreams and enabling her to see a future which perhaps, before that typing class, had become obscured by clouds of drugs and the accompanying criminal lifestyle. That vision of a better future was rekindled by a dedicated, demanding teacher who dreamed better dreams for her student than the student was able to dream for herself.

Correctional educators refer to themselves as math teachers, history teachers, G.E.D. educators, plumbing instructors, computer instructors, counselors, administrators, and school psychologists. I humbly suggest that in addition to the subject matter they teach, their real job is to change the self-image of their students and, consequently, the way they think, act and feel.

Biographical Sketch

Drafted into the U.S. Army in 1969 Richard Dackow was assigned as a military policeman at the Fort Dix stockade. There he became interested in correctional psychology and treatment. After discharge he attained a Master's degree in Clinical/Counseling Psychology. He did an internship at Massachusetts' Westfield detention center Division of Youth Services, and was later hired by New York City Department of Corrections. Richard worked at the Manhattan House of Detention—the Tombs—and on Rikers Island. He was assigned Director of Classification at the Adolescent Reception and Detention Center and later at the Correctional Center for Women. In 1977 he was appointed Director of Classification and Treatment at the Suffolk County, New York Sheriff's Office, where he surveyed the educational needs of entering juvenile inmates. This information was used by the State of New York to develop the Education of Incarcerated Youth legislation, applying special education principles to provide a consistent funding stream for the education service throughout New York State. Richard earned his Doctorate in Psychology from Fordham University. He served as a founding board member of the American Red Cross Community Service Program, Eastern Suffolk BOCES Jail Education Advisory Board, Director of Suffolk County Jail's Overcrowding Study, and Director of a school-based intervention/prevention program for at-risk students. Dr. Dackow is now a clinical supervisor for a DBT treatment program in a women's correctional facility.

Chapter XV

European Prison Rules:
Correctional Education as a Human Right

by Bill Muth

Note: This essay originally appeared in Gehring and Rennie, 2008, pp. 61-64.

To the current writer, an educator with 25 years experience in American prisons, the Council of Europe's Recommendation No. R(89)12 of the Committee of Ministers To Member States on Education in Prison, known as the European Prison Rules (EPR), provides a stark contrast to the reigning U.S. corrections paradigm. Advocates of the Responsibility Model (Seiter & Fleiser, 1999), endorsed by many U.S. correctional systems, argue for expert interventions that incorporate top-down diagnostic-prescriptive methods. They view prisoners as deficient in pro-social and pro-vocational skills and aspire to measure "criminogenic risk factors" in terms of deviance from social norms (Gaes, Flanagan, Motiuk, & Stewart, 1999; Gendreau & Andrews, 1990).

The current EPR start from a radically different set of assumptions. Characterized by Kevin Warner as "the Human Dignity Approach" (1998, p. 118), the Rules are grounded in the human rights tradition as embodied in a declaration passed by the United Nations Educational, Scientific and Cultural Organization (UNESCO) at the 4th International Conference on Adult Education—that learning is an inherent human right (Council of Europe, 1990). Rather than top-down, the EPR view adult learning as student-directed. "Prisoners should be listened to and their agreement or willingness should be sought in connection with decisions. This means. . .that the prisoner should no longer be seen as an object of treatment but as a responsible subject" (Hans Tulkens, former Director-General of the Dutch Prison Service, in Warner, 1998, p. 119).

Differences between the U.S. Responsibility Model and the Council of Europe's EPR extend beyond ideas of prisoners and prison education, to beliefs about punishment, social justice, aims of education and the role of social science. This brief Appendix, however, is limited to a short historical explanation, followed by the current Rules—Council of Europe Recommendation No. R(89)12—which are printed in their entirety.

Historical Context For The Current EPR

In 1984, the European Committee on Crime Problems created a Select Committee of Experts on Education in Prisons, and charged the Committee to study prison education systems in all member states of the Council of Europe and to recommend changes to existing Rules. Between 1984 and 1988 the Select

Committee met seven times in Strasbourg. Despite diverse social, cultural, and programmatic differences, the members found common ground in a number of areas, including (a) a broad definition of prison education that addressed formal and non-formal activities, "library services, vocational education, cultural activities, social education, physical education and sports, as well as the academic subject[s]. . ." (Council of Europe, 1990, p. 8); (b) a belief that prison education should equate in quality with "the best adult education in the society outside" (p. 12); and (c) an emphasis on linking prisoners with the outside community.

The Select Committee justified the costs of prison education with three claims. First, prisons are destructive of personality; education can help normalize prisons and offset their destructiveness. Second, prison education helps to address the societal injustice that renders poorer educational opportunities to poorer people—e.g., the high numbers of prisoners that grew up in poverty. Third, education may encourage individuals to take on new, crime-free ways of living. (This last rationale is similar in ends, if not means, to the primary rationale for the U.S. Responsibility Model.)

In 1987 the Committee of Ministers of the Council of Europe, supportive of the recommendations of the Select Committee, issued the first version of the EPR with Recommendation No. R(87)3.

> The Committee of Ministers is the Council of Europe's decision-making body. It is. . .a governmental body, where national approaches to problems facing European society can be discussed on an equal footing. . . .It is the guardian of the Council's fundamental values, and monitors member states' compliance with their undertakings. (Council of Europe, 2007, para.1).

Although the new Rules, like older versions going back over 50 years, were regarded as principles rather than law, the Committee of Members regarded them as having a serious and powerful international role:

> Whilst the rules have no binding legal status in international law, they have been widely recognised as constituting a virtual code of practice in prison administration and treatment. Furthermore, the domestic legal status of the rules, although it varies from country to country, is such that in one form or another they have an important influence on the moral and practical standards that govern prison administration. Over the period, now more than half a century, during which the rules have been internationally valid, they have directly, or indirectly, encouraged higher standards and served to ensure the minimum conditions of humanity and decency in the prison systems. Although, therefore, the formal status of the rules is that of guidance to prison administrations, they impose powerful moral and political obligations on those

member states that have accepted them. (Council of Europe, 1990, p. 22).

In addition to the ethical imperative, the Rules carry the prestige of the Committee of Ministers, which is responsible for guarding "the Council of Europe's fundamental values." The current EPR were drafted in 1989, in Council of Europe Recommendation No. R(89)12.

COUNCIL OF EUROPE RECOMMENDATION No. R(89)12 OF THE COMMITTEE OF MINISTERS TO MEMBER STATES ON EDUCATION IN PRISON

(adopted by the Committee of Ministers on 13 October 1989 at the 429th meeting of the Ministers' Deputies)

The Committee of Ministers, under the terms of Article 15.b of the Statute of the Council of Europe—

- Considering that the right to education is fundamental;

- Considering the importance of education in the development of the individual and the community;

- Realising in particular that a high proportion of prisoners have had very little successful educational experience, and therefore now have many educational needs;

- Considering that education in prison helps to humanise prisons and to improve the conditions of detention;

- Considering that education in prison is an important way of facilitating the return of the prisoner to the community;

- Recognising that in the practical application of certain rights or measures, in accordance with the following recommendations, distinctions may be justified between convicted prisoners and prisoners remanded in custody;

- Having regard to Recommendation No. R(87)3 on the European Prison Rules and Recommendation No. R(81)17 on Adult Education Policy,

—recommends the governments of member States to implement policies which recognise the following:

1. All prisoners shall have access to education, which is envisaged as consisting of classroom subjects, vocational education, creative and cultural activities, physical education and sports, social education and library facilities;

2. Education for prisoners should be like the education provided for similar age groups in the outside world, and the range of learning opportunities for prisoners should be as wide as possible;

3. Education in prison shall aim to develop the whole person bearing in mind his or her social, economic and cultural context;

4. All those involved in the administration of the prison system and the management of prisons should facilitate and support education as much as possible;

5. Education should have no less a status than work within the prison regime and prisoners should not lose out financially or otherwise by taking part in education;

6. Every effort should be made to encourage the prisoner to participate actively in all aspects of education;

7. Development programmes should be provided to ensure that prison educators adopt appropriate adult education methods;

8. Special attention should be given to those prisoners with particular difficulties and especially those with reading or writing problems;

9. Vocational education should aim at the wider development of the individual, as well as being sensitive to trends in the labour market;

10. Prisoners should have direct access to a well-stocked library at least once per week;

11. Physical education and sports for prisoners should be emphasised and encouraged;

12. Creative and cultural activities should be given a significant role because these activities have particular potential to enable prisoners to develop and express themselves;

13. Social education should include practical elements that enable the prisoner to manage daily life within the prison, with a view to facilitating the return to society;

14. Wherever possible, prisoners should be allowed to participate in education outside prison;

15. Where education has to take place within the prison, the outside community should be involved as fully as possible;

16. Measures should be taken to enable prisoners to continue their education after release;

17. The funds, equipment and teaching staff needed to enable prisoners to receive appropriate education should be made available.

Biographical Sketch

Bill Muth is an Assistant Professor of Adult and Adolescent Literacy at Virginia Commonwealth University. Until August 2005, Bill was the Education Administrator for the Federal Bureau of Prisons (FBOP). Other positions with the FBOP included: reading teacher, principal, and Chief of the Program Analysis Branch. In 2004 Bill earned his Doctorate in Adult Literacy from George Mason University. His research interests include Thirdspace and Reading Components theories, especially as these apply to prison-based family literacy programs and children of incarcerated parents.

References

A neural network guide to teaching. (1998). *Phi Delta Kappa Fastbacks*, (431), 7-50.

ACTE (2008). *Career and technical education's role in workforce readiness credentials*. The Association for Career and Technical Education. Alexandria, VA. Retrieved March 26, 2008, from http://www.acteonline.org.

Adams, K., Bennett, K., Flanagan, T., Marquart, J, Cuvelier, S., Burton, V. Fritch, E., Gerber, J., & Longmire, D. (1994). A large-scale multidimensional test of the effect of prison education programs on offenders' behavior. *The Prison Journal, 74,* 433-449.

Alemagno, S. & Dickie, J. (2005). Employment issues of women in jail. *Journal of Employment Counseling, 42,* 67-74.

Andrews, D., & Bonta, J. (1994). *The psychology of criminal conduct.* Cincinnati, Ohio: Anderson.

Aos, S., Phipps, P., Barnoski, R. & Lieb, R. (2001). *The comparative costs and benefits of programs to reduce crime.* Olympia: Washington State Institute for Public Policy.

Batiuk, M.E. (2005). Disentangling the effects of correctional education. *Criminal Justice, 5*(1).

Bazos, A., & Hausman, J. (2004). *Correctional education as a crime control program.* Los Angeles: University of Los Angeles.

Bell, J.A. (1998). Problems in statistics: Learning style, age, and part-time students. *Education, 118*(4), 526-528.

Benda, B.B. (2005). Gender differences in life-course theory of recidivism: A survival analysis. *International Journal of Offender Therapy and Comparative Criminology, 49*(3), 325-342.

Bertrand, M. (1996). Women in prisons: A comparative study. *Caribbean Journal of Criminology and Social Psychology, 1*(1), 38-58.

Billington, D. D. (1998). *Seven characteristics of highly effective adult learning programs.* New Horizons for Learning: The adult learner, [On-line newsletter]. Available FTP: http://newhorizons.org/articlebillington1.html.

Blitz, C.L. (2006). Predictors of stable employment among female inmates in New Jersey: Implications for successful reintegration. *Journal of Offender Rehabilitation, 43*(1), 1-22.

Bloom, B., Owen, B., & Covington, S. (2003). *Gender-responsive strategies: Research, practice, and guiding principles for women offenders.* Washington, D.C.: National Institute of Corrections (#018017).

Bloom, B., & Steinhart, D. (1993). *Why punish the children? A reappraisal of the children of incarcerated mothers in America.* San Francisco: National Council on Crime and Delinquency.

Bouffard, J., MacKenzie, D., & Hickman, L. (2000). Effectiveness of vocational education and employment programs for adult offenders: A methodology-based analysis of the literature. *Journal of Offender Rehabilitation, 31*(1/2), 1-42.

Bowen, J. (1965). *Soviet education: Anton Makarenko and the years of experiment.* Madison, Wisconsin: The University of Wisconsin Press.

Bransford, J. D., Brown, A.L. & Cocking, R. R. (Eds.). (2000). *How people learn: brain, mind, experience, and school.* Washington, DC: National Academy Press.

Brewster, D. R., & Sharp, S. F. (2002). Educational programs and recidivism in Oklahoma: Another look. *The Prison Journal, 82*(3), 314-334.

Brookfield. S. (1987). *Developing critical thinkers: Challenging adults to explore alternative ways of thinking and acting.* Buckingham, Alabama: The Open University Press.

Bushway, S., & Reuter, P. (1997). Labor markets and crime risk factors. Chapter 6 in *Preventing Crime: What Works, What Doesn't, What's Promising,* edited by L.W. Sherman, Gottfredson, D., MacKenzie, D., Eck, J., Reuter, P., & Bushway, P. Washington, D.C.: U.S Department of Justice, Office of Justice Programs.

Cameron, M. (2001). No. 194 Women prisoners and correctional programs. *Australian Institute of Criminology trends & issues in crime and criminal justice,* 1-6.

CDCR (California Department of Corrections and Rehabilitation). (August 19, 2010). Weekly population report (chart). Retrieved 8-19-10 from http://www.cdcr.ca.gov/Reports_Research/Offender_Information_Services_Branch/WeeklyWed/TPOP1Ad08022.pdf.

Comings, J., Garner, B. & Smith, C. (Eds.). *The Review of Adult Learning And Literacy: Connecting Research, Policy, and Practice (Vol. 4).* National Center for the Study of Adult Learning and Literacy. Mahwah New Jersey: Lawrence Erlbaum.

Comings, J.P., Parrella, A., & Soricone, L. (1999, December). *Persistence among adult basic education students in pre-GED classes*. Cambridge Massachusetts: National Center for the Study of Adult Learning and Literacy. Report #12.

Corey, G., & Corey, M.S. (1997). *I never knew I had a choice (6ᵗʰ ed.)* (1-38). Pacific Grove, California: Brooks/Cole Publishing Company.

Council of Europe (COE). (1990). *Education in prison*. Recommendation No. R (89) 12 adopted by the Committee of Ministers of the Council of Europe on 13 October 1989 and Explanatory Memorandum. Strasburg: COE.

Council of Europe (COE). (2007). *What is the Committee of members?* Retrieved on October 24, 2007, from: http://www.coe.int/t/cm/aboutCM_en.asp.

Covey, S. (1989). *The 7 habits of highly effective people*. New York: Free Press.

Covington, S.S. (1998). The relational theory of women's psychological development: Implications for the criminal justice system. In R. T. Zaplin (Ed.), *Female offenders: Critical Perspectives and Effective Interventions* (113-131). Gaithersburg, Maryland: Aspen Publishers.

Covington, S.S., & Bloom, B.E. (2006). Gender responsive treatment and services in correctional settings. *Women & Therapy, 29*(3/4), 9-33.

Crutchfield, R., & Pitchford, S. (1997). Work and crime: the effects of labor stratification. *Social Forces, 76*(1), 93-118.

D'Amico, D. (2004). Race, class, gender and sexual orientation in adult literacy: Power, pedagogy, and programs. In J. Comings, B. Garner, & C. Smith (Eds.). *The Review of Adult Learning And Literacy: Connecting Research, Policy, and Practice (Vol. 4)*. National Center for the Study of Adult Learning and Literacy. Mahwah New Jersey: Lawrence Erlbaum.

Dewey, J. (1997). *Experience and education*. New York: Touchstone.

Dewey, J. (1907). *School and society*. Chicago: University of Chicago Press.

Di Clemente, C.C., & Gordon, J.R. (1982). Developing a self-efficacy scale for alcoholic treatment. *Alcoholism: Clinical and Experimental Research, 6*(1).

Ditton, P.M. (1999). *Mental health and treatment of inmates and probationers*. (U.S. Department of Justice Publication No. NCJ 174463). Washington, DC: U.S. Government Printing Office.

Dryer, R., Beale, I. L., & Lambert, A. J. (1999). The balance model of dyslexia and remedial training: An evaluative study. *Journal of Learning Disabilities, 32*(2), 174-186.

Dunn, R. (1998). Timing is everything. *Momentum, 29*(4), 23-25.

Dunn, R., Griggs, S.A., Olson, J., Beasley, M., & Gorman, B.S. (1995, July / August). A meta-analytic validation the Dunn and Dunn model of learning-style preferences. *The Journal of Educational Research, 88*(6), 353-362.

Ellis, D.B. (1991). *Becoming a master student instructor guide (6th ed.).* Rapid City, South Dakota: College Survival, Inc.

Encyclopedia of Business. (2006). On the job training. Retrieved March 26, 2008, from http://www.referenceforbusiness.com/encyclopedia/Oli-Per/On-the-Job-Training.html.

Erisman, W., & Contardo, J.B. (2005, November). *Learning to reduce recidivism: A 50-state analysis of postsecondary correctional education policy.* Washington, DC: Institute for Higher Education Policy.

Esler, W. K. (1984). The new learning theory: Brain physiology. *The Clearing House, 58,* 85-89.

Fine, M., Torre, M.E., Boudin, K., Bowen, I., Clark, J., Hylton, D., Martinez, M., "Missy," Roberts, R.A., Smart, P., & Upegui, D. (2001, September). *Changing: The impact of college in a maximum security prison.* New York: The Graduate School and University Center, City University of New York.

Gaes, G.G., Flanagan, T.J., Motiuk, L.L. & Stewart, L. (1999). Adult correctional treatment. In M. Tonry & J. Petersilia (Eds.), *Prisons* (361-426). Chicago: University of Chicago Press.

Gardner, H. (1993). *Multiple intelligences: The theory in practice.* New York: BasicBooks.

Gardner, H. (1999). *The disciplined mind: What all students should understand.* New York: Simon & Schuster.

Gee, J. (2005). Education in rural county jails: Need versus opportunity. *Journal of Correctional Education, 57*(3), 12-25.

Gehring, T. (1988). Five principles of correctional education. *Journal of Correctional Education, 39*(4), 164-169.

Gehring, T. (1999). *Three phases of Kuhn's paradigm change model.* Unpublished manuscript. San Bernardino: California State.

Gehring, T. (2000). Compendium of material on the pedagogy-andragogy issue. *Journal of Correctional Education, 51*(1), 151-162.

Gehring, T., & Rennie, S. (2008). *Correctional education history from A to Z.* San Bernardino: California State University.

Gehring, T., & Wright, R. (March, 2003). Three ways of summarizing correctional education progress, trends. *Journal of Correctional Education 55*(1), 5-13.

Gendreau P., & Andrews D.A. (1990). What the meta-analyses of the offender treatment literature tells us about "what works." *Canadian Journal of Criminology, 32,* 173-184.

Goswami, S. (2002). *Unlocking options for women: A survey of women in Cook County Jail.* Chicago: Coalition for the Homeless.

Grant, N. (2008). *Helping dropouts break the cycle of poverty.* National Public Radio. FTP: http://www.npr.org/about/.

Greenfeld, L.A., & Snell, T.L. (1999). *Women offenders.* (U.S. Department of Justice Publication No. NCJ 175688). Washington, DC: U.S. Government Printing Office.

Guild, P.B., & Chock-Eng, S. (1998). Multiple intelligence, learning styles brain-based education: Where do the messages overlap? *Schools in the Middle, 7*(4), 38-40.

Hairston, C.F. (1991). Family ties during imprisonment: Important to whom and for what? *Journal of Sociology and Social Welfare, 18*(1), 87-104.

Halpern, D.F. (1996). *Thought & knowledge: An introduction to critical thinking (3rd ed.).* Mahwah, New Jersey: Lawrence Erlbaum Associates.

Hamlyn, B., & Lewis, D. (2000). *Women prisoners: A survey of their work and training experiences in custody and on release.* London: Home Office, Research Development and Statistics Directorate.

Harlow, C.W. (2003). *Education and correctional populations.* (U.S. Department of Justice Publication No. NCJ 195670). Washington, DC: U.S. Government Printing Office.

Harm, N.J., & Phillips, S.D. (2001). You can't go home again: Women and criminal recidivism. *Journal of Offender Rehabilitation, 32*(3), 3-21.

Harrison, P.M., & Beck, A.J. (2005). *Prison and jail inmates at midyear 2004.* Washington, DC: Bureau of Justice Statistics (NO 208801).

Harrison, B., & Schehr, R.C. (2004). Offenders and post-release jobs: Variables influencing success and failure. *Journal of Offender Rehabilitation, 39*(3), 35-68.

Hernandez, V.R., & Franklin, C. (2008). Theory and practice of social work with individuals, families, and groups. In D.M. DiNitto & C.A. McNeece (Eds.), *Social Work Issues and Opportunities in a Challenging Profession* (29-50). Chicago: Lyceum Books.

Holy Bible. (King James Version). (1977). Nashville, Tennessee: Thomas Nelson, Inc.

Hunsinger, I. (1997). Austin MacCormick and the education of adult prisoners: Still relevant today. *Journal of Correctional Education, 48* (4), 160-165.

Indiana State University. (1999a). *Brief summary of select learning style models*. CTL learning styles site. [Web page]. Available FTP: http://web.indstate.edu/ctl/styles/model2.html.

Indiana State University. (1999b). *On-line inventories of learning styles*. CTL learning styles site. [Web page]. Available FTP: http://web.indstate.edu/ctl/styles/invent.html.

Insel, P., & Roth, W. (2002). *Core concepts in health*. Boston: McGraw Hill Press.

James, D. J. (2004). *Profile of jail inmates, 2002*. Washington, DC: Bureau of Justice Statistics (No 201932).

Judelson, K., Kuleshov, V., and Kumarin, V. (1976). *Anton Makarenko: His life and his work in education*. Moscow: Progress Publishers.

Kaplan, L. S. (1998). Using the 4MAT instructional model for effective leadership development. *NASSP Bulletin, 82*(599) 83-92.

Kirst-Ashman, K.K., & Hull, G.H. (1993). *Understanding generalist practice*. Chicago: Nelson-Hall.

Kling, J., Weiman, D.F., & Western, B. (2000, October). *The labor market consequences of "mass" incarceration*. Paper presented for the Reentry Roundtable, Urban Institute, Washington DC.

Knowles, M.S. (1987). *Andragogy in action: Applying modern principles of adult learning*. San Francisco: Josey-Bass.

Knowles, M.S. (1998). New perspectives on andragogy. In M.S. Knowles, E.F. Holton III, & R.A. Swanson, (Eds.) *The adult learner: The definitive classic in adult education and human resource development (5th Ed.)* (133-152). Woburn, Massachusetts: Butterworth-Heinemann.

Koshmanova, T. (1997). *Teacher education and social transition in independent Ukraine*. MCIES Conference Report.

Lahm, K.F. (2000). Equal or equitable: An exploration of educational and vocational program availability for male and female offenders. *Federal Probation, 64*(2), 39-46.

Langan, P.A., & Levin, D.J. (2002). *Recidivism of prisoners released in 1994*. (U.S. Department of Justice Publication No. NCJ 193427). Washington, DC: U.S. Government Printing Office.

Lawrence, S., Mears, D., Dubin, G., & Travis, J. (2002). *The practice and promise of prison programming*. Washington, DC: Urban Institute Justice Policy Center.

Learnativity. (Site Map). (1997-1999). *The Learnativity, Co.* [Web page] Available FTP: http://learnativity.com/sitemap.html.

Lindeman, E.C. (1926). *The meaning of adult education*. New York: New Republic.

Lineham, M.M. (1993). *Cognitive-behavioral treatment of borderline personality disorder*. New York: Guilford Press.

Lyman, M. & LoBuglio, S. (2007, March/April). "Whys" and "hows" of measuring jail recidivism. *American Jails*, 9-18.

MacCormick, A. (1976/1931). *The education of adult prisoners: A survey and a program*. New York: AMS Press.

MacGillis, A. (2001). Union plumbing for new members: The United Association taking novel steps to fill its ranks. *Baltimore Sun* newspaper, Telegraph Section, p. 1A. (Retrieved September 3, 2001, from the *Baltimore Sun* website www.SunSpot.net.)

Martin, D., Potter, L. (1998, summer). How teachers can help students get their learning styles met at school and at home. *Education, 118*(4), 549-555.

Mattucci, R.F., & Johnson, M.W. (2003). Teaching hands-on plumbing in a county facility: A working plumbers experience. *The Journal of Correctional Education, 54*(1), 15-18.

Mauer, M., & Chesney-Lind, M. (Eds.). (2002). *Invisible punishment: The collateral consequences of mass imprisonment*. New York: New Press.

McKeachie, W.J. (1995, November). Learning styles can become learning strategies. *NTLF [On-line journal featured article], 4*(6), 1-4. Available FTP: http://www.ntlf.com/html/pi/9511/article1.htm.

McKenzie, W. (1999). Multiple intelligences inventory. *The one and only surfaquarium*. FTP:http://surfaquarium.com/MI/inventory.htm.

Merriam, S.B., Caffarella, R.S., & Baumgartner, L.M. (2007). *Learning in adulthood (3rd ed)*. San Francisco: Jossey-Bass.

Morash, M., Bynum, T.S., & Koons, B.A. (1998). *Research in brief—Women offenders—Programming needs and promising approaches*. Washington, DC: United States Department of Justice (No 171667 full report).

MTC Institute. (2003). *The challenge of teaching (and learning) in prison*. FTP:http://www.mtctrains.com/institute/publications/RP-TheChallengeofTeachingandLearninginPrison.pdf.

Mumola, C.J. (2000). *Incarcerated parents and their children*. (U.S. Department of Justice Publication No. NCJ 182335). Washington, DC: U.S. Government Printing Office.

O'Brien, L. (1989, October). Learning styles: Make the student aware. *NASSP Bulletin*, 85-89.

O'Brien, P., & Bates, R. (2005). Women's post-release experiences in the U.S.: Recidivism and reentry. *International Journal of Prisoner Health, 1*(2), 1-15.

O'Brien, P., & Young, D.S. (2006). Challenges for formerly incarcerated women: A holistic approach to assessment. *Families in Society: The Journal of Contemporary Human Services, 87*(3), 359-366.

Office of the Governor. (August 19, 2010). Retrieved 8-19-10 from http://gov.ca/index.php?/fact-sheet/1084/.

Ornstein, A.C. & Levine, D.U. (1997). *Foundations of education. (6th ed.)*. New York: Houghton Mifflin Company.

Patchin, J.W. & Keveles, G.N. (2004). *Alternatives to incarceration: An evidenced-based research review*. Northwest Wisconsin Criminal Justice Management Conference. Cable, Wisconsin. 10 March 2006.

Petersilia, J. (2005). *Understanding California corrections*. Berkley, California: University of California Policy Research Center. http://www.seweb.uci.edu/users/joan/images/CPRC.pdf.

Pogorzelski, W., Wolff, N., Pan, K., & Blitz, C. (2005). Behavioral health problems, ex-offender reentry policies, and the "Second Chance Act." *American Journal of Public Health, 95*(10), 1718-1724.

...

Prochaska, J.O. & DiClemente, C.C. (1982). Transtheoretical therapy: Toward a more integrative model of Change. Psychotherapy: *Theory, Research, and Practice, 19,* 276-288.

Reasoner, R.W. (2007). *Review of self-esteem research.* Retrieved from <u>www.self-esteem-international.org/content/5-research.htm</u>.

Reentry Policy Council. (2010). *Charting the safe and successful return of prisoners to the community.* Retrieved on February 22, 2010 from: <u>http://reentrypolicy.org/government_affairs/second_chance_act</u>.

Reinert, H. (1986). Learning style identification exercise. [Reproduced in *Becoming a master student,* see Ellis, 1991 entry above]. Lynnwood, Washington: Edmonds School District No. 15.

Ritberger, C. (2007). *Managing people: What's personality got to do with it.* Carlsbad, California: Hay House, Inc.

Rogers, C. (1986). Client-centered therapy. In I.L. Kutash & A. Wolf (Eds.), *Psychotherapist's casebook* (197-208). San Francisco: Jossey-Bass.

Rose, C. (2004). Women's participation in prison education: What we know and what we don't know. *The Journal of Correctional Education, 55*(1), 78-100.

Ross, R.R., & Fabiano, E. (1985). *Time to think: A cognitive model of delinquency prevention and offender rehabilitation.* Johnson City, Tennessee: Institute of Social Sciences and Arts, Inc.

Ruddell, R. (2005). *Expand or expire: Jails in rural America.* Unpublished manuscript.

Sabol, W.J., Couture, H., & Harrison, P.M. (2007). *Prisoners in 2006.* (U.S. Department of Justice Publication No. NCJ 219416). Washington, DC: U.S. Government Printing Office.

Sabol, W.J., Minton, T.D., & Harrison, P.M. (2007). *Prison and jail inmates at midyear 2006.* (U.S. Department of Justice Publication No. NCJ 217675). Washington, DC: U.S. Government Printing Office.

Saylor, W., & Gaes, G., (1997). Training inmates through industrial work participation and vocational and apprenticeship instruction. *Corrections Management Quarterly, 1*(2), 32-43.

Seiter, R. & Fleisher, M. S. (1999). The responsibility model: Teaching pro-social values to inmates. *Corrections Management Quarterly, 3,* 57-65.

Seiter, R, & Kadela, K. (2003). Prisoner reentry: What works, what does not, and what is promising. *Crime & Delinquency, 49*, 360-78.

Shaughnessy, M. F. (1998). An interview with Rita Dunn about learning styles. *The Clearing House, 71*(3), 141-145.

Sherman, L., Gottfredson, D., MacKenzie, D., Eck, J., Reuter, P., & Bushway, S. (1998). Preventing crime: What works, what doesn't, what's promising. Washington, DC: U.S. Department of Justice, Office of Justice Programs, Bureau of Justice Statistics.

Smith, C.J., & Young, D.S. (2003). The multiple impacts of TANF, ASFA, and mandatory drug sentencing for families affected by maternal incarceration. *Children and Youth Services Review, 25*(7), 535-552.

Snedden, D. (1907). *Administration and educational work of American juvenile reform schools.* New York: Teachers College, Columbia University.

Sonnier, I.L. (Ed.). (1985). *Methods and techniques of holistic education.* Springfield, IL: Charles C. Thomas Publisher.

Spark, C., & Harris, A. (2005). Vocation, vocation: A study of prisoner education for women. *Journal of Sociology, 41*(2), 143-161.

Spoon, J.C., & Schell, J.W. (1998). Aligning student learning styles with instructor teaching styles. *Journal of Industrial Teacher Education, 35*(2) 41-56.

Stephan, J.J. (1997). *Census of state and federal correctional facilities, 1995.* Washington, DC: U.S. Department of Justice, Bureau of Justice Statistics.

Steurer, S.J., & Smith, L.G. (February, 2003). *Three-State recidivism study: Executive summary.* Correctional Education Association (Lanham, MD) and Management & Training Corporation Institute (Centerville, Utah).

Steurer, S., Smith, L., & Tracy, A. (2001). *Three state recidivism study.* Correctional Education Association. Retrieved 15 October, 2005 from http://www.ceanational.org/documents/3StateFinal.pdf.

Stites, R. (2004). Implications of the new learning technologies for adult literacy and learning. In J. Comings, B. Garner, & C. Smith (Eds.). *The Review of Adult Learning And Literacy: Connecting Research, Policy, and Practice (Vol. 4).* National Center for the Study of Adult Learning and Literacy. Mahwah New Jersey: Lawrence Erlbaum.

Tonkin, P., Dickie, J., Alemagno, S., & Grove, W. (2004). Women in jail: "Soft skills" and barriers to employment. *Journal of Offender Rehabilitation, 38*(4), 51-71.

Tracy, C., & Johnson, C. (1994). *Review of various outcomes studies relating prison education to reduced recidivism*. Austin, Texas: Windham School System.

Walter, T.L. & Siebert, A. (1996). *Student success (7th ed.)*. Orlando, Florida: Harcourt Brace & Company.

Warner, K. (1998). The "prisoners are people" perspective—and the problems of promoting learning where this outlook is rejected. *The Journal of Correctional Education, 49*(3), 118-132.

Weaver, R. (2006). *Sounding the alarm. The school dropout crisis has devastating effects on young people*. NEAToday FTP: http://www.nea.org/columns/presview11-06.html.

Webster, A. (December 28, 2007). - Publications: Let's Talk. *Mental Health Services for Women Offenders, 32*(1). Ottawa: Correctional Service of Canada.

Wikipedia. (August 19, 2010). Incarceration in the United States. Retrieved 8-19-10 from http://wikipedia.org/wiki/Incarceration_in_the_United_States.

Williamson, R.D. (1998). Designing diverse learning styles. *Schools in the Middle, 7*(4) 28-31.

Wilson, D.B., Gallagher, C.A., & MacKenzie, D.L. (2000). A meta-analysis of corrections-based education, vocation, and work programs for adult offenders. *Journal of Research in Crime and Delinquency, 37*(4), 347-368.

Winifred, M. (1996). Vocational and technical training programs for women in prison. *Corrections Today, 58*(5), 168-170.

Wright, R. (Ed.), (2008). *In the borderlands: Learning to teach in prisons and alternative settings (3rd ed)*. San Bernardino, CA: California State University.

Yochelson, S., & Samenow, S. (1977). *The criminal personality, Volume II: A profile for change*. New York: Jason Aronson, Inc.

Young, D.S., & Mattucci, R.F. (2006). Enhancing the vocational skills of incarcerated women through a plumbing maintenance program. *The Journal of Correctional Education, 57*(2), 126-140.